THE ART OF CHILDREN'S PICTURE BOOKS

GARLAND REFERENCE LIBRARY
OF THE HUMANITIES
(VOL. 1636)

THE ART OF CHILDREN'S PICTURE BOOKS

A Selective Reference Guide
Second Edition

Sylvia S. Marantz
and
Kenneth A. Marantz

GARLAND PUBLISHING, INC.
NEW YORK & LONDON / 1995

Library of Congress Cataloging-in-Publication Data

Marantz, Sylvia S.
  The art of children's picture books : a selective reference guide /
Sylvia S. Marantz and Kenneth A. Marantz.—2nd ed.
      p. cm. — (Garland reference library of the humanities ; vol.
1636)
    Includes index.
    ISBN 0-8153-0937-6
    1. Picture books for children—History—Bibliography.
    2. Illustrated books, Children's—History—Bibliography.
    3. Children's literature—Illustrations—Bibliography. I. Marantz,
Kenneth A. II. Title. III. Series.
  Z1037.1.M37 1995
  [PN1001.A1]
  011.62—dc60   94-16308

Printed on acid-free, 250-year-life paper
Manufactured in the United States of America

Contents

Preface to the First Edition   vii

Preface to the Second Edition   ix

Introduction   xi

Reflections for the Second Edition   xix

Part I: History of Children's Picture Books   3

Part II: How a Picture Book Is Made   29

Part III: Criticism of Children's Picture Books,
Including Their "Use" with Children   45

Part IV: Artists Anthologized   133

Part V: Books, Articles, and Audiovisual Materials
on Individual Picture Book Artists   165

Part VI: Guides and Aids to Further Research   235

Part VII: Some Collections and/or Repositories of
Materials on Picture Books and Their
Creators   245

Index of Artists   251

Index of Authors, Editors, and Compilers   257

Index of Titles   269

Preface to the First Edition

This publication began at least six years ago as a search for material for another book entirely. As the notes and references accumulated, patterns began to emerge. It was then that Gary Kuris of Garland made us aware that what we were gathering might be of interest to other researchers, and we made the fatal error of agreeing to compile it. As anyone who has attempted any bibliography on anything already knows, the task is endless. Almost every reference leads to several more. Friends mutter half-recalled titles; partial xeroxes of periodical articles surface with dates missing or blurred; promising titles yield nothing relevant but mention other possibilities; decisions on how far to pursue must be made constantly. We found ourselves snatching moments at the card catalogs of libraries as diverse as that in the Tate Museum in London or in the center of Canberra, Australia, while on other business entirely. All too often the vital page or the entire bound volume containing the relevant issue was missing. This search has proved exhausting but cannot claim to be exhaustive. Our last computer search was done in the fall of 1985, but we have included books and articles that have come to our attention as particularly relevant from 1986 and 1987 as well. As I write, someone somewhere is printing another article we will unfortunately miss. We hope that this bibliography will serve as a springboard to carry others farther and faster in their quests. We welcome the calling of omissions and additions to our attention.

Sylvia Marantz
October 1987

Preface to the Second Edition

The pool of materials about the picture book has, since 1987, expanded to a lake, or perhaps even a sea, with waves rising higher each year. We began collecting for this update as soon as the manuscript for the first edition was completed, finding the task ever more difficult. We soon gave up on traveling to obtain anything from beyond the United States, and concentrated on American sources.

The improvements in technology and indexing have made both library book and periodical searching incredibly faster and easier. But the problems of missing volumes, lost articles, torn-out pages continue to plague us. The cooperation of publishers in making materials available also varies enormously.

The increasing interest in the art of the picture book is gratifying. Materials will probably continue to multiply. But perhaps the ease of finding information on the growing "information highway" will make a third edition of this bibliography unnecessary. In any case, we leave the collection to others in the future.

Sylvia Marantz
December 1993

Introduction

With These Lights

Which such Book, and in such a dress may (I hope) serve to entice witty children to it, that they may not conceit a torment to be in the school, but dainty fare. For it is apparent, that children (even from their infancy almost) are delighted with Pictures, and willingly please their eyes with these lights: And it will be very well worth the pains to have once brought to pass, that scare-crows may be taken away out of Wisdom's Gardens.

The Orbis Pictus,
John Amos Comenius, 1657

In the 300 years since Comenius created what has been frequently noted as "the first children's picturebook" our gardens have not yet been cleared of all scarecrows. Despite increasing attention to the illustrations in children's books in this century, most of the concerns seem to be about the shape, size, and clothing of these scarecrows rather than with speculation about their placement in the garden. For me picture books should be perceived and valued as a form of visual art, *not* literary art. To insist on valuing them as literature makes us appreciate the pictures primarily in relationship to the text, more as handmaidens than as symbols having unique personalities. In remaining textbound we fail to exploit sufficiently the visual qualities of books that Comenius astutely identified as those that cause us delight.

Humans have created pictures for thousands of years, have chosen to make visible some of the feelings and fears and desires that inhabited their psyches. They made marks on cave walls, on bones and boulders, on dried animal skins, and on the plaster-coated walls of their tombs. These pictures tell us stories, in other words, they illuminate or illustrate dreams or lived experiences. Whether an Italian Renaissance painting depicting the adoration of the Magi or an Amerindian drawing on an animal hide of a battle with paleface soldiers, the marks made are intended to be a visual narrative. As books evolved in the Western world pictures have also been used to help tell stories, to make specifically visual what the text could only more generally suggest.

The history of the book, like any history of a human enterprise, is a complex one that properly demands investigation of economic, political, artistic, and technological forces operating within cultures. Obviously, without the development of movable type, mass production would not be possible, and without the Industrial Revolution there wouldn't be the kind of literate and relatively affluent audience for the flood of books that technology made possible. And without emancipation of the young from the world of adult work there would have been no need to create books for children. The many histories of children's literature depict an evolution from books designed to train the moral faculties, to produce the proper behavior needed in adult society, to those, toward the end of the nineteenth century, that began to understand the value of esthetic joy for youngsters, the delight that Comenius wrote of. Randolph Caldecott, rather than Comenius, is properly the father of the picture book, because unlike *The Orbis Pictus*, which was an illustrated language textbook, his books partnered lively drawings with simple story texts created to entertain, not instruct. Victorian England was the cultural engine that drove this book form into our century, with Caldecott and artists like Crane and Potter at the throttle.

The initial momentum behind picture books waned as the *illustrated book* grew in importance, with such artists as Rackham and Pyle and N.C. Wyeth and Shepard producing stacks of enticing volumes. Although difficult to pinpoint the exact year, it was some time during the churning decades between the World Wars that the picture book regained the vitality of the earlier Golden Age, an energy that exploded into a second gilded, if not 18-carat gold, age of productivity. It is the "nowness" of this productivity with its profound unrealized potential that continues to stimulate our curiosity, to provoke our speculations about these art objects. These inquiries have, over a score of years, helped identify characteristic qualities of the genre that make it possible to be more constructively critical than most current writers have been.

One must begin with a point of view, a psychological set, a conscious frame of reference. When one goes to an art museum, one is prepared to respond to the objects as if they were whatever you may define as "art" objects. In a real sense we create "rules" for appreciating them that are different from those we use for responding to other sets of objects, for example, tools, automobiles, postage stamps. Therefore it is important to be as clear as possible about what sort of thing a picture book is. To sort it out from other related things, it might be useful to imagine a line that has at one end a typical novel, that is, a book whose pages are filled exclusively with the printed word. At the other end of this imaginary line is the totally textless book, one that conveys its message (mainly a story) using only pictures. In between are volumes that have a single illustration (a frontispiece), some that employ chapter-heading or concluding vignettes, others that provide occasional full-page pictures that highlight particular events or delineate characters in the narrative, and a few that interlard a variety of illustrations throughout the entire book. In all of these examples it is possible to remove all the pictures and be left with a coherent, completely satisfying piece of literature. Artists like Dore, Picasso, Matisse, Eichenberg, Moser, Shahn, and Baskin have all contributed drawings, etchings, and woodcuts to illustrate poems and stories. Indeed, the history of the book is replete with examples of illustrated works, and, of course, the practice continues.

In responding to these kinds of books we have been conditioned by our cultural conventions to read the texts as literature, with its appropriate critical criteria, and to appreciate the visual art separately, as individual esthetic objects. It has become common practice for collectors to remove the pictures from some of these works and treat them as one would any other picture from an artist's studio: to mat, frame, and hang them on the wall. They do not lose artistic value by being separated from the text they illustrated. In recent years a parallel practice has evolved to treat the "original" studio products of picture book artists in the same way. If the artist created a series of watercolor paintings as illustrations for a retelling of a traditional fable, for example, each one could be matted, framed, and hung on the wall. But in this case what is displayed is the fragment of something, as when a broken head of a marble statue is mounted for exhibition in a museum. The painting and the head surely have qualities that may evoke esthetic responses, but they are still incomplete; they have been removed from the context of their original design. A picture book, unlike an illustrated book, is properly conceived of as a unit, a totality that integrates all the designed parts in a sequence in which the relationships among them—the cover, endpapers, typography, pictures—are crucial to understanding the book. In a significant sense, each book, like each etching pulled from the artist's copper plate, is an original artwork. All that preceded its printing—and there are many steps in the process—are but means to that end.

Therefore, to appreciate a picture book one must take a point of view that is based on an understanding of it as the composite set of qualities that differentiates it from other objects. However, to complicate matters a bit, within the family of "picture books" there are several relatives that skew this viewpoint. There are collections of poems and fables whose organizational logic is quite different from that of a single story. Similarly those collections of notions ("concepts") like colors or tools or wildflowers do not have as structured a framework as a narrative demands. Alphabets and counting books may or may not have such a framework, depending on the organizing principle or their generation, but they do have a sequential logic based on their definitions as linguistic or numerical components. Then there are the collections of puzzles and fact books that tell how things work or take us into the fields to learn about nature. All have in common the twin narratives in the form of words and pictures that characterize the picture book.

All picture books tell stories. And all stories began as things told by a storyteller. When transcribed onto the silent page the voice is lost and with it the idiosyncratic manner each teller has in making the story special. The illustrator replaces the speaker and the pictures become, symbolically, the voice that conveys some of the special qualities of meaning that language frequently cannot. Conjure up images of the many mice who have been the central characters of picture books as an example of how the artist's vision can take a word—"mouse"—and create brave leaders, artistic speakers, and orators by the use of line and color. In evaluating picture books, we attend to the qualities of that symbolic voice just as we attend to the "interpretation" by the vocalist or group of yet another performance of a popular musical composition. What makes that rendition special and how does it affect us?

Because the picture book is much more a visual art object than a piece of literature, book selection should focus more on the visual attributes than on the text. Clearly, I must hedge this statement, because story line, even in a textless work, is important, and, indeed, separates the routine from the seductive book. Yet picture books are such rich repositories of visual art, so readily available compared with the resources housed in galleries and museums, that I believe we must take the fullest advantage of them. Probably the most immediate quality of a picture book is its craftsmanship. Are you convinced by the way figures are rendered that they can do the things asked of them? This is not at all a matter of naturalism. Lionni's use of relatively simple cut-paper shapes to create birds and mice and alligators is very convincing. Although at times we may admire the patterned papers he uses, we look through the means of production and become believers in the reality of his characters, just as we do when we take Sendak's magic sailboat to visit the "Wild Things." In picking books you will want those that can carry you beyond the surface recognition of medium and the naming of objects represented into the spiritual realm of the story.

What I am referring to here is the expressive content of the book, the stuff of effect that deals more with the "how" of communication than the "what." Beyond the bare bones of plot, how are details used in the illustrations to add a texture, even a subplot, so that the eye looks for clues in later pages based on earlier visual hints? Knight's *Twelve Days of Christmas* interweaves the escapades of a raccoon into the classical rhyme to supplement the main character's playing out of the text's events. The effect is to add even more fun to a lively retelling (i.e., visual interpretation). Color manipulates our emotions as a puppeteer's strings move a marionette's limbs. Shulevitz's changing shades of blue in his *Dawn* create major mood shifts hardly hinted at in the text. And unusual angles are devices used by Van Allsburg in drawing us into his surreal worlds. Such artistic tools are available to all, but only some illustrators think to use them.

Although it is tempting to rely on formal rules for evaluating picture books to create canons of picturemaking and design in order to categorize and then measure each work, to do so would sap the vital juices of personal response. Most current reviewing, however, not only avoids this deathtrap but also sidesteps the necessary attention to those qualities that contribute to the esthetic impact of the book. As a visual narrative one should expect to find humor, pathos, excitement, mystery, beauty, repulsion—the expressive content that one picks up a book to get. There is a layer of meaning that Anthony Browne instills into his version of *Hansel and Gretel* when he depicts the mother and witch looking very much alike. Further, his use of vertical elements throughout is a symbolic motif that acts upon our subconscious to add further texture to the visual meanings of the tale. The audacity of setting the piece in modern times forces us to deal with the content in nontraditional ways. These are examples of an artist consciously packing his work with clues that we must unpack if we are to derive more than a superficial reading. The "what" of the story remains basically within the traditional track. But it is "how" he goes about visualizing it, that is, creating the visual narrative, that makes all the difference. Of course there is no reason to believe that one must like a picture book after the unpacking has been done. Taste remains one of the most personal rights we have.

As with any art form, response (call it appreciation or evaluation or even criticism) is a complex affair that demands experience to make it a personal value. Because so many of us have been raised to perceive books as temples of the word, our visual-art sensibilities have not had a decent chance to develop. The sorts of analyses suggested above are not automatic and, as simple as they seem, can only hint at the extensive opportunities that picture books offer. They are available for all to become involved with, to learn from, and, hence, to enjoy. And many books have been created to help those who desire to become educated.

I am one with Comenius when he writes that "it will be very well worth the pains to have once brought to pass" the involvement with the picture books that can so delight not only "witty children" but all of us.

Kenneth Marantz
1987

Reflections for the Second Edition

There's been no change in our delighted involvement with picture books since the first edition. But there has been a marked increase in the number published each year. This rise has been accompanied by an intensified interest shown by scholars in the historical and theoretical qualities of the genre, as seen in some of the new entries below.

Both the professional and the popular journals have discovered that artists and authors can speak very well for themselves. More writing by and about the artists has perhaps contributed to the creation of a sort of star system for these previously uncelebrated creators. Exhibitions of their original art work in museums and in galleries, from which collectors have begun to purchase, have added to their prestige. The fact that other people, like editors and art directors, play a major role in the shaping of picture books seems also to be attracting the attention of the journals at last.

Meanwhile, motivated by a "multicultural" trend in education, the volume of titles dealing with geographical locations beyond our borders as well as with the diversity of our current population has increased dramatically. Many picture books now appear in bilingual texts or simultaneously in different languages. Unfortunately reviewers, although more numerous, have not for the most part begun to engage the qualities of the artwork in the picture book as seriously and as effectively as necessary to help the interested appreciators.

Although the business of picture book publishing has tended to avoid some of the innovative practices of the 1960s and 1970s, and has pushed the publication of perhaps too many "fast food"–type titles, there are still extensive numbers of imaginatively conceived and handsomely produced books that have caught the attention of many more commentators. These writings we herein call to your attention.

December 1993

The Art of Children's Picture Books

PART I

History of Children's Picture Books

1. Adams, Bess Porter. *About Books and Children: Historical Survey of Children's Literature.* New York: Holt, 1953. 573pp.

   Pages 363–83 give the history of illustrations in children's books through Howard Pyle, plus a few b & w reproductions. Some notes on illustrations occur *passim.*

2. Alderson, Brian. *Sing a Song for Sixpence: The English Picture Book Tradition and Randolph Caldecott.* Cambridge: Cambridge University, 1986. 112pp.

   Profusely illustrated in b & w and color. Prepared on the occasion of an exhibit at the British Library (October 1986–January 1987) on the centennial of Caldecott's death to "place his work within the tradition of narrative illustration" and show his role in the "English style" of picture books. Notes on woodcuts and other techniques of historic illustration, on Hogarth, Blake, Rowlandson, Cruikshank, Bennett, and Evans. Discussion of Caldecott and his work begins on p. 79. Homage and examples from illustrators who followed him are on pp. 84–106.

3. Arnold, Arnold. *Pictures and Stories from Forgotten Children's Books.* New York: Dover, 1969. 169pp.

   Chiefly, 485 b & w illustrations. Pages 1–8 give the history of children's literature and the attempts to change it. Sections on "morals and manners," "nursery rhymes," "street cries," "fairy tales," "anthropomorphism," "Robinsonads," "humor and riffles," "books on sports, games and pastimes," "periodicals" and "books that teach" have brief explanatory introductions before the reproductions of words and pictures.

4. Bader, Barbara. *American Picture Books from Noah's Ark to the Beast Within.* New York: Macmillan, 1976. 615pp.

Prodigious in scope, impressive in scholarship, yet a delightfully readable history. Chapters are sometimes devoted to significant illustrators (Wanda Gag, Dr. Seuss, Maurice Sendak); to subject matter (of the American Indian; Negro identification, Black Identity); to stylistic changes (the Dynamics and Fun of the Form, the Japanese Advent); and sometimes to the effects of cultural conditions (the American Line, Social Change, Foreign Background). Six hundred sixty-three reproductions (130 in color) provide visual examples for her critical analysis. Without a doubt, this is the major reference to use for a sense of the sweep of the American scene up to the mid-1970s.

5. Barr, John. *Illustrated Children's Books.* London: British Library, 1986. 89pp.

A brief, but sharply perceptive, 200-year history of English publications from Newbery to Rackham, to those in the Library's collection. Notes that the "special attraction" is that the illustrations had to be original graphics transferred by artist or craftsman to block or plate. "Techniques of reproduction," pp. 6–9, describes methods used and their influence on style. Carefully and fully illustrated with b & w and full-color reproductions along with discussions of the most important books and illustrators of this period.

6. Barry, Florence. *A Century of Children's Books.* New York: George H. Doran, 1923. 257pp.

A British history from chapbooks on.

7. Bator, Robert, ed. *Masterworks of Children's Literature; Volumes Three and Four: The Middle Period, 1740–1836.* 2 vols. New York: Stonehill Publishing with Chelsea House, 1983.

   Complete texts with some b & w illustrations for historic study.

8. Bingham, Jane. *Fifteen Centuries of Childrens' Literature: An Annotated Chronology of British and American Works in Historical Contexts.* Westport, Conn.: Greenwood, 1980. 540pp.

   It is necessary to look under the individual name of the author or illustrator to find picture book information. A straight chronology. Concise listing of major works. Short essays on each century.

9. Bland, David. *A History of Book Illustrations: The Illuminated Manuscript and the Printed Book.* Berkeley: University of California, 1969. 459pp.

   Profusely illustrated (436 illustrations) in b & w and color. Begins with Egyptian papyrus; codex continues with medieval and oriental illumination. From introduction of printing to 1520, country-by-country; from 1520 to 1600, country-by-country; eighteenth century, country-by-country; nineteenth century, country-by-country; and twentieth century, country-by-country. Children's books discussed in each period and country. Information well indexed. Includes Poland, Russia, etc.

10. Boston Museum of Fine Arts. *The Artist and the Book 1860–1960, in Western Europe and the United States.* Catalog of an exhibition. Cambridge, Mass.: Harvard University and the Boston Museum of Fine Arts, 1961.

    Children's books are barely represented since more celebrated artists, especially painters and sculptors, "seldom touched them."

11. Bravo-Villasante, Carmen. *Historia de la Literatura Infantil Espanola.* Madrid: Revista de Occidente, 1959. 270pp.

    Includes magazines for children, pp. 75–86. Some illustrations reproduced in color.

12. Brenni, Vito J., comp. *Book Illustration and Decoration: A Guide to Research.* Westport, Conn.: Greenwood, 1980. 191pp.

    Includes sections on reference works, book decoration, manuals of illustration and other writings on technique (e.g., etching, lithography, color printing). Also includes the history of illustration methods in individual countries from ancient times to present (in general and by time period), science and technology, medicine, music, geography and history. Part 7, "Illustration and Decoration in Children's Books," pp. 121–136, includes art, techniques, and principles on pp. 121–122, early history to 1900 on pp. 123–124, twentieth century on pp. 124–126, and in individual countries on pp. 126–136. Includes references to early sources not repeated in this bibliography.

13. Butler, Francelia, ed. *Masterworks of Children's Literature, Volumes One and Two: The Early Years, 1550–1739.* 2 vols. New York: Stonehill Publishing with Chelsea House, 1983.

    Complete versions of the texts of selected works, with some b & w illustrations.

14. Caradec, Francois. *Histoire de la ltterature enfantine en France.* Paris: Albin Michel, 1877. 271pp.

    Discusses the history of children's literature in France with references to some other countries. Pp. 129–139 cover illustrators.

15. Cott, Jonathan, gen. ed. *Masterworks of Children's Literature.* New York: Stonehill Publishing with Chelsea

House, 1983. See editors of individual volumes: Francelia Butler, *The Early Years, 1550–1739;* Robert Bator, *The Middle Period, 1740–1836;* Robert Lee Wolff, *The Victorian Age, 1837–1900;* Jonathan Cott, *Victorian Color Picture Books;* William T. Moynihan, and Mary E. Shaner, *The Twentieth Century.*

16. ———, *Masterworks of Children's Literature, Volume Seven: Victorian Color Picture Books.* New York: Stonehill Publishing with Chelsea House, 1983. 184pp.

Selections of text and color illustrations from works of Caldecott, Crane, Greenaway, Doyle, Ballantyne, and others. "A Dialogue with Maurice Sendak," pp. ix–xxi has detailed criticism of the artists and works included.

17. Cox, Alfred John. *The Making of the Book: A Sketch of the Book-Binding Art.* New Castle, Del.: Oak Knoll Books, 1986. 88pp.

From p. 37 on, simply a reprint of Cox's 1878 treatise, which discussed the book-binding art with "a few hints"; covered book-binding in Chicago at the time, gave a price list of books, and "commendations" from people who appreciated his binding work. Paul S. Koda's introduction discusses Cox's life, work, and its importance.

18. Crane, Walter. *Of the Decorative Illustration of Books Old and New.* London: Bracken, 1984, 1896. 243pp.

Many b & w illustrations. Crane's historic account of book design and illustration and what he considers a "revival" of printing as an art. His comments on children's books, pp. 126–132, include toy books.

19. Dalby, Richard. *The Golden Age of Children's Book Illustration.* New York: Gallery Books, 1991. 144pp.

More than 150 illustrations in b & w and color. Brief summaries of the artists' lives and careers are followed by descriptions of the books they illustrated. More than fifty artists are included, mostly English with a few Americans—lesser-known and famous—from Caldecott and Greenaway to Harry Clarke and Margaret Tarrant.

20. Darton, Frederick J. Harvey. *Children's Books in England: Five Centuries of Social Life.* Cambridge: Cambridge University, 1932. 2d ed., 1958. 3d ed. with extensive revisions by Brian Alderson, 1982. 398pp.

Some b & w illustrations. Although he does not deal with picture books specifically, he includes them in his historic survey. His comments on them and the processes used for them can be found in the index under "illustration" and "illustrations."

21. De Vries, Leonard. *Flowers of Delight.* New York: Pantheon Books, 1965. 232pp.

From the Osborne Collection of Early Children's Books. "An agreeable garland of prose and poetry for the instruction and amusement of little masters and misses and their distinguished parents. Embellished with some 700 elegant woodcuts and engravings on wood and copper of which upwards of 125 are neatly colored. Selected with the greatest care from books for juvenile minds, 1765–1830." Includes a note on the Osborne collection in Toronto, an anthologist's note on the history of children's books, some notes on the original books and on the writers, illustrators, and publishers. Bibliography.

22. Doyle, Brian, ed. *The Who's Who of Children's Literature.* New York: Schocken, 1968. 380pp.

One hundred and four plates of b & w illustrations. Emphasis is on English language authors and early classics from 1800 to 1968. "The Illustrators," pp. 304–357, is an alphabetical dictionary of illustrators with biographical information and their chief works listed. Medal winners are included.

23. *Early Children's Books and Their Illustration.* New York: Pierpont Morgan Library, and Boston: David R. Godine, 1975. 263pp.

Illustrated in b & w and color with facsimile pages and illustrations. Beginning with historical background, 225 outstanding examples of these books have been chosen from the library's collection to be discussed by type (Aesop's Fables, ABC's, primers, etc.) including comments on the illustration. Separate chapters cover Edward Lear, pp. 242–246, and Beatrix Potter, pp. 247–249. Other illustrators are accessible from the Index; e.g., Kate Greenaway.

24. *Fabulous and Familiar: Children's Reading in New Zealand, Past and Present.* Catalogue of an exhibition. New Zealand: National Library of New Zealand, 1991. 57pp.

Many book illustrations reproduced in color. Catalog of an exhibition commemorating twenty-five years of the library's service. An introductory chapter on children's reading from the 1890s to the 1940s by Mary Atwool mentions the important illustrators (pp. 10–11). Mary Hutton covers children's reading from 1940 to 1990 (pp. 21–41), with discussion of picture books from the U. S. (pp. 22–28), those from England (pp. 29–33), from Australia (pp. 36–37), and from New Zealand (p. 39).

Athol McCredie, in "Growing up with the *School Journal*: The Illustrations Since 1940" (pp. 42–47), covers trends and changes in illustration and raises provocative questions about the importance of quality art and its effect on young children. The publication is issued periodically by the government as a text each child owns.

Judy Taylor covers "Beatrix Potter and New Zealand" (pp. 48–52).

25. Feaver, William. *When We Were Young: Two Centuries of Children's Book Illustration.* New York: Holt, 1977. 96pp.

Chiefly color and b & w illustrations. A comprehensive international survey of techniques, sources, influences, and styles of the best-known illustrators from William Blake to Maurice Sendak.

26. Field, Louise Frances (Story). *The Child and His Book: Some Account of the History and Progress of Children's Literature in England.* London: W. Gardner, Darton and Co., 1891. 2nd ed., 1892. Reissued Detroit: Singing Tree, 1968. 358pp.

A few b & w illustrations. Includes history from "Before the Norman Conquest," and a discussion of the life of the child. Chapter XIV, "Some Illustrators of Children's Books," pp. 293–315, discusses the early illustrators from Bewick to the author's time. A very interesting comparison is drawn between the "too good" results of the improved technology and the "directness and simplicity of the older illustrations," and the effect on the reader.

27. Fraser, James H. *Society and Children's Literature: Papers Presented on Research, Social History, and Children's Literature.* Sponsored by the School of Library Science, Simmons College, and the Committee on National Planning for the Special Collections of the Children's Services Division of the American Library Association. May 14–15, 1976. Boston: Godine, 1978. 209pp.

Chapter 9, "Manuscripts of Children's Literature in the Beinecke Library" by Marjorie G. Wynne, pp. 139–149, includes descriptions of the letters of Edward Lear with illustrations, many works of Walter Crane, and Arthur Rackham's original illustrations for *Peter Pan in Kensington Gardens* in the collection at Yale.

28. Georgiou, Constantine. *Children and Their Literature.* Englewood Cliffs, N.J.: Prentice-Hall, 1969. 501pp.

Includes some b & w illustrations. Chapter 2, pp. 15–43, is a history of children's books. Chapter 4, pp. 61–

105, "Picture Books and Story Books," discusses nursery rhymes, alphabet and counting books, concept books, books for easy reading, and books on other cultures. Lists criteria, including design, but does not spend much time discussing or analyzing the illustrations. His annotations for his list of books include mention and description of illustrations.

29. Gobels, Hubert. *Hundert Alte Kinderbucher, 1870–1945: Eine Illustrierte Bibliographie.* Germany: Harenberg, 1981. 436pp.

Contains a page of information on each book, a b & w reproduction of each title page and two more pages, usually of illustrations, reproduced in b & w. "Nachwort," pp. 411–430.

30. Harthan, John. *The History of the Illustrated Book, The Western Tradition.* London: Thames and Hudson, 1981. 465pp.

Thirty-three pages are in color. For general historic background, some children's book illustrators are mentioned, such as Quentin Blake on p. 279, and Sendak, Macaulay, and Chwast on pp. 280–281. Examples of others' works are included.

31. Haviland, Virginia, and Margaret N. Coughlan, eds. *Yankee Doodle's Literary Sampler of Prose, Poetry and Pictures: Being an Anthology of Diverse Works Published for the Edification and/or Entertainment of Young Readers in America before 1900.* New York: Thomas Crowell, 1974. 466pp. Selected from the Rare Book Collections of the Library of Congress.

A brief introduction followed by reproductions of the books. Bibliography.

32. Hewins, Caroline Maria. *A Mid-Century Child and Her Books.* New York: Macmillan, 1926. Reprint, Detroit, Mich.: Singing Tree, 1969. 136pp.

Some small b & w illustrations. Describes her childhood and the books she remembers from the late nineteenth century, with some comments on the pictures. A reproduction of an old alphabet, pp. 123–136.

33. Huck, Charlotte S., with Susan Hepler and Janet Hickman. *Children's Literature in the Elementary School.* 4th ed. New York: Holt, Rinehart and Winston, 1987. 753pp. 5th ed. San Diego, Calif.: Harcourt Brace Jovanovich, 1993. 866pp.

Illustrated in b & w and color. All editions of this book have chapters on the history of children's books and on picture books, their art, and artists. In the 4th ed., chapter 3, "Changing World of Children's Books," pp. 94–142, covers the history here. Chapter 5, "Picture Books," pp. 195–249, including a multi-page color insert of illustrations, covers a definition, the art and the artists, the language, the content, guides for evaluation, and themes and subjects.

The 5th ed., chapter 5, "Picture Story Books" has expanded to pp. 238–304. "Art and Artists" are covered in pp. 241–264.

34. Hurlimann, Bettina. *Three Centuries of Children's Books in Europe*, translated and edited by Brian W. Alderson. Cleveland: World Publishing Co., 1967. 297pp.

Some b & w and color illustrations and photographs. This comprehensive historical picture includes: chapter 10, "Education Through Pictures," pp. 127–144, which covers the history of pictures in books. Chapter 11, pp. 145–151, "Photography," briefly discusses this type of illustration. Chapter 12, "Colour Prints," pp. 152–159, covers the historic addition of color. Chapter 13, "Wham! Sok! Thinks!" pp. 160–172, covers comic strips from Wilhelm Busch to Walt Disney. Chapter 15, "Jean de Brunhoff," pp. 195–200. Chapter 16, "Picture Books in the Twentieth Century," pp. 201–245, covers books from all countries and their production.

35. *Illustrators of Children's Books.* Catalog published yearly in conjunction with the Bologna International Children's Bookfair, 1980 to present. Publisher varies.

   Catalog of invited artists with examples of work and biographical information. From 1980 to present available. Picture Book Studio published the 1991 and 1992 editions, with two full pages of color reproductions of the illustrations of each selected artist.

36. *Images a la Page: Une Histoire de l'image dans les livres pour l'enfants.* Paris: Gallimard, 1984. 128pp.

   In conjunction with two exhibitions in Paris in 1984 and 1985, a group of writers have summarized the history of children's book illustration, with emphasis on France, and have discussed current changes in technology and their effects on the art and artists of today. Authors include Jean Claverie, Christiane Clerc, Etienne Delessert, Catherine Gendrin, Claude Lapointe, Yves Lebrun, Laura Noesser, Claude-Ann Parmegiani, Patrick Roegiers, Roland Topor, and Francois Vie. A list of active illustrators, with their works, is appended.

37. International Board On Books For Young People. Section française. *Dictionnaire des ecrivains pour la jeunesse—auteurs de la langue français.* Paris: Seghers, 1969. 214pp.

   A dictionary-like list of authors with their dates, brief notes, and list of their works, including a few illustrators. List of prize winners.

38. Jagusch, Sybille A., ed. *Stepping Away from Tradition: Children's Books of the Twenties and Thirties: Papers from a Symposium.* Sponsored by the Children's Literature Center and the Center for the Book in the Library of Congress. Nov. 15, 1984. Washington, D.C.: Library of Congress, 1988. 139pp.

   Four papers presented at the symposium. Of particular interest is Abe Lerner's "Designing Children's

Books: A Look at the Twenties and Thirties," pp. 37–49, which discusses this design as not a mystery but a craft, which he analyzes. He notes the freedom available because of the revolution in art, the new type, paper and improvements of the off-set process, and covers examples, challenges, and his own history in the field.

39. James, Philip Brutton. *Children's Books of Yesterday.* London/New York: Studio, 1933. Reprinted, Detroit, Mich.: Gale Research, 1976. 128pp.

   In addition to a brief introduction on the history of picture books, pp. 11–15, the book consists of reproduced half-page to full size pages of pictures from nineteenth-century children's books, in b & w, with notes on content, author, illustrator, etc.

40. Johnson, Diana L. *Fantastic Illustration and Design in Britain, 1850–1930.* Catalog of an exhibition with an essay by George P. Landow. Providence: Rhode Island School of Design, Museum of Art, 1979. 240pp.

   Chiefly illustration, some in color. Catalog of an exhibition at Museum and at Cooper-Hewitt Museum of the Smithsonian. Essay, pp. 9–27, discusses the nature and role of fantastic illustration and design and its relation to the political and social life of the times and artistic climate. The relationship between children's literature and fantasy and how the world of imagination in childhood is carried into maturity is discussed on pp. 15–16. Realms of literary fancy are covered in pp. 28–43. A list of items on exhibit with information on the object and the artist, if known, follows to p. 97. The rest of the book consists of plates.

41. Jones, Linda Harris. "A Comparison of the Works of Walter Crane, Randolph Caldecott and Kate Greenaway and Their Contributions to Children's Literature." Master's thesis, University of North Carolina, Chapel Hill, 1965. 57pp.

Thesis for Master's in Library Science. Following a brief historical summary, Jones summarizes the life and the work of Crane, pp. 9–23, Caldecott, pp. 24–29, and Greenaway, pp. 30–38, with some analysis of the style of individual works. Chapter V, "Comparisons of the Characteristics of the Artists' Work," pp. 39–46, finds many similarities in both their lives and their work. Chapter VI, pp. 47–52, shows Jones' appreciation of their contributions to the field of children's book illustration, including a discussion of children's preference studies. The bibliography includes works not covered in this selected bibliography.

42. Lewis, John. *The Twentieth Century Book.* New York: Van Nostrand Reinhold, 1967. 270pp.

Profusely illustrated in b & w and color. Chapter 7, pp. 176–241, deals with "The Illustration and Design of Children's Books." After a review of the popular books and illustrators of the late nineteenth century (adventures, fairy tales, Beatrix Potter) Lewis moves to the acceptance of the three- and four-color half-tones at the start of the twentieth century. The French added a "new look" in color lithography with Boutet de Monvel and others. Lewis discusses other artists such as de Brunhoff, Artzybasheff, Ardizzone, and new editions of classics. P. 216 begins "The Graphic Designer's Book," including a discussion of Ben Shahn. Finally, he discusses the design of books for schools.

43. Lima, Carolyn W., and John A. Lima. *A to Zoo: Subject Access to Children's Picture Books.* 3d Edition. New York: Bowker, 1989. 939pp.

Catalogs nearly 12,000 titles under 700 subjects. "Introduction: Genesis of the English-Language Picture Book," pp. xiii–xxiv, gives a succinct summary of picture book history with an extensive bibliography. The book itself offers access to picture books by way of a wide variety of subjects listed in the front. For use in libraries without key word search possibility or for quick personal memory-jogging. A title and an illustrator index are also helpful. No analysis or even discussion of text or illustrations.

44. Lystad, Mary. *From Dr. Mather to Dr. Seuss: 200 Years of American Books for Children.* Boston: Hall, 1980. 264pp.

Despite fifty b & w reproductions of illustrations from all periods, it is remarkable in its lack of attention to illustration, illustrators, and picture books. There is no index and no reference to illustrations in the table of contents. Includes social history and changing social values for children.

45. MacDonald, Ruth K. *Literature for Children in England and America from 1646 to 1774.* Troy, N.Y.: Whitston, 1982. 204pp.

Several cogent remarks (approx. twelve) about key people and books. Helps explain the role of pictures, qualities, techniques.

46. Madura, Nancy L. "The Impact of Phototechnology on the Illustrations in Picturebooks." Master's thesis, Ohio State University, Columbus, 1986. 93pp.

An exploration of the Victorian period's incorporations of the newly invented photographic reproduction capabilities as they affected the works of such illustrators as Crane, Greenaway, Potter, Dulac, etc. A summary timeline superimposes Processes, Inventions, Publications and Illustrators.

47. Mahoney, Bertha E., and Elinor Whitney. *Contemporary Illustrators of Children's Books.* Boston: Bookshop for Boys and Girls, 1930. 135pp. Reprinted, Detroit, Mich.: Gale, 1978.

Alphabetical listing of illustrators with a paragraph or two of bio-bibliographic information, some provided by the person; criticism also quoted. Small b & w illustrations throughout. Final section contains essays on types of illustrated children's literature in Germany and France, introduction on illustration by Lynd Ward, and essays on past influences: "The Bewicks: Thomas and John" by Wilbur Macy Stone, pp. 99–100. "The Fairies Come into Their Own" (on Cruikshank, Doyle, Tenniel, and Hughes) by Jacqueline Overton, pp. 101–109. "Tuppence Colored" (on Crane, Caldecott and Greenaway) by Jacquelene Overton, pp. 110–125. "The Brandywine Tradition: Howard Pyle and N.C. Wyeth" by Dudley Cammett Lunt, pp. 126–130. "About Lovat Fraser" by Rachel Field, pp. 131–132.

48. Mahony, Bertha E., Louise Payson Latimer, and Beulah Folmsbee, comps. *Illustrators of Children's Books, 1744–1945*. Boston: Horn Book, 1947. 527pp.

Contains many small and full-page b & w illustrations. Part I, "History and Development," includes articles on the history of children's books, on nineteenth-century British illustrators, on early American illustration, on "Howard Pyle and His Times" by Robert Lawson, pp. 103–122, on foreign picture books, on graphic processes, illustrators, animation, twentieth-century developments, and "The Book Artist: Yesterday and Tomorrow" by Lynd Ward, pp. 247–262. Part III, "Biographies," gives a dictionary listing of living illustrators with a paragraph of biographical information, names of works, and in some cases, quotations. Part IV, "Appendix," gives a bibliography of sources for each chapter of each section.

49. McCulloch, Lou. *Children's Books of the 19th Century*, photographic illustrations by Thomas R. McCulloch. Des Moines, Iowa: Wallace-Homestead, 1979. 152pp.

"An informative reference with prices, tracing the early history of children's books." Has some examples in color of many types of books, with related books and current values of each.

50. McLean, Ruari. *Victorian Book Design and Colour Printing.* 2d ed. Berkeley: University of California, 1972. 241pp.

   Many b & w illustrations and sixteen color plates. Larger format and different plates from earlier British edition. Includes information on the radical changes taking place at the time. Chapter 6, pp. 47–63, covers "Children's Books up to 1850."

51. Meyer, Susan E. *A Treasury of the Great Children's Book Illustrators.* New York: Abrams, 1983. 271pp.

   Profusely illustrated in b & w and color on almost every page. All of the illustrators discussed were born in the nineteenth century. The introduction gives details of the art, literature and technology of the period, and of the lives of children. Pp. 9–47 compare Britain and the United States. This handsome book is as valuable for its visual quality as it is for its verbal quality.

   The illustrators included are: Edward Lear, pp. 49–63; John Tenniel, pp. 65–77; Walter Crane, pp. 79–93; Randolph Caldecott, pp. 95–107; Kate Greenaway, pp. 109–125; Beatrix Potter, pp. 127–141; Ernest H. Shepard, pp. 143–155; Arthur Rackham, pp. 157–175; Edmund Dulac, pp. 177–193; Kay Nielsen, pp. 195–209; Howard Pyle, pp. 211–231; N. C. Wyeth, pp. 233–247; W.W. Denslow, pp. 249–265.

52. Morris, Charles Henry. *The Illustration of Children's Books.* London: Library Association, 1957. 18pp.

   Brief summary of history and techniques, including important names, pp. 1–16, is followed by notes on "the kinds of pictures which appeal to children," pp. 16–18.

53. Moynihan, William T., and Mary E. Shaner, eds. *Masterworks of Children's Literature, Volume Eight: The*

Twentieth Century. New York: Stonehill Publishing with Chelsea House, 1983. 333pp.

Actual texts not needed in this volume since they are readily available. Chapters summarize developments in major genres. Of particular interest: Ann Devereaux Jordan, "Small Wonders: Baby Books and Picturebooks," pp. 193–220, summarizes the developments in this area and analyzes what is currently available for the very young (baby books) and gives a quick overview of important figures and trends in picture books. Full-page b & w illustrations.

54. Muir, Marcie. *A History of Australian Children's Book Illustration.* New York: Oxford University Press, 1982. 160pp.

Relates the history of Australian children's books to that of books and illustrations in general and to Australian history. Chapters cover emerging Australian illustrators, special stories for boys and for girls, books about imaginary creatures as well as those peculiar to Australia. Traces developments between the wars and their flourishing after the second world war to the present. Mostly descriptive, rather than interpretive, criticism or analysis of illustrations. Many b & w and some color examples of the illustrations amplify the text.

55. Muir, Percy. *English Children's Books, 1600–1900.* New York: Praeger, 1954. 255pp.

Chapter 7, "The Importance of Pictures," pp. 172–204, includes the important names in picture books and illustrated books. The bibliography, pp. 192–196, is loaded with references for further study. List of books by date and artist, pp. 197–203. Technical processes, the work of Greenaway and Evans, Caldecott and Crane, are covered, with reproductions in b & w and elegant color. Chapter 8, "Nick-Nacks," pp. 204–217, discusses toy books, paper dolls, etc. "Three R's," pp. 217–226 covers didactic books.

56. ———. *Victorian Illustrated Books.* New York: Praeger, 1971. 287pp.

Chapter 2: "Catnachery, Chapbooks and Children's Books," sets the stage for the books that came later. Picture books and their illustrators are mentioned or discussed along with other illustrated books. Foreign influences, including American, are also discussed. Illustrated with b & w and a few color examples.

57. Pellowski, Anne. *The World of Children's Literature.* New York: Bowker, 1968. 538pp.

Comprehensive worldwide bibliography. Introductory essays on the state of children's literature in each area and country are followed by an annotated bibliography for that place. Access through the "Illustrations of Children's Books" entry in the index, country-by-country.

58. Peppin, Brigid. *Fantasy: The Golden Age of Fantastic Illustration.* New York: Watson-Guptill, 1975. 192pp.

"Introduction," pp. 7–22, covers the artists, their work and technique. Work for children is included, from artists Walter Crane, Edmund Dulac, Rudyard Kipling, Edward Lear, Kay Nielsen, Arthur Rackham, John Tenniel, and others. Chiefly color and b & w illustrations.

59. Peterson, Linda Kauffman, and Marilyn Leathers Solt. *Newbery and Caldecott Medal and Honor Books: An Annotated Bibliography.* Boston: G.K. Hall, 1982. 427pp.

Includes history of the medals, notes on characteristics and trends. Each book is listed with summary and critical commentary. Complete list to 1981. Appendix: terms, definitions, criteria, pp. 399–401.

60. Pickering, Samuel F. *John Locke and Children's Books in Eighteenth-Century England.* Knoxville: University of Tennessee, 1981. 286pp.

   Includes analysis of chapbooks, pp. 104–137. Clear b & w reproductions in original size.

61. Pitz, Henry Clarence. *Illustrating Children's Books: History, Technique, Production.* New York: Watson-Guptill, 1963. 207pp.

   Part I, "History," pp. 13–102, begins with Comenius in the seventeenth century; discusses the British graphic tradition from which children's illustrators emerged; covers European developments from 1800 on; covers America from early history through Pyle and the Brandywine tradition to the artists and techniques of the mid-twentieth century. Part II, "Technique and Production," begins with a division of the segments of children's books by age level and characteristics of each. He then describes the physical structure of the book and how to set up pages, discusses typography and design and the methods of reproduction of illustrations, plus the way to prepare for reproduction. Final tips are on the handling of an illustrating assignment. Includes b & w and color illustrations.

62. Poltarnees, Welleran. *All Mirrors Are Magic Mirrors: Reflections on Pictures Found in Children's Books.* La Jolla, Calif.: Green Tiger, 1972. 60pp.

   Thoughts on the purpose of children's books, descriptions and discussion of the work of many illustrators, including Maurice Sendak, Arthur Rackham, Kate Greenaway, and others, as he treats the "Realm of faerie," the relation between pictures and words, between author and illustrator, "domestic happiness" and "looking at pictures of animals." Profusely illustrated with b & w drawings and tipped-in color plates.

63. Prentice, Jeffrey, and Bettina Bird. *Dromkeen: A Journey into Children's Literature*. New York: Holt, 1987. 175pp.

   After describing Dromkeen, the "old homestead" near Melbourne, Australia, where two Australian booksellers began a collection of materials on Australian books for children, the authors give a history of Australian children's literature, with pp. 87–102 emphasizing "picture-story books." The ongoing educational activities at Dromkeen are delineated, including visits by illustrators such as Helen Oxenbury and John Burningham, Jeannie Baker, and Michael Foreman. Future plans are listed. An appendix lists the artwork in the collection as of January 1, 1985, along with the prepublication materials. Profusely illustrated in b & w and color with photos and reproduced art.

64. Ray, Gordon N. *The Illustrator and the Book in England from 1790–1914*. Catalog of an exhibition, March–April 1976. New York: Pierpont Morgan Library, 1976. 336pp.

   Discussion of the subject is included in this catalog of an exhibition of the author's collection at the Morgan Library. Among the illustrators whose works were in the exhibit and who have their lives and work described briefly are Edward Lear, pp. 59–62; Sir John Tenniel, pp. 116–117; Walter Crane, pp. 151–154; Randolph Caldecott, pp. 154–155; Kate Greenaway, pp. 156–157; and Arthur Rackham, pp. 203–206. Works by Beatrix Potter, Edmund Dulac, and Kay Nielsen are mentioned on pp. 208–209. Profusely illustrated, chiefly in b & w.

65. Reed, Walt, and Roger Reed. *The Illustrator in America, 1880–1980: A Century of Illustration*. New York: Madison Square, 1984. 355pp.

   A decade-by-decade survey listing artists with some information on their life and work. A few illustrators for children are included; e.g., Jessie Willcox Smith, N.C. Wyeth, Maurice Sendak. The index must be searched name-by-name. Profusely illustrated on every page, mainly in color.

66. Rosenbach, A.S.W. *Early American Children's Books with Bibliographic Descriptions of the Books in his Private Collection.* New York: Dover, 1971. 354pp.

    Describes the kinds of books historically available to children. Information on the illustrations must be derived from the individual descriptions and introduction. B & w illustrations.

67. Sale, Roger. *Fairy Tales and After: From Snow White to E.B. White.* Cambridge, Mass.: Harvard University Press, 1978. 280pp.

    Literary analysis of some fairy tales and other children's books and their authors. Part of the discussion of Beatrix Potter concerns her art. B & w illustrations.

68. Smith, Dora V. *Fifty Years of Children's Books, 1910–1960: Trends, Backgrounds, Influences.* Champaign, Ill.: National Council of Teachers of English, 1963. 149pp.

    Includes "Golden Age of Children's Books, 1925–1940," p. 32; the American picture book, p. 34; photographic picture books, p. 37; children's books in World War II and beyond (1940–1949); the picture book, pp. 55–56; children's books in a bursting world (1950–1960); more good picture books, pp. 67–70; "Summary: the Perfecting of the Picture Book," pp. 92–93. Many bibliographies; many small b & w reproductions.

69. Smith, Janet Adam. *Children's Illustrated Books.* London: Collins, 1948. 50pp.

    Gives a brief history. Covers toy books, boxes. "Illustrated Story Books" from p. 21 discusses Tenniel, MacDonald, Lear, and other Victorians, then Evans who made Crane, Greenaway, and Caldecott possible. P. 39 begins discussion of the twentieth century, Rackham,

Dulac, and others. Compares the best of modern books with contemporary posters and advertising lithography. With four plates in color and thirty-three b & w illustrations.

70. Targ, William, ed. *Bibliophile in the Nursery: A Bookman's Treasury of Collector's Lore on Old and Rare Children's Books.* Cleveland, Ohio: World, 1957. 503pp.

"Illustrators in the Nursery," pp. 468–487, by Richard Williamson Ellis, includes several paragraphs of notes on the life and works of illustrators from Caldecott, Crane, Greenaway, Pyle, and Rackham to Van Loon, de Angeli, Lawson, Sewell, Pitz, Artzybasheff and Duvoisin. A few b & w illustrations.

71. Thorpe, James. *English Illustration: The Nineties.* New York: Hacker Art Books, 1975. 268pp.

Establishes the environment of general illustration in which the talents of illustrators for children flourished, including periodicals as well as books. Individual illustrators are indexed. Illustrated with many b & w examples.

72. Thwaite, Mary F. *From Primer to Pleasure in Reading: An Introduction to the History of Children's Books in England from the Invention of Printing to 1914 With an Outline of Some Developments in Other Countries.* Boston: The Horn Book, 1963. 340pp.

In the context of a general history of children's literature, the section on "Picture Books and Books for Young Children," pp. 188–200, covers important names. The summary of other countries includes mention of important picture books. Contains twenty-eight pages of b & w illustrations.

73. Townsend, John Rowe. *Written for Children.* 3d ed. New York: Lippincott, 1987. 364pp.

Covers the history of all children's literature, including some b & w illustrations. "Picture Books in Bloom: USA," pp. 304–316, discusses and analyzes the top American illustrators; includes notes on their books. "Picture Books in Bloom: Britain," pp. 317–325, offers the same analysis of British illustrators.

74. Trignon, Jean de. *Histoire de la ltterature enfantine, de la Mere l'Oye au Roi Babar.* Paris: Hachette, 1950. 241pp.

This historic discussion includes both magazine and book illustrators, non-French (Crane, Rackham, Bilibin, Disney) and French, from Boutet de Monvel on. Illustrators are accessible in the index.

75. Tuer, Andrew W. *Pages and Pictures from Forgotten Children's Books.* London: Leadenhall, 1898, 1899. Reprinted, Detroit, Mich.: Singing Tree, Book Tower, 1969. 510pp.

Brief introduction, pp. 5–10, describes some of the books and how they were colored, followed by b & w reproduced pages from nearly a hundred old books.

76. Wakeman, Geoffrey. *Aspects of Victorian Lithography: Anastatic Printing and Photozineography.* Wymondham, Eng.: Brewhouse. 1970. 63pp.

Descriptions of these technical processes used for duplication of facsimiles in the nineteenth century. Inserted facsimiles.

77. Weinstein, Frederic D. *Walter Crane and the American Book Arts, 1880–1915.* New York: Columbia University, 1970. 271pp.

Useful bibliography primarily of pre-1925 references. A thoughtful, though less than totally convincing, analysis of Crane's influence on the design and illustration of American books. Children's books are given some special emphasis. Most useful for its total coverage of Crane's work.

78. Weitenkampf, Frank. *The Illustrated Book*. Cambridge, Mass.: Harvard University, 1938. 314pp.

    Historical approach, century-by-century, detailing technique and important people and places. Gives many examples in b & w of whole pages with lettering and illustration. Illustrators of children's books not important. Chapter 10, "Color Work and Children's Books," pp. 213–224 discusses the technique of color development especially in nineteenth-century England (Crane, Greenaway) and other countries (Boutet de Monvel, Pyle, Parrish, Bilibin), with some comments on adult attitudes about illustrations for children.

79. Whalley, Joyce Irene. *Cobwebs to Catch Flies: Illustrated Books for the Nursery and Schoolroom, 1700–1900*. Berkeley: University of California, 1974. 163pp.

    After a summary of the early history of pictures in books and of the techniques used, Whalley discusses didactic books by type: Alphabet, Counting, Religious Instruction, Moral Improvement, History, Geography and Travel, Street Cries and Occupations, Natural History and Science, Grammar, Music, Languages. The bibliography lists more books for study in each area in addition to books about these early books.

80. ———, and Tessa Rose Chester. *A History of Children's Book Illustration*. London: J. Murray with the Victoria and Albert Museum, 1988. 268pp.

    A remarkably complete and insightful history of the illustrations in English-speaking children's literature. Starting with a brief chapter entitled "In the Beginning," which shows seventeenth-century examples, the remaining eleven chapters focus on developments from "The Later 18th Century" into the 1980s. The British authors have used the extensive holdings of the Victoria and Albert Museum for examples, thus British titles dominate. The discussion includes chapters on chapbooks and toy books, and a chapter on the covers of children's books. "Reproduction Techniques of Book Illustration," pp. 245–248, adds valuable information. An unannotated bibliography, mostly British, and a "List of Early Publishers," useful in dating titles, extends the utility of this major reference work.

Note: An American edition entitled *The Bright Stream*, is scheduled for publication in 1994 by David Godine.

81. Wolff, Robert Lee, ed. *Masterworks of Children's Literature, Volumes Five and Six: The Victorian Age, 1837–1900*. 2 vols. New York: Stonehill Publishing with Chelsea House, 1983.

Texts of historic interest. See volume seven edited by Jonathon Cott for the color picture books of this period.

PART II

How a Picture Book Is Made

82. Aliki. *How a Book Is Made.* New York: Crowell, 1986. 32pp.

   A picture book for children which details the steps in the production of a picture book from the author's idea to arrival in the bookstore. Shows the role of the editor, artist, designer, copyeditor, typesetter, proofreader, production director. Details how the art is reproduced and the other steps of printing and production.

83. Althea (Althea Braithwaite). *Making a Book.* Cambridge, Eng.: Dinosaur, 1980. Unpaginated.

   This picture book for children simply and succinctly describes how a typical book is produced, from typesetting to bookshop.

84. Bang, Molly. *Picture This: Perception & Composition.* Boston: Little, Brown, 1991. 141pp.

   Bang provides a ready access to the structure of picture books by "Building a Picture" using cut paper geometric shapes and the *Little Red Riding Hood* story. Subsequent sections deal with "The Principles" (of design) "Some Remarks about Space," and "Arranging Shapes on a Rectangle." Suggested for use by adolescents, this book's insights and many strikingly clear color illustrations make it valuable for anyone who wants to understand how pictures tell stories.

85. Behrmann, Christine. "The Media Used in Caldecott Picture Books: Notes toward a Definitive List." *Journal of Youth Services in Libraries* 1, No. 2 (Winter 1988): 198–212.

   The author has attempted to list the original art media used for all Caldecott Medal and Honor books. A list of useful art definitions is included.

86. Brookfield, Karen. *Book.* New York: Knopf, 1993. 64pp.

   Chiefly color photographs and some drawings with paragraphs of information and captions. Covers origin of writing, paper, and books in different formats from all over the world. Describes the materials and methods of printing and binding, plus other areas of writing and the book market. Illustrated books are discussed on pp. 48–49, and children's books on pp. 54–55.

87. Clarke, Grace Dalles. "A Publisher's Perspective." *Horn Book* 68, no. 3 (May–June 1992): 365–368.

   Grudgingly acknowledging the "supremacy of the text," the former illustrator and art director, now editor, describes the ever-changing role of the art director and/or designer of a picture book.

88. Colby, Jean Poindexter. *Writing, Illustrating and Editing Children's Books.* New York: Hastings House, 1967. 318 pp.

   Includes some b & w photographs, diagrams and illustrations. Part I discusses writing. Part II, pp. 91–207, discusses illustration and production. The qualities that are necessary for each age group through high school are listed and defined with examples. Requirements for the illustrator, given here, may be outdated by current technology. Includes setting fees and getting started. Pp. 131–148 give a timetable for a picture book, what really happens in the course of producing the book among all those concerned (editor, production manager, printer) from start to printing. Pp. 149–172 discuss typography and book design with examples; pp. 173–186 detail printing methods; and pp. 187–198 discuss binding and jackets, with examples. Pp. 199–208 covers "Production Close Calls: What Can Go Terribly Wrong," and Part III, "Editing," is of general interest. Covers awards and the Children's Book Council.

* Cox, Alfred John. *The Making of the Book: A Sketch of the Book-Binding Art.* Cited above as item 17.

89. *Creating Jack and the Bean Tree: Tradition and Technique.* Sound filmstrip. Weston, Conn.: Weston Woods, 1987. 95 frames, 17½ min.

  In addition to placing her book about Jack (Crown, 1986) into its folklore tradition and North Carolina mountain setting, Gail Haley discusses her research and demonstrates how she created the illustrations.

90. Edwards, Michelle. *Dora's Book.* Minneapolis, Minn.: Carolrhoda, 1990. 32pp.

  Using the picture book format and story-telling form, Edwards tells the tale of Dora and her friend Tom. They hand print and bind copies of a book she has written and illustrated. With her color illustrations, Edwards shows all the steps needed to produce a book by hand.

91. *Evolution of a Graphic Concept: The Stonecutter.* Sound filmstrip. Weston, Conn.: Weston Woods, 1977. 1 filmstrip, 1 cassette. 71 frames, 15 min.

  The artist, Gerald McDermott, describes his background and his choice to tell this tale to film and then to illustrate. His research, step-by-step development process, including decisions made, and all steps of the art world are described and shown.

92. Fakih, Kimberly Olson. "Tying up the Talent: Exclusivity
    Deals and Brand Name Publishing." *Publishers Weekly*
    235, no. 20 (May 19, 1989): 39–43.

    Covers some of the picture book artists who have
    signed exclusive contracts and some who have not, with
    comments from the publishers and notes on the
    advantages and disadvantages.

93. Frank, Jerome P. "Children's Books: Coming Home to
    Print?" *Publishers Weekly* 235, no. 8 (February 24, 1989):
    199–206.

    Individual publisher's decisions are noted, such as
    Greenwillow's decision to stay abroad, in this discussion
    of the move of children's book printing back from Pacific
    Rim countries. Other publisher's choices are covered, as
    is the current use of a scanner, rather than color
    separation, for reproducing illustrations.

94. *Gail E. Haley: Wood and Linoleum Illustration.* Sound
    filmstrip. Weston, Conn.: Weston Woods, 1978. 1
    Filmstrip, 1 Cassette. 72 frames, 17 min.

    The artist herself tells something of the history of
    printmaking. Then she uses her work for *A Story A Story*
    as an example to show how her illustrations evolved
    from her inspirations in African art, how she did the
    illustrations from drawings, and joined paper figures
    through linoleum blocks and watercolor painting.

95. Garrett, Caroline S. "A Fairytale Book: Exploration into
    Creating an Art Form." Master's thesis, Ohio State
    University, Columbus, 1985. 68pp.

    Evolution of a theory of fairytales and the testing of
    the relationship of text and illustration through the
    creation of an illustrated original story.

96. Gates, Frieda. *How to Write, Illustrate and Design Children's Books.* Monsey, N.Y.: Lloyd-Simone, 1986. 155pp.

   A comprehensive manual full of practical wisdom. Sections include a very brief history, analysis of categories of books, details of techniques and media, specifications for step-by-step production, marketing procedures, and contract advice. The 276 b & w illustrations and fifty-three color reproductions provide crucial information. An elaborate glossary is useful in defining the many technical terms.

97. Goldenberg, Carol. "The Design and Typography of Children's Books." *Horn Book* 69 no. 5 (September–October 1993): 559–567.

   Covers the role of the book designer, specifically information on the picture book, from first encounter through all the decisions that must be made from type face to jacket and binding.

98. Gordon, Stephan F. *Making Picture-Books: A Method of Learning Graphic Sequence.* New York: Van Nostrand Reinhold, 1970. 96pp.

   Chiefly b & w illustration. Discusses subject, style, theme, page design, and materials and gives examples, not necessarily for children's books. Especially good for demonstrating sequential techniques, needed for picture books, beyond just the design of individual pages.

99. Greenfeld, Howard. *Books from Writer to Reader.* New York: Crown, 1976. 211pp.

   B & w and color examples of illustrations. Clear analysis of literary agent, publishing house, role of the editor, how an illustrator prepares work for publication, what the copy editor, designer, jacket designer, production supervisor, compositor, proofreader and indexer do. Includes how the book is printed, how color work is done, the binding, the trip from publisher to warehouse to bookstore, and, finally, the publicity and reviews that bring it to the attention of the reader. Glossary.

"The Completely Revised and Updated Edition," dated 1989, updates all the valuable information noted above. It has also added a chapter on "Desk-Top Publishing." 197pp.

100. Gross, Gerald, ed. *Editors on Editing*. Rev. ed. New York: Harper & Row, 1985. 373pp.

In addition to information on all kinds of editing, it also contains: Ann Beneduce, "Planting Inflammatory Ideas in the Garden of Delight: Reflections on Editing Children's Books," pp. 258–264, which includes some comments on picture books and their makers.

101. Hands, Nancy S. *Illustrating Children's Books: A Guide to Drawing, Printing, and Publishing*. Englewood Cliffs, N.J.: Prentice-Hall, 1986. 166pp.

Some b & w illustrations and a four-page color insert. Provides useful examples for would-be illustrators. The writing is simple with frequent exercises, questions, and practical advice to assist the user. Chapters cover such logical topics as "Looking at Artists at Work," "Types of Children's Books," "Preparing Art for Printing," and "Publishing." A glossary, four pages of resources, and a brief history of illustrated books are useful supplements.

102. Harms, Jeanne McLain, and Lucille J. Lettow. "Book Design: Extending Verbal and Visual Literacy." *Journal of Youth Services in Libraries* 2, no. 1 (Winter 1989): 136–142.

A detailed analysis of all aspects of book design from format through jacket, end papers, front matter, half-title and title page, and finally, the whole body. Many examples from picture books are included. Shows how to "expand meaning" and "develop aesthetic appreciation." Includes a bibliography of well-designed picture books.

103. Hart, Thomas L. "Delinquent Youth Write and Illustrate their Own Books." *American Libraries* (November 1990): 998–1000.

    Describes a project in the Dade County (Miami) Juvenile Justice Center School where Phyllis Segor, a library media specialist, inspired delinquent youths to write and illustrate their own books using Apple computers.

104. Holtze, Sally Holmes. "One Man's Art of Bookmaking." *The Five Owls* (September–October 1988): 15–16.

    Describes the work of Vincent Torre at the Inkwell Press, where he publishes the books that he has written, hand-set in type, cut the illustrations from wood blocks, then hand-cranked through a press. Small b & w illustrations.

105. *How a Picture Book Is Made: The Making of* The Island of the Skog *from Conception to Finished Book.* Sound filmstrip. Weston, Conn.: Weston Woods, 1976. 66 frames, 10 min.

    Steven Kellogg tells how he became a picture book artist. He describes, from first ideas to printed book in hand, all the steps taken and people involved in the production of his picture book.

106. Irvine, Joan. *How to Make Pop-Ups.* Barbara Reid, illus. New York: Morrow, 1987. 93pp.

    Irvine carefully explains the materials and methods used to make pop-ups, fold-outs, slides, and other devices that can be used for books or cards. She also shows how to combine them into a book. B & w drawings throughout.

107. ———. *How to Make Super Pop-Ups*. Linda Hendry, illus. New York: Morrow, 1992. 96pp.

More ideas for bigger and better constructions than her earlier book cited in item 106. No books, as such, are shown. B & w drawings throughout.

108. Jacques, Robin. *Illustrators at Work*. London: Studio Books, 1963. 112pp.

Although only a few children's book artists are included among the succinct biographies in this practical reference, the sections on the historical influences and technical information of "processes of reproduction" and the business of illustration provide relevant insights. This book is limited to b & w artists working "in the main English illustrative tradition." Over seventy illustrations.

109. Jenkins, Patrick. *Flipbook Animation and Other Ways to Make Cartoons Move*. Ontario: Kids Can Press, 1991. 96pp.

Includes instructions on how to make a flipbook, some cinemagraphic techniques that demonstrate picture sequencing, and several early "motion-picture devices," with b & w illustrations.

110. Jennett, Se-an. *The Making of Books*. 4th ed. London: Faber and Faber, 1967. 512pp.

Includes b & w photos and illustrations. Although the first part on printing and binding is out of date, part two, "The Design of Books," pp. 199–476 shows principles that still apply.

111. Jensen, Virginia Allen. "A Picturebook for the Blind." *Bookbird* (January 1980): 7–12.

An account of the creation of *What's That*, a picture book for blind youngsters, with much on the technical problems of printing a book that appeals to all sorts of children and can be produced economically.

112. Johnson, Paul. *A Book of One's Own: Developing Literacy Through Making Books*. Portsmouth, N.H.: Heinemann, 1990. 119pp.

Includes many b & w photos and drawings. After a chapter on "The Book as Art" pp. 7–14, in which he discusses books as art objects, including some one-of-a-kind books, Johnson starts by helping children to find a story to tell. Subsequent chapters demonstrate ways of making books with children, clearly showing processes and many examples of children's books.

113. Kehoe, Michael. *A Book Takes Root: The Making of a Picture Book*. Minneapolis, Minn.: Carolrhoda, 1993. 48pp.

A step-by-step depiction (filled with color photograph illustrations), of the production of the picture book *Green Beans* from the author's original idea through the editorial process to the designer's choice of illustrator. The artist is then shown developing the story's illustrations from sketches and the dummy to full color art. The role of the designer, the choice of typeface, the work of the typesetter and of the keyliner are noted. A clear explanation of the four-color printing process is followed by printing and binding. A glossary of terms is included.

114. ———. *The Puzzle of Books*. Minneapolis, Minn.: Carolrhoda, 1982. Unpaginated.

B & w photographs on every page of this children's book make clear the people and the operations involved in making a particular book, from the arrival of the author's manuscript at the editor's desk, through the work of the artist, designer, typesetter, keyliner, cameraperson, stripper, platemaker, printer, and binder to produce the book for library or bookstore. Note the updated version of this information in Kehoe's newer book cited above.

115. Kurth, Heinz. *Print a Book.* Baltimore, Md.: Penguin, 1975. 32pp.

    A picture book for children which discusses the production process, shows tone block and color separation, and finally encourages the reader to make a flip-book, giving full instructions.

116. "A Look at the Creative Process." *Publishers Weekly* 234, no. 5 (July 29, 1988): 134–140.

    With photos and small reproductions. The authors and illustrators who discuss the problems and challenges of their current publication include Barry Moser on *In the Beginning,* John Agee on *The Incredible Painting of Felix Clousseau,* Anthony Browne on *Alice's Adventures in Wonderland,* and Barbara Cooney on *Island Boy.*

117. Lucas, Barbara. "Picture Books for Children Who Are Masters of Few Words." *School Library Journal* 19 (May 1973): 31–35; and *Library Journal* 98 (May 15, 1973): 1641–1645.

    In showing why picture books "cost so much," Lucas details how a book is made, including the role of the editor and some of the costs of color processes, paper, etc.

118. Martin, Douglas. *Book Design: A Practical Introduction.* New York: Van Nostrand Reinhold, 1991. 206pp.

    With many b & w illustrations, chapters cover text, typeface, format, book anatomy, and materials. Chapter 7, "Working with Illustrators," is of particular interest. A very extensive glossary and a useful annotated bibliography are included.

119. Martin, Rodney. *The Making of a Picture Book.* John Siow, illus. Milwaukee, Wisc.: Gareth Stevens, 1989. 32pp.

Profusely illustrated, mainly in color, with photographs, drawings, and reproductions of illustrations. Demonstrates the evolution of an actual picture book, *There's a Dinosaur in the Park* (published in Australia and done by this team) from the notes on an idea and a photo taken later through the editing of text and selection of illustrator. Then we are shown the work at the publishing house of the editor, the designer, the keyliner, the film house where the color proofs are made, the production director, and the printer. Finally the pages are cut, sewn, bound, and there is a production party to celebrate.

120. Marzollo, Jean. "Bookmaking Made Simple." *Instructor* (May–June 1991): 36–42.

    Step-by-step instructions with color illustrations for making blank books. This can help demonstrate how books are put together.

121. Mestrovich, Marta. "Perestroika and Picture Books." *Publishers Weekly* 238, no. 10 (February 22, 1991): 128–131.

    Discusses the difficulties encountered when Russian-American co-publishing is attempted. Covers several examples of successful collaboration, with color and b & w illustrations. Separate notes on Gennady Spirin.

122. Mitgutsch, Ali. *From Picture to Picture Book.* Minneapolis, Minn.: Carolrhoda, 1986. 24pp.

    In words simple enough for very young children to understand, Mitgutsch describes how a picture book comes to be, from the idea, through production, to story time at home. Humorous color illustrations alternate with text pages.

123. Montanaro, Ann R. *Pop-up and Movable Books: A Bibliography.* Metuchen, N.J.: Scarecrow, 1993. 559pp.

"A record of nineteenth and twentieth century (1850s–1991) English-language books containing movable illustrations." Clear definitions of terms describing types of books, such as "lift-the-flap," "double-page pop-up," etc. After a brief history, a list by title includes annotations. Other indexes by name of author, illustrator, consultant, series, and date.

124. Olmert, Michael. *The Smithsonian Book of Books*. Washington, D.C.: Smithsonian, 1992. 319pp.

Profusely illustrated with more than 350 photographs and reproductions in b & w and color. A stunning example of book art using large, glossy pages that capture the nuances of the replicated works, and a comprehensive treatment of the worldwide history of books, bookmaking, and libraries. "A Picture's Worth . . ." pp. 235–253 deals specifically with book illustrations (including some for children), and with the history and development of various technologies for their reproduction. "Mother Goose and Company" pp. 254–265 discusses a few of the key figures in children's books from Potter to Sendak.

   * Pitz, Henry Clarence. *Illustrating Children's Books: History, Technique, Production*. Cited above as item 61.

125. Rixford, Ellen. "Making Dimensional Illustrations." *American Artist* 53, no. 568 (November 1989): 70–74.

Discusses many techniques of making illustrations in three dimensions, using a wide variety of materials including paper, clay, wood, fabric, and assemblages in boxes. Color illustrations.

126. Roback, Diane. "I Spy: More Than Meets the Eye." *Publishers Weekly* 240, no. 15 (April 12, 1993): 26–28.

The team of Walter Wick and Jean Marzollo, who together create the "I Spy" books for Scholastic, discuss with Roback how they work together. Color photos show how Wick puts the scenes together for Marzollo to write the rhymes.

127. Roberts, Ellen E. M. *The Children's Picture Book: How to Write It, How to Sell It.* Cincinnati, Ohio: Writer's Digest, 1981. 189pp.

Although mainly concerned with the writing, Roberts defines the picture book, describes the structure and types, covers the essential elements and the basic steps from idea to production. Also covers the business and how to enter it, with information on contracts, agents, royalties, etc. Some small b & w illustrations, and 28pp. of color plates.

128. Ryder, John. *The Case for Legibility.* New York: Moretus, 1979. 77pp.

Profusely illustrated with b & w examples and diagrams. Discusses how the design of a book can aid in its legibility, with the various steps to be taken, the choices to be made; i.e., typeface, paper, margins, spaces, up to jacket design.

129. See, Lisa. "The Art of Children's Books: Every Picture Tells a Story." *Publishers Weekly* 237, no. 30 (July 27, 1990): 212.

Describes the establishment and current operation of the Los Angeles art gallery Every Picture Tells a Story including the artists represented and current prices.

130. Shulevitz, Uri. *Writing with Pictures: How to Write and Illustrate Children's Books.* New York: Watson-Guptill, 1985. 271pp.

Profusely illustrated in b & w and color. Large and handsomely designed. Part I defines picture books and story books and shows actual story telling picture sequences, good and poor, and defines elements of story and the refining of it. Part II begins with the storyboard and dummy. Elements of size, shape, and scale are shown with many examples, as are the parts of a book from jacket to sewing. Part III, "Creating the Pictures," gives examples and contrasts others to show the purpose of illustration (decoration, expressiveness, etc.). Lessons in drawing figures and objects include examples of many kinds and demonstrate how to use reference sources, including nature, for some details. Notes on elements of composition also include many examples. Drawing techniques are demonstrated, as are steps toward a personal style. Part IV details steps necessary to prepare artwork for reproduction, including the nature of the printing process, color preparation, and examples from his own work on different techniques to reproduce for the effect desired.

131. Stan, Susan. "Conversations: Susan Hirschman." *The Five Owls* 2, no. 1 (September–October 1987): 7.

Brief summaries of how the editor at Greenwillow works with the artist/author, especially her experiences with alphabet books. B & w photos.

132. Stone, Bernard, and Arthur Eckstein. *Preparing Art for Printing.* Rev. ed. New York: Van Nostrand Reinhold, 1983. 194pp.

A detailed explanation of the processes of modern commercial printing and how the graphic artist must work with them to prepare artwork for printing. Includes tools and equipment and covers one-color and multi-color printing. All terms are explained in detail. Profusely illustrated in b & w and color.

133. *Story of a Book.* Series 1. Literature for Children. Sound filmstrip. Verdurgo City, Calif.: Pied Piper, 1970. 1 filmstrip, 1 cassette.

Tells how Holling C. Holling created *Pagoo* from idea through research, writing, and illustrating, to printing and publishing.

134. Weiss, Ava. "The Artist at Work: The Art Director." *Horn Book* 61, no. 3 (May–June 1985): 269–279.

Describes how she became an art director and details her work on picture books throughout their production. Some small b & w illustrations.

135. *The Well-Built Book: Art and Technology.* Video. Film. Stamford, Conn.: Book Manufacturers Institute, 1990. 28 min.

Covers manual construction of a book: signatures, collation, sewing, or gluing and covering. Then describes process of production through shipping.

136. Wells, Rosemary. "Words and Pictures: The Right Order." *Publishers Weekly* 231, no. 8 (February 27, 1987): 146.

In her call for good stories for picture books, Wells discusses both the writing and the illustration, with her conviction that the words are primary. Photo.

* Whalley, Joyce Irene, and Tessa Rose Chester. *A History of Children's Book Illustration.* Cited above as item 80.

137. Wilson, Rodger B. "The Genesis of a Picturebook: A Personal Journal of the Creation of a Children's Picturebook from the Conception to Final Printing." Master's thesis, Ohio State University, Columbus. 1979. 123pp.

A brief history, with particular attention to the technical means of printing illustrations, sets up a thorough chronological analysis of the varied experiences involved in creating and having a picture book published.

138. Yokoyama, Tadashi. *The Best of 3–D Books.* Tokyo: Rikuyo-sha Publishing, 1989. 155pp.

Except for a few pages in English and Japanese describing the different types of 3–D books and how they are constructed, this is all chiefly color photos of about 100 recent outstanding 3–D books of all kinds.

139. Zwicker, Marilyn. "Creating Children's Books at the Rochester Folk Art Guild." *Wilson Library Bulletin* 55, no. 2 (October 1980): 118–122.

Description of the process used by the guild in designing and processing general picture book titles.

PART III

Criticism of Children's Picture Books, Including Their "Use" with Children

140. Abrahamson, Richard F., and Robert Stewart. "Movable Books—A New Golden Age." *Language Arts* 59, no. 4 (April 1982): 342–347.

    A discussion of some of the new "toy" or movable books, how they are made, and their authors. Reproductions of old books are noted.

141. Alderman, Belle, and Lauren Harman, eds. *The Imagineers: Writing and Illustrating Children's Books.* Canberra, Australia: Reading Time, 1983. 171pp.

    Collection of papers given at the Children's Book Council of Australia ACT Branch October Seminars 1981–1982. Illustrators discussing their work include: Bruce Treloar, pp. 41–53, on the development of *Bumble's Dream* from gestation to finished book. Pamela Allen, pp. 133–148, tells how she does picture books in general and of some problems with particular books. Elizabeth Honey, pp. 155–168, discusses how she became an illustrator and how she works. Brief biographical sketches and references are included for all. The work of the editor is covered by Kay Ronai, pp. 113–125. Information on judging for the Book of the Year awards is given by Diana Page and Belle Alderman on pp. 69–99. Some b & w illustrations and photographs.

142. American Institute of Graphic Arts. *Children's Books* (*AIGA Journal* III, no. 3. 1967/1968) 74pp.

A series of short articles covers the judging of this America Institute of Graphic Arts exhibition of children's books; problem of designing for the preschool group; illustrations in school textbooks; designing books for practical uses; and a review of foreign picture books.

143. Andersen, Anne. "Teaching with Picture Books" (The Literature-Based Classroom). *The Five Owls* VII, no. 2 (November–December 1992) : 31.

Summarizes ways to incorporate study of picture books into the teaching of sixth graders, with many examples.

144. Andreae, Christopher. "Artists' Adventures in Wonderland." *Christian Science Monitor* (May 23, 1989): 16–17.

An analysis of Anthony Browne's *Alice's Adventures in Wonderland* includes comments and references to the versions of several other illustrators, with b & w illustrations.

145. Apseloff, Marilyn. "Books for Babies: Learning Toys or Preliterature." *Children's Literature Association Quarterly* 12, no. 2 (Summer 1987): 63–66.

Analyzes both text and illustration of some of the many new books for the very young, and questions their educational value, with a mention of the qualities of illustration.

146. Arakelian, Paul G. "Text and Illustration: A Stylistic Analysis of Books by Sendak and Mayer." *Children's Literature Association Quarterly* 10, no. 3 (Fall 1985): 122–127.

Comparison of Mayer's *There's a Nightmare in My Closet* with Sendak's *Where the Wild Things Are* using page layouts and sentence structures. Combines formal techniques with considerable descriptive information.

147. *Art and Man* 21, no. 6 (April–May 1992): 16pp.

Published for young people by Scholastic under the direction of the National Gallery of Art, this issue of the art magazine is concerned with "The Art of Illustration," with a special feature on Maurice Sendak. Profusely illustrated in color, the entire issue covers illustrations and their relationship with story-telling, including an article on animation.

148. Aubrey, Irene Elizabeth. *Notable Canadian Children's Books*. Ottawa: Ministry of Supply and Services, yearly.

The 1983 supplement, for example, reviewed thirty-two books in sixty-two pages.

149. Avery, Gillian. "The Cult of Peter Pan." *Word and Image* 2, no. 2 (April–June 1986): 173–185.

An analysis of British children's literature focuses on its illustrators' depiction of fairies, with an emphasis on the Edwardian years. Such artists as Margaret Tarrant, Mabel L. Atwell, and Ernest Shepard are included in this sociological survey of the Peter Pan type of childhood they exemplified.

* Bader, Barbara. *American Picture Books from Noah's Ark to the Beast Within*. Cited above as item 4.

* Bang, Molly. *Picture This: Perception & Composition*. Cited above as item 84.

150. Barclay, Donald A. "Interpreted Well Enough: Two Illustrators' Visions of *Adventures of Huckleberry Finn*." *Horn Book* 68, no. 3 (May–June 1992): 311–319.

Of course *Huckleberry Finn* is not a picture book, but Barclay's analysis and comparison of the illustrations done by Edward Windsor Kemble (the first illustrator of the book), with those of Barry Moser are of interest. The design and relationship of text and illustration, the illustrations themselves, the fact that they appear at all in a novel today, are all analyzed, with three b & w illustrations.

* Barr, John. *Illustrated Children's Books.* Cited above as item 5.

151. Barron, Pamela, and Jennifer Q. Burley, eds. *Jump over the Moon: Selected Professional Readings.* New York: Holt, Rinehart and Winston, 1984. 512pp.

A collection of reading from many sources on the "concerns of the literature for early childhood" expressing many points of view. Made to accompany a television course co-produced by the University of South Carolina and the South Carolina Educational Television Network.
Many articles are directly concerned with illustration and picture books; some appear separately listed in this bibliography. Of particular interest are part 6, "Illustrations," pp. 157–192; and part 11, "Sharing Picture Books," pp. 348–491.

152. Bator, Robert. *Signposts to Criticism of Children's Literature.* Chicago: American Library Association, 1983. 345pp.

This collection of articles, speeches, etc. on aspects of children's literature includes a section entitled "Picture books," pp. 149–165. After an introduction, the articles included are: Kenneth Marantz, "The Picture Book as Art Object: A Call for Balanced Reviewing," pp. 152–156; Blair Lent, "There's Much More to the Picture Than Meets the Eye," pp. 156–161; including the role of the artist as well as discussion of picture books. Margaret Matthias and Graciela Italiano, "Louder Than a Thousand Words," pp. 161–165, analyze the importance of illustration and style.

153. *Beginning with Excellence: An Adult Guide to Great Children's Reading.* Cambridge, Mass.: Sound Advantage, 1992. 3 audio-cassettes, 6, 30-min. programs.

> *Horn Book* and twenty-five writers and illustrators offer comments and information about themselves and their work. Artists include: Chris Van Allsburg, Tomie dePaola, David Macaulay, James Marshall, and Maurice Sendak.

* Behrmann, Christine. "The Media Used in Caldecott Picture Books: Notes toward a Definitive List." *Journal of Youth Services in Libraries*. Cited above as item 85.

154. *The Ben Yitzak Award for Distinguished Illustration of a Children's Book.* Pamphlet. Jerusalem: The Israel Museum, printed every two years starting 1986.

> A pamphlet with information in English and Hebrew is issued including information about the award-winning book and the Honor books, with color illustrations.

155. Benedict, Susan, and Lenore Carlisle, eds. *Beyond Words: Picture Books for Older Readers and Writers*. Portsmouth, N.H.: Heinemann, 1992. 142pp.

> Illustrations by children. The aim is to demonstrate how picture books can and have been used with older students for enjoyment, inspiring book-making, and inviting discussion on many subjects. Many examples of student reaction are given. Unfortunately, the art of the book and its illustration are seldom dealt with. Chapters that do deal seriously with the visual include:
> Bishop, Rudine Sims, and Janet Hickman. "Four or Fourteen or Forty: Picture Books Are for Everyone" pp. 1–10. A discussion of the definition of a picture book, some notes on quality of illustration, and an analysis of some notable picture books are included.
> Rynerson, Barbara Bagge. "'Whoa! Nigel, You're a Wild Thing,'" pp. 21–32. Among other discussions with

a class of grades 1 and 2, the author includes "A Closer Look at Illustrations," with comparisons and contrasts.
Le Tord, Bijou. "Research: An Adventure," pp. 123–124;
Councell, Ruth Tietjen. "Illustrating Handel: A View from the Drawing Board," pp. 125–128. Two illustrators talk about research and decisions made for particular books.

156. Benson, Ciaran. "Art and Language in Middle Childhood: A Question of Translation." *Word and Image* 2, no. 2 (April–June 1986): 123–140.

A thoughtful examination of the relationships between words and pictures, two distinct "symbol systems," and the ramifications of "translation" when we speak of the "experience of a picture." What distortions in meaning occur in the transformation from picture to word? Both psychological and philosophical sources are exploited and the concept of "inner speech" is explored.

157. Berridge, Celia. "Illustrators, Books, and Children: An Illustrator's Viewpoint." *Children's Literature in Education* 2, no. 1 (Spring 1980): 21–30.

Review of a range of studies relating to children's responses to pictures which indicated inconclusive or erroneous findings. Comments by some major illustrators point out their alienation from any child audience. The question of consciously creating illustrations to meet the tastes of children remains a matter of "splendid controversy."

158. Bingham, Jane M., ed. *Writers for Children: Critical Studies of Major Authors Since the Seventeenth Century.* New York: Scribner, 1988. 661pp.

Critical essays, biographies, and bibliographies which include some illustrators; all deceased. The space devoted to their art varies from a lot to nothing. The authors and the artists analyzed include Marilyn F. Apseloff on Edward Ardizzone (pp.15–20); Ethel Heins on Ludwig Bemelmans (pp. 55–61); Roderick McGillis on William Blake (pp. 69–76), with nothing on his art; Ann M. Hildebrand on Jean de Brunhoff (pp. 91–96); Karen Nelson Hoyle on Virginia Burton (pp. 111–115); Elaine A. and Edward C. Kemp on James Daugherty (pp. 155–161), with no art included; Karen Nelson Hoyle on Wanda Gag (pp. 241–246); Avi on Robert Lawson (pp. 345–349); Myra Cohn Livingston on Edward Lear (pp. 351–356); Ruth K. MacDonald on Beatrix Potter (pp. 439–446); and Jill P. May on Howard Pyle (pp. 447–454).

159. Bishop, Rudine Sims. "Books from Parallel Cultures: New African-American Voices." *Horn Book* 68, no. 5 (September–October 1992): 616–620.

Along with discussion of chapter books, Bishop includes comments on new picture books by African-Americans Dolores Johnson and James Ransome, among others.

160. Bitzer, Lucy. "The Art of Picture Books: Beautiful Treasures of Bookmaking." *Top of the News* 38, no. 3 (Spring 1982): 226–232.

The Art Director of Four Winds Press analyzes media, style, and expressive content of many historic and contemporary illustrators. Also details what to look for from dust jacket through end papers, half-titles, etc. An appreciation of the qualities evident in the best. Six small b & w illustrations.

161. Blumenthal, Eileen Polley. "Picture Books For Chinese Children." *Intellect* 106 (March 1978): 357–358.

With photographs of examples. From her dissertation at the University of Michigan, shows how moral models are reinforced in the children's books, which cost little or nothing, and are issued in editions of a million.

162. Bodner, George R. "The Post-Modern Alphabet: Extending the Limits of the Contemporary Alphabet Book from Seuss to Gorey." *Children's Literature Association Quarterly* 14, no. 3 (Fall 1989): 115–117.

    A rather rapid overview of both Seuss and Gorey, with focus on their ABC production, using these as examples of a shift from didacticism to entertainment.

163. *Books for Children: Bibliography.* Wheaton, Md.: Association for Childhood Education International, 1989. 128pp.

    This puzzling collection includes sixteen pages of annotations of picture books with no criteria for selection other than "only certain titles of some excellent but prolific authors." Comments almost totally neglect the pictures.

164. Bornens, Marie-Therese. "Problems Brought About by 'Reading' a Sequence of Pictures." *Journal of Experimental Child Psychology* 49, no. 2 (April 1990): 189–226.

    A study of about 150 French children, ages 3–7, using several methods for testing their understanding of how pictures create narratives. Examples used were created for the study (b & w drawings reproduced). Findings suggest that Piaget's theory of "active interiorized imitation" is faulty and that Chomsky's concept of "pre-existing structures" is more useful. This study shows the evolution of visual narrative comprehension from earliest age to the six-year-old.

165. Bosma, Bette. *Fairy Tales, Fables, Legends and Myths: Using Folk Literature in Your Classroom.* New York: Teachers College, 1987. 116pp.

    Three pages call attention to the values of illustrations in some books and suggest a few projects for appreciation and making pictures. Although no criteria are given, illustrations "worthy of note" are starred in the extensive list of recommended books.

166. ———. *Fairy Tales, Fables, Legends, and Myths.* 2nd ed. New York: Teachers College Press, 1992. 189pp.

The annotated bibliography, "A Guide to Recommended Folk Literature for Children," pp. 111–159, makes brief mention of the art while an asterisk again marks illustrations "Worthy of Note." "Visual Art," p. 91, simply suggests related art activities.

167. Bostian, Frieda F. "On Using Balloons Sparingly." *Children's Literature Association Quarterly* 15, no. 1 (Spring 1990): 13–16.

A thoughtful analysis of the uses of balloons in picture books: for dialogue, for emphasis, to add interest, and as a form of stage whisper. The author perceives them as a "semiotic device . . . the perfect bridge between the visual and the verbal."

168. Brown, Marcia. *Lotus Seeds: Children, Pictures and Books.* New York: Scribner, 1985. 224pp.

Fourteen speeches and other pieces written by Brown in the years from 1949–1984, including her three Caldecott speeches. Covers such topics as the world of children's books, her own techniques of work, and her reflections on people, life, and art. She writes from the heart of the picture book renaissance, bringing to facts and names a special sense of spirituality.

169. Busbin, O. Mell, and Susan Steinfirst. "Criticism of Artwork in Children's Picture Books: A Content Analysis." *Journal of Youth Services in Libraries* 2, no. 3 (Spring 1989): 256–266.

A statistical analysis of five major reviewing periodicals seeking answers to five fundamental questions about reviewers' attention to the visual components of picture story books for children in grades K–3. Findings indicate that "reviewers are [not] knowledgable about . . . illustrations of picture books."

170. Butler, Francelia, ed. *Children's Literature Volume 1.* Philadelphia: Temple University Press, 1972. 186pp.

Includes Julie Carlson McAlpine, "Sendak Confronts the 'Now' Generation," pp. 138–142, covering Sendak's answers to questions about his work at the University of Connecticut, December 10, 1970.

171. ———. *Children's Literature Volume 2.* Philadelphia: Temple University Press, 1973. 256pp.

Includes Annabelle Simon Cahn's "Leo Lionni, Artist and Philosopher," pp. 123–129, which discusses his life, studio, technique, works, and philosophy; includes quotations. Two b & w illustrations.

172. ———. *Children's Literature Volume 3.* Philadelphia: Temple University Press, 1974. 256pp.

Includes Justin G. Schiller's "Artistic Awareness in Early Children's Books," pp. 175–185, historic notes read at the Second Children's Book Showcase, Drexel, March 19, 1973.

173. ———. *Children's Literature Volume 6.* Philadelphia: Temple University Press, 1977. 298pp.

Includes: Christa Kamenetsky's "Arthur Rackham and the Romantic Tradition: The Question of Polarity and Ambiguity," pp. 115–129, with b & w illustrations; Jennifer R. Waller's "Maurice Sendak and the Blakean Vision of Childhood," pp. 130–141; and reviews of Newbery and Caldecott winners, 1975–76, by David L. Greene, pp. 191–194.

174. ———. *Children's Literature Volume 12.* New Haven: Yale University, 1984. 255pp.

Includes Geraldine DeLuca's "Exploring the Levels of Childhood: The Allegorical Sensibility of Maurice Sendak," pp. 3–24, with some discussion of the visual aspects of his work.

175. -———. *Children's Literature Volume 13*. New Haven: Yale University, 1985. 228pp.

Includes Ruth B. Bottligheimer's "Iconographic Continuity in Illustrations of *The Goosegirl*," pp. 49–71, which analyzes many versions in the history of the tale; Michael Steig's "Reading *Outside Over There*," pp. 139–153, analyzes several reviews of the book and gives Steig's own interpretation including the illustrations.

176. Callaghan, Linda Ward. "Caldecott Citations: A Selective Bibliography." *Journal of Youth Services in Libraries* 1, no. 2 (Winter 1988): 160–167.

Brief annotations on materials on all aspects of the Caldecott medal, including the history, acceptance speeches, illustrators, and the art of illustration.

177. Callahan, Joan F. "The Picturebook as the Central Focus of an Elementary Art Curriculum." Master's thesis, Ohio State University, Columbus. 149pp.

Using Bruner's "spiral curriculum" model as a jumping off point, this study makes a case for picture books as esthetic objects which can help children learn about the structure of art history as well as the methods of the professional artist to develop critical and appreciative skills needed in all esthetic enterprises.

178. Carroll, Joyce Armstrong. *Picture Books: Integrated Teaching of Reading, Writing, Listening, Speaking, Viewing, and Thinking*. Leann Mullineaux, illus. Jackdaws Series no. 1. Englewood, Colo.: Teacher Ideas Press/Libraries Unlimited, 1991. 64pp.

Twenty-eight relevant picture books are presented to demonstrate how they may be exploited for a series of connection and extension activities focussed around themes in various subjects in grades 1–12. Subject matter rather than artistic qualities are exploited even in the "Art Connections" suggestions. Extensive, but unannotated, bibliography.

179. ———. *Story Books: Integrated Teaching of Reading, Writing, Listening, Speaking, Viewing, and Thinking.* Leann Mullineaux, illus. Jackdaws Series no. 2. Englewood, Colo.: Teacher Ideas Press/Libraries Unlimited, 1992. 64pp.

More connection and extension activities. Although most of the books used are picture books, there is an almost total neglect of their visual qualities. No mention of the illustrators is given in the bibliographic credits. "Art Connections," where they exist, lack any esthetic function. Extensive, but unannotated, bibliography.

180. Cascardi, Andrea E. *Good Books to Grow On: A Guide to Building Your Child's Library from Birth to Age Five.* New York: Warner, 1985. 130pp.

An annotated list, including mainly picture books, by age level, with brief notes on the illustrations. Illustrators are indexed.

181. Cass, Joan E. *Literature and the Young Child.* 2d ed. England: Longman, 1984. 130pp.

Combines quality books with children ages 2–8. Chapter 2, "Picture Books and Their Illustrators," pp. 4–15, covers phases of perceptual development and how the needs for the familiar, for color, for pictures "strong and clear in outline" can be met. Also discusses the role of the illustrator with examples of children's preferences, design, and typography.

182. Chambers, Nancy, ed. *The Signal Approach to Children's Books*. Metuchen, N.J.: Scarecrow, 1980. 352pp.

Selections from the publication *Signal* include: "Signal quote" from Edward Ardizzone, pp. 32–33, an analysis of what the good illustrator does and what skills are needed. "Picture books and verse," pp. 64–65, lists important contemporary British author-illustrators. "The Cinderella story, 1724–1919," by Irene Whalley on p. 144, describes early illustrations. Some b & w illustrations.

183. Chapman, Diane L. "The New Look of Children's Picture Books." Paper presented at the annual meeting of the International Reading Association, St. Louis, Mo. May 1980. ERIC Microfiche ED 189607 80. 29pp.

Summarizes innovations of style and media used, lists some artists and styles, and how the media used reflects character. Discusses photography, wordless books, "problem books," and gives lists of some of these with some evaluation.

184. "Children's Book Illustrators Play Favorites." *Wilson Library Bulletin* 52, no. 2 (October 1977): 165–173.

Arnold Lobel, Karla Kuskin, Trina Hyman, and Tomie dePaola talk about their favorite illustrators and why they like them.

185. *Children's Books International 1*. Proceedings of a conference. Boston: Boston Public Library, 1976. 134pp.

The proceedings of a conference include an interview with a Japanese artist (Kazue Mizumura); an illustrated talk on illustrators of Grimm tales; and a panel discussing some issues of illustrating in "The Business of Books." Sixty pages are devoted to a catalog of titles exhibited. There are no illustrations of books reproduced.

186. *Children's Books International 2.* Proceedings of a conference. Boston: Boston Public Library, 1977. 154pp.

   The proceedings of a conference include an illustrated talk mainly about the animated books of Meggendorfer (late nineteenth century); a history of the Biennale of Illustrations in Bratislava; and a catalog (65pp.) of displayed books. No reproductions included.

187. Cianciolo, Patricia. "Developing the Beginning Reading Process with Picture Books." Paper presented at the meeting of the "Five Year Olds in School" Conference, East Lansing, Mich. January 9–10, 1987. ERIC Document ED 280013. 26pp.

   Research, especially in the 1970s, has shown the importance of picture books, especially those of quality, to a child's early reading process. Of five qualities listed by the author, of special interest are #3: Relation of text and illustration, and #4: Illustration quality beyond the literal, pp. 2–3. Includes analysis of some picture books and a fine professional bibliography.

188. ———. *Illustrations in Children's Books.* 2d ed. *Literature for Children* series. Dubuque, Iowa: Wm. C. Brown, 1976. 210pp.

   Designed mainly for teachers, but librarians and parents should also learn from the large quantities of information provided. Chapters describe how to appraise illustrations; identify styles (taken from the art world) which she feels illustrated books have in common; explain many of the media and techniques illustrators use; and finally, offer a variety of means for the illustrations to be used in schools. Half the book is devoted to an annotated bibliography of illustrated books, a list of some wordless books, and basic information about Caldecott titles and those from the Children's Book Showcase. Some b & w illustrations.

189. ———. *Picture Books for Children.* 2d ed., rev. and enl. Chicago: American Library Assn., 1981. 237pp.

Introduction, pp. 1–29, discusses what a picture book is, her criteria for selections, some notes on styles of art in general and of that in picture books, and categories of response and subjects. The remaining pages are an annotated bibliography arranged in categories from "Me and My Family," out to others, the world and imaginary worlds. Index of authors, illustrators and titles. Some b & w illustrations.

190. ———. *Picture Books for Children.* 3d ed. Chicago: American Library Assn., 1990. 230pp.

Most titles in this edition are new entries, published through March 1989. Of particular interest are chapter 1, "Choosing Picture Books," pp. 1–40; "The Picture Book as Art," pp. 25–28; and "Criteria for Evaluating a Picture Book," pp. 29–38. The annotated bibliography follows.

191. ———. "Use Wordless Picture Books to Teach Reading, Visual Literacy and to Study Literature." *Top of the News* 29 (April 1973): 226–234.

Along with analysis of the literary devices and elements in these books, there is some analysis of style. There is also a bibliography of useful books. Also in Mary Lou White's *Children's Literature.*

192. *Collected Perspectives: Choosing and Using Books for the Classroom.* Edited by Hughes Moir, Melissa Cain, and Leslie Prosak-Beres. Boston: Christopher-Gordon in association with Cooperative Services for Children's Literature at the University of Toledo, 1990. 280pp.

Collected from *Perspectives,* a book review journal written by teachers and librarians on "how to use new books in schools and libraries." Includes "best books" of 1984–1988. "Picture Story Books," pp. 1–67, includes a good selection of 128 titles, but the comments are inconsistent and weak on illustration.

193. Considine, David M. "Visual Literacy and Children's Books: An Integrated Approach." *School Library Journal* 33, no. 1 (September 1986): 38–42.

After defining visual literacy and stating its importance to young people today, the author shows how illustrations in children's books can help develop these skills. Unannotated resources listed include picture books, videos, filmstrips, and a few curriculum projects. Some b & w illustrations.

194. Cott, Jonathan. *Pipers at the Gates of Dawn: The Wisdom of Children's Literature.* New York: Random House, 1983. 327pp.

Introduction has personal reflections on the importance of children's literature. "The Good Dr. Seuss," pp. 3–37, includes a visit, interview, and critical discussion, plus two-page history of first children's book. "Maurice Sendak, King of All Wild Things," pp. 41–84, includes biographical information, criticism, and commentary. "William Steig and his path," pp. 88–133, includes an interview, an analysis of early cartoons and detailed discussion of books. Some b & w illustrations and photographs.

*   ———, gen. ed. *Masterworks of Children's Literature, Volume Seven: Victorian Color Picture Books.* Cited above as item 16.

195. Crago, Maureen, and Hugh Crago. *Prelude to Literacy: A Preschool Child's Encounter with Picture and Story.* Carbondale, Ill.: Southern Illinois University, 1983. 294pp.

Reports on, but also attempts to interpret, one child's comments on color and other aspects of pictures in books from age twelve months to five years. Art examples from "fine art" are included. Discusses picture preference in light of previous research.

196. Cross, Jennifer Lynn. "Artistic Interpretation in the Fairytale Picturebook." Master's thesis, Ohio State University, Columbus, 1987. 234pp.

First the study establishes the symbolism and form of traditional Western fairy tales, then it investigates the problems of illustration within this tradition by means of analysis of several versions of Grimm's tales, and through creating an original picture book.

197. Cullinan, Bernice E., ed. *Children's Literature in the Reading Program*. Newark, Del.: International Reading Assn., 1987. 171pp.

Chapter 8, "Enriching the Arts and Humanities through Children's Books," by Sam Leaton Sebesta, pp. 77–81, is concerned with artists of both "fine art" and picture books, and discusses ways to introduce and discuss their work with children.

198. ———, with Mary K. Karrer, and Arlene M. Pillar. *Literature and the Child*. New York: Harcourt Brace Jovanovich, 1981. 594pp.

Basically a textbook for Children's Literature classes. Includes "Historical View of Children and Books," pp. 35–69. The chapter on picture books is by subject, with a few pages on art techniques, and on criteria for selection. Profiles of book authors and illustrators with quotations and critical analyses are throughout the book. Useful teaching suggestions and appendices. Includes some photographs and some color illustrations.

199. ———. *Literature and the Child*. 2d ed. San Diego, Calif.: Harcourt Brace Jovanovich, 1988. 730pp.

Update with newly published titles and illustrator profiles.

200. Darling, Harold, and Peter Neumeyer, eds. *Image and Maker: An Annual Dedicated to the Consideration of Book Illustration*. La Jolla, Calif.: Green Tiger, 1984. 56pp.

Profusely illustrated in b & w with tipped-in color plates. Contents include:

"How Picture Books Work," by Perry Nodelman, pp. 1–12, tries to show "how very much pictures control our responses to words" by analyzing some examples.

"What Manner of Beast? Illustrations of *Beauty and the Beast*," by Stephen Canham, pp. 13–25, compares several versions and their effect.

"Luther Daniels Bradley: Guide to the Great Somewhere-or-Other," by Helen Borgens, pp. 26–36, is an appreciation of Bradley's life and work.

"Jessie Willcox Smith," by Carolyn Haywood, pp. 37–42, covers Smith's life and work.

"The Great Catalogs: An Alternate Way to Study Early Children's Book Illustration," by Kenneth E. Luther, pp. 43–54, describes catalogs from several sources and gives order information.

201. Darton, Frederick Joseph Harvey. *Modern Book Illustration in Great Britain and America*. London/New York: The Studio Limited/William Edwin Rudge, 1931. 144pp. (Special Winter number of "The Studio," edited by C. Geoffrey Holme.)

Almost every other page has a full-page b & w illustration up to p. 79, seven in color. Pp. 80–144 are all illustrations. Some discussion of the history of technique, mainly in adult books, with children's books on p. 75.

202. dePaola, Tomie. "From Lascaux to Hi-Tech." Fourth Annual Naomi Chase Lecture, June 2, 1983. *New Books for Young Readers*. Minneapolis: University of Minnesota, 1984: 18–23.

A personal view of the role of the artist-illustrator through history.

203. Dirda, Michael. "The New Golden Age of Kids' Books." *Connoisseur* (September 1990): 75–83.

 A personal overview of some of "the field's finest fabrications, new and old"; includes some notes on the good picture book as "the artistic artifact" with an analysis of the qualities of current books and classics.

204. Dondis, Donis A. *A Primer of Visual Literacy.* Cambridge: Massachusetts Institute of Technology, 1973. 194pp.

 Useful for acquiring vocabulary for approaching and analyzing two-dimensional graphic imagery. Chapter VI, pp. 104–127, uses simple contrasts to point out techniques used by designers; e.g., transparency vs. opacity.

205. Dooley, Patricia. "The Window in the Book: Conventions in the Illustration of Children's Books." *Wilson Library Bulletin* 55, no. 2 (October 1980): 108–112.

 Some history of the appearance of illustrations and their points of view, and how technology has led to some changes.

206. Doonan, Jane. "The Object Lesson: Picturebooks of Anthony Browne." *Word and Image* 2, no. 2 (April–June 1986): 159–172.

 A close-reading analysis of several of Browne's works, presenting evidence of the "liberating power of his art," an art that deals with aspects of the human condition. Surrealism and focus on gorillas are two major themes. B & w illustrations.

207. Dorfman, Ariel. *The Empire's Old Clothes: What the Lone Ranger, Babar, and Other Innocent Heroes Do to Our Minds.* New York: Pantheon, 1983. 225pp.

 Nothing on illustration, but a fascinating sociopolitical analysis of Babar, among others.

208. Dressel, Janice Hartwick. "Abstraction in Illustration: Is It Appropriate for Children?" *Children's Literature in Education* 15, no. 2 (Summer 1984): 103–112.

An argument that first sketches the twentieth-century evolution of "abstract" art and then makes a case for its suitability for picture book illustration. "Abstract art must be interpreted on the basis of its existence alone . . . "

209. Driesson, Diane Z. "A Description of a Select Group of Six Fifth Grade Students' Response to Picturebooks." Ph.D. diss., Ohio State University, Columbus, 1984. 190pp.

How do children with several years of picture-book school experience respond to picture books in terms of preferences and varying attributes of book design? An open-ended questioning procedure is used in small group and individual settings.

210. Durand, Marion, and Gerard Bertrand. *L'image dans le livre pour enfants.* Paris: L'Ecole des Loisirs, 1975. 220pp.

Profusely illustrated in color and b & w with examples from many countries. This comprehensive treatment of children's book illustration deserves the wide readership only a translation into English could deliver. The analysis of style, the discussion of the role of word and text and their interrelationship, the treatment of the principal characters, human or animal, realistic or caricature, serious or humorous, are all done with a keen analytic eye and many examples. The discussion of the variety of contemporary styles, including photography, is of particular interest. Political and social connotations are also covered.

211. ———. "One Hundred Years of Illustrations in French Children's Books," translated by Diana Wormuth. *Yale French Studies*, no. 43 (1969): 85–96.

Demonstration of the claim that children's book illustration has suffered "a gradual impoverishment" by critical analysis of several exemplars. Speculation that the low status of illustrators today, compared with a hundred years ago, may be a major cause of the decline.

212. Duvoisin, Roger. "Children's Book Illustration: The Pleasures and the Problems." *Top of the News* 22, no. 1 (November 1965): 299–316.

His views on "what is an illustration and what makes it beautiful" from an "artistic point of view." He discusses the design problems involved and how they relate to the audience of children, the role of abstraction, some history of illustration and its relation to art history and painting.

213. Egoff, Sheila A., ed. *One Ocean Touching: Papers from the First Pacific Rim Conference on Children's Literature.* New York: Scarecrow, 1979. 252pp.

Includes: Margaret Johnston, "Surprised by Joy: The World of Picture-Books," pp. 147–154. Picture books are shown as the " . . . basis of all literature, so also . . . the basis of art criticism." Discusses briefly what makes a good picture book, and mentions some books that she feels have the important qualities from the U.S., England, and Canada.

Graham Booth, "The Price of Being an Artist," pp. 155–163, relates how he became a book illustrator; the reality of working as an illustrator; his problems and fears; his working methods and the economics of the business.

Elizabeth Cleaver, "Picture Books as Artform," pp. 195–196, discusses the influences on her work; her personal feelings and method of working; and the economic hardship of the business.

214. ———. *The Republic of Childhood: A Critical Guide to Canadian Children's Literature in English.* 2d ed. Toronto: Oxford University Press, 1975. 335pp.

Chapter 9, "Illustration and Design," pp. 255–270, covers some Canadian illustrators of the past plus newer illustrators and their techniques. Chapter 10, pp. 271–291, "Picture-Books and Picture Storybooks," discusses these as a more recent and independent development from illustration alone; "A Separate Genre," distinguishes between picture books and picture storybooks and gives many examples of current books and their creators in Canada. Lists of titles and award winners for illustration included.

215. Eisner, Elliot W., ed. *Reading, the Arts, and the Creation of Meaning.* Washington, D.C.: National Art Education Association, 1978. 160pp.

Includes Kenneth Marantz, "On the Mysteries of Reading and Art: The Picture-book as Art Object," pp. 71–87, which investigates some of the problems that differentiate written language and pictures as symbol systems. Denies the reasonability of art as a language and points out that the reading process is still a mysterious one because there are no "global equivalents of word signs."

216. Elleman, Barbara. "Caldecott Winners Are Picture Perfect." *Gifted Children Monthly* 7, no. 6 (June 1986): 16–17, 20.

Summarizes Caldecott Medal background and analyzes current winners and some of the best from the past.

217. ———. "Discovering Art Through Picture Books." *Gifted Children Newsletter* 4, no. 12 (December 1983): 16–17.

Giving many examples of picture books to use, Elleman shows how to introduce the art to children.

218. ———. "Picture-Book Art: Evaluation," "Sources." *Booklist* (June 15, 1986): 1548–1549.

Elleman briefly summarizes the challenge of evaluating the art of a picture book, with suggestions of a method to do so, and a list of sources she has found helpful.

219. England, Claire, and Adele M. Fasick. *ChildView: Evaluating and Reviewing Materials for Children.* Littleton, Colo.: Libraries Unlimited, 1987. 207pp.

After some discussion of child development, "Materials for Early Childhood" are covered on pp. 53–77, including formats. Details of characteristics of "sophisticated picture books" for older children and adolescents on pp. 60–61, of "picture art books," p. 62, illustrations specifically, pp. 62–71, design and typography, pp. 71–73, with a "Checklist" on pp. 74–75.

220. *Enjoying Illustrations.* Sound filmstrip. *Literature for Children* series 3. Verdugo City, Calif.: Pied Piper, 1971. 1 Filmstrip, 1 cassette.

Covers forty artists. Discusses the role of the illustrations and encourages comparisons of versions of the same story.

221. Estes, Glenn E., ed. *American Writers for Children Since 1960: Poets, Illustrators, and Nonfiction Authors.* Detroit, Mich.: Gale, 1987. 430pp.

There is a brief biography for each person, an analysis of their work, a list of books, original art sketches, and sources for further information. Artists are;
Marcia Brown, by Mary Ann Heffernan, pp. 7–14;
Tomie dePaola, by Anne Sherrill, pp. 15–26;
William Pene du Bois, by Susan Garness, pp. 27–37;
Roger Duvoisin, by Agnes D. Stahlschmidt, pp. 38–49;
Leonard Everett Fisher, by Mell Busbin, pp. 57–67;

Theodor Seuss Geisel, by Myra Kibler, pp. 75–86;
M. B. Goffstein, by Janice Alberghene, pp. 87–98;
Edward Gorey, by Douglas Street, pp. 99–107;
Trina Schart Hyman, by Hugh Crago, pp. 108–115;
Ezra Jack Keats, by Richard Seiter, pp. 116–125;
Steven Kellogg, by Millicent Lenz, pp. 126–132;
Leo Lionni, by Lesley S. Potts, pp. 139–152;
Arnold Lobel, by Jacqueline Gmuca, pp. 165–176;
David Macaulay, by Nellvena Duncan Eutsler, pp.
177–188;
James Marshall, by Hugh T. Keenan, pp. 189–199;
Mercer Mayer, by P. Gila Reinstein, pp. 200–209;
Evaline Ness, by Philip A. Sadler, pp. 234–242;
Richard Scarry, by Bobbie Burch Lemontt, pp. 248–
257;
Maurice Sendak, by John Cotham, pp. 258–272;
Uri Shulevitz, by Sue Lile Inman, pp. 273–281;
Peter Spier, by M. Sarah Smedman, pp. 282–296;
William Steig, by Joy Anderson, pp. 297–305;
Chris Van Allsburg, by Laura Ingram, pp. 306–313;

"Afterword: Children's Book Illustration in the Twentieth Century," by Anne Devereaux, pp. 315–322, a historical survey, briefly analyzes some artists' techniques, including some not in this book.

Book Awards and Prizes are discussed on pp. 325–365, with a Bibliography, pp. 367–370.

222. Evans, Dilys. "An Extraordinary Vision." *Horn Book* 67, no. 6 (November–December 1991): 712–715.

Discusses the art of illustration thirty years ago, with its use of black and white and pre-separated colors, and the artists who did it well. Then both the art world and the printing industry went through great changes which affected book illustration. Evans introduces here her interest in these changes that will continue to concern her.

223. ———. "An Extraordinary Vision: Picture Books of the Nineties." *Horn Book* 68, no. 6. (November–December 1992): 759–763.

Describes the "unique look" of current picture books with particular reference to the art of Lane Smith and Jeannie Baker.

224. ———. "Wordless Picture Books—The Medium Is the Message." *Booklinks* (March 1992): 46–49.

Analyzes five top-quality wordless or almost wordless picture books; all but one published in 1991. Offers suggestions for further activities after reading them with children. One illustration from each book is reproduced.

225. Eyre, Frank. *British Children's Books in the Twentieth Century.* New York: E.P. Dutton, 1971. 153pp.

"Books with pictures" discusses what illustration should be and what makes a successful picture book. Also gives the history of picture books in Britain and mentions many books, both familiar and unfamiliar, to Americans. His appendix on books from Commonwealth countries mentions some regional picture books, authors and illustrators. "Award Winners" includes those from Britain, Australia, New Zealand, and Canada.

* *Fabulous and Familiar: Children's Reading in New Zealand, Past and Present.* Cited above as item 24.

226. Ford, Elizabeth A. "Resurrection Twins: Visual Implications in *Two Bad Ants*." *Children's Literature Association Quarterly* 15, no. 1 (Spring 1990): 8–10.

An analysis, somewhat amplified by the responses of "two five-year-olds I shared the book with," which concludes that the pictures desensitize the reader to the ant as a living creature by depicting these in violently destructive situations similar to some popular cartoons.

227. Fox, Geoff, and Graham Hammond, eds. *Responses to Children's Literature: Proceedings of the Fourth Symposium of the International Research Society for Children's Literature Held at the University of Exeter, September 9–12, 1978.* New York: K.G. Saur, 1980. 141pp.

Includes: Stuart Amor, "A Functional Approach to Illustrations in Children's Books—The Work of Frantisek Holesovsky," pp. 76–80. Summarizes the approach of the Czech theorist as a possible spur to analysis or further research.

Agnia Barto, "Children's Responses to Illustrations of Poetry," pp. 81–87, contains personal experiences and reflections on these responses.

Carmen Bravo-Villasante, "Text and Illustration in Emblem Books," pp. 88–91, contains historical information on these symbolic images.

Patricia Cianciolo, "Children's Responses to Illustrations in Picture Books," pp. 102–108, summarizes studies of responses and references and relates them to children's previous experience.

Janine Despinette, "Modern Picture Books and the Child's Visual Sense," pp. 109–116, discusses the importance of the illustration beyond simply the didactic, and the psychological and aesthetic effects of the picture on the child, giving some examples from specific books.

Joseph Schwarcz, "The Continuous Narrative Technique in Children's Literature," pp. 117–126, gives an analysis of illustration of time passing and research on its psychological effect on children of different ages.

Bela Toth, "Psychological Relationships Between Text and Illustration," pp. 129–130, describes experiments on eight- to ten-year-olds' reactions to the interaction of text and picture, and the effect of the illustration.

228. Freeman, Graydon La Verne, and Ruth Sunderlin Freeman. *The Child and His Picture Book*. Watkins Glen, N.Y.: Century House, 1933. Updated 1967. 111pp.

   Original nine chapters discuss "function" of picture books; some existing books of the time; adult opinion of picture books; and the choices children make in picture books and illustrations. The updated section rechecks some of the data from the earlier study. Appendix lists facts on some illustrators. Illustrations in b & w.

229. Gagnon, Andre. "French Canadian Picture Books in Translation." *Children's Literature Association Quarterly* 15, no. 4 (Winter 1990): 212–217.

   Five French-Canadian authors whose work has been translated into English with success are discussed: Ginette Anfousse, who is also an illustrator; Bertrand Gauthier, whose works with Daniel Sylvestre's illustrations have descriptions here of the art as well; Marie-Louise Gay, who also illustrates; Stephane Poulin and Gilles Tibo, also author-illustrators. The art in many of their books is discussed.

230. Gainer, Ruth Strays. "Beyond Illustration: Information About Art in Children's Picture Books." *Art Education* (March 1982): 116–119.

   How to use picture books to show a variety of ways artists deal with problems to help children in art classes solve theirs. Values in using these books are delineated. Includes a list of particularly rich sources.

231. Garrett, Jeffrey. "'With Murderous Ending, Shocking, Menacing . . .': Sarah Moon's *Little Red Riding Hood* 10 Years After." *Bookbird* 31, no. 3 (September 1993): 8–9.

   Summarizes and quotes from the wide variety of critical opinions voiced concerning the "stark rendering" of the fairy tale in Sarah Moon's photographs. Two b & w illustrations.

* Georgiou, Constantine. *Children and Their Literature.*
  Cited above as item 28.

232. Giff, Patricia Reilly, Martha Belden, and Mary Jane
     Mangini Rossi. "Look Again: Picture Books Are More
     Than Pictures." *Instructor* (September 1985): 56–62.

     Analysis of picture books with special qualities of
     format, story, or added meaning for use with students.

233. Gill, Bob, and John Lewis. *Illustration: Aspects and
     Directions.* New York: Reinhold, 1964. 96pp.

     General discussion of the qualities all illustration
     should possess. A dozen pages devoted to "children's
     books" provide a jet plane's eye-view of the history and
     an equally brief, but barbed, critique of the current
     scene. More illustrations than text in b & w and color.

234. Glazer, Joan I., and Linda Leonard Lamme. "Poem
     Picture Books and Their Uses in the Classroom." *Reading
     Teacher* 44, no. 1 (October 1990): 102–109.

     Discusses several illustrated editions of poems along
     with the question of whether poems should be
     illustrated or whether children should be allowed to
     make their own pictures. Stating that there are times to
     use such books, the authors give examples of ways to do
     this with children, attending to both the words and the
     illustrations. A long list of books to use is included.

235. Golden, Joanne M., and Annyce Gerber. "A Semiotic
     Perspective of Text: The Picture Story Book Event."
     Journal of Reading Behavior 22, no. 3 (1990): 203–219.

     A semiotic framework involving "sign, interpreters,
     interpretants, signification and context," is used to
     analyze the reading of Sendak's *Where the Wild Things
     Are* with a group of second graders in an attempt to
     examine how pictures and words relate in picture books.

236. Goldsmith, Evelyn. "Learning from Illustrations: Factors in the Design of Illustrated Educational Books for Middle School Children." *Word and Image* 2, no. 2 (April–June 1986): 111–121.

Although the focus is on "fact books" from a design point of view, much of the author's analysis is applicable to picture book concerns. Such factors as color, typographic considerations, layout, and semantic characteristics are among those listed as crucial for picture book appreciation. B & w illustrations.

237. ———. *Research into Illustration: An Approach and Review.* Cambridge: Cambridge University Press, 1984. 487pp.

A valuable compilation and analysis of current—mainly post-1970—research studies "applicable to educational illustration in general," are gleaned from visual communication, psychology, and education. Sections include: "Use of Illustration," pp. 9–120; "Analysis of Illustration" (the major section), pp. 121–390; and "Research into Illustration," pp. 391–424. Focus is on the pragmatics of communicating information rather than the esthetics of pictures. Excellent use is made of 205 b & w illustrations and over two hundred studies.

238. ———, ed. *Research into Illustration 2.* Proceedings of a conference held at the Sallis Benney Theatre, Faculty of Art and Design, Brighton Polytechnic, Grand Parade, Brighton. February 16–17, 1984. Brighton, Eng.: Brighton Polytechnic, 1984. 153pp.

The general question raised was "Do illustrations for children need specific considerations . . .?" Are they different? Includes "Some Research Findings" by Evelyn Goldsmith, pp. 3–11, her concerns about how children perceive the illustrations, in part or as a whole, alone or in sequence.

"Deceptive Beetles" by Tony Potter, pp. 13–28, discusses how children perceive pictures at various ages;

and the differences between illustrations for picture books and those for informational books.

"Hang the Children—What About the Books?" by Brian Alderson, pp. 29–35, analyzes Errol LeCain's version of the *Snow Queen* to show the importance Alderson places on the relation of illustration to text. Also raises concerns about the paucity and difficulty of research into picture book illustration.

"Child as Parent to the Illustrator: Drawing and Painting with Words," by John Vernon Lord, pp. 37–108, analyzes in detail how many illustrators work with concerns of text and picture composition regardless of the age of the child consumer.

Summary of "Illustration from a Publisher's Point of View," by Tom Maschler, p. 104.

"Books, Illustrations and Child Development: How Much Are We Ever Likely to Know?" by Nicholas Tucker, pp. 111–119, covers areas of research related to how children perceive illustrations and how limited our ability to find out is.

"How Does Perception Develop?" by Richard Gregory, pp. 121–122.

"A Very Brief Talk . . . ?" by Raymond Briggs, pp. 123–132, is a personal account of his feelings about his life as author-illustrator, the style of his books, and some letters to and from children.

Reports from leaders of discussion groups on the main subject and chair's summary, pp. 133–148. Some b & w illustrations. Conference delegates listed in appendix.

239. "Graphic Gallery." *Horn Book* 62 (November–December 1986): 695–723.

A jury of Richard Bartlett, David Macaulay, and Ed Young chooses fourteen picture books (1980–1984) and presents them with their "observations about the visual aspects of the genre."

Graphis magazine. "International Journal of Graphic Art and Applied Art" (Zurich: Walter Herdag, The Graphis Press) has occasional issues on "children's book illustration." Some have also been issued as separate expanded volumes numbered 1, 2, 3, and 4, covering the international world of children's book illustration. Some of these are described here. All are profusely illustrated in both b & w and color.

240. *Graphis* 23, no. 131 (1967): 206–315.

Includes: Arsen Pohribny, "New Trends in Czechoslovak Children's Books," pp. 208–215, 310, describes a new artistic freedom and analyzes some winners at the Bologna Book Fair.

Robert F. Klein, "Children's Books in France," pp. 216–223, 304, mainly gives examples.

Hans A. Halbey, "The German Picture-Book Gains Ground," pp. 224–231, 306, discusses some illustrators, German and not, and credits modern art with opening children to less traditional illustration.

Judy Taylor and John Ryder, "Children's Book Illustration in England," pp. 232–241, 306, covers a rising new wave of British illustrators to challenge United States domination.

Bettina Hurlimann, "Notes on Japanese Picturebooks," pp. 242–249, 304, discusses artists and typical qualities.

Olga Siemaszkova, "Thoughts on Children's Books in Poland," pp. 250–261, 304, covers the current, rapid development and booming business, and suggests that they may prepare children for the adult world while educating parents' tastes.

Bettina Hurlimann, "The Swiss Picture-Book Today," pp. 262–271, 307, covers current producers.

Harlan Quist, "Children's Book Production in the U.S.A.," pp. 272–295, 312–313, covers the current "boom" but is concerned with the quality of what is published.

241. *Graphis* 27, no. 155 (1971–1972).

Contains articles by Franz Casper on "Children's Picture Books Today," pp. 301–303, in Italy; pp. 306–312, in Scandinavia; pp. 296–297, in Russia; pp. 298–300, in Hungary; pp. 304–305, in Austria; also includes:

Horst Kunnemann, "Present and Future Evolution of the German Picture-Book," pp. 228–241.

Bettina Hurlimann, "Notes on Japanese Picturebooks," pp. 268–273, updates her last report.

Zbigniew Rychlicki, "Children's Book Illustration in Poland," pp. 274–283, with examples.

242. *Graphis* 31, no. 177 (July 1975), also called "Third International Survey of Children's Book Illustration." 136pp.

Includes a special introduction by Virginia Haviland and the following articles:

Bettina Hurlimann, "German Picture-Books of the 19th Century," pp. 2–11 (not in magazine), an illustrated survey.

Jerome Snyder, "U.S. Children's Books in a Changing World," pp. 12–28, covers the effects of the unsettled society with examples.

John Ryder, "Children's Book Illustration in Britain," pp. 30–37, feels there is little new, except from Australia, but shows more from old favorites.

Christine Chagnoux, "New Children's Books—Or Parents' Books?—in France," pp. 38–47, feels children have not been consulted enough, and that Babar is "still king."

Ingeborg Ramseger, "New Trends in Children's Books in Germany," pp. 48–59, feels 1969 was a turning point, when facts and realism (as well as beauty) were demanded for all classes of children, but quality was not to be sacrificed. New names noted.

Jurg Schatzmann, "Tradition and Internationalism in the Swiss Children's Book," pp. 60–75, covers both co-productions and purely Swiss artists, old and new, with examples.

Tadashi Matsui, "The Japanese Picture-Book in Past and Present," pp. 76–83, gives a brief history, some Western influences, and examples of current works.

Mieczyslaw Piotrowski, "Polish Illustrators and the Children's Book," pp. 84–93, covers the continuation of high standards.

Dusan Roll, "Contemporary Children's Book Illustration in Czechoslovakia," pp. 94–99, discusses high standards set by the art school of Bratislava and the many artists doing book illustration.

Anna Katharina Ulrich, "The Future Evolution of the Art of the Picture-Book," pp. 100–115, raises questions about the handsome, expensive picture book with "sketchy content," in a future of reduced publishing and co-publishing, and whether any but established authors will find publishers.

Walter Abegg, "ABC and Counting Books," pp. 116–123 (not in magazine), gives brief survey. Short biographies of illustrators are included in book only.

243. *Graphis* 34, no. 200 (April 1979), also called "Fourth International Survey of Children's Book Illustration." Edited by Walter Herdeg. Pp. 468–615.

Includes notes on 1979 as the Year of the Child by Hans Conzett and "The Rights of the Child." Also:

Michael Patrick Hearn, "Ivan Y. Bilibin: The Leading Illustrator of Children's Books in Pre-Revolutionary Russia," pp. 472–481 (not in magazine), a brief summary with many examples.

"Current Picture-Book Publishing in the United States of America," pp. 482–501, covers lower sales and the revival of interest in fantasy and fairy tale.

Brian Alderson, "Children's Books in Britain: Divergent Styles and Occupational Highlights," pp. 502–515, discusses the very wide range and the importance of the whole, rather than individual pictures.

Christine Chagnoux, "French Children's Books: Cult of the New v. the Old Favorites," pp. 516–525, discusses what is popular, notes higher quality of paper, and color production.

Hildegard Krahe, "German Picture-Books—A Ray of Hope for Children in an Unkind Age?," pp. 526–541, reflects on the continuing production of some artists, the lack of new experimenters, but some growth in fantasy, and the fun of toy books.

Bettina Hurlimann, "The International Palette of Swiss Children's Books," pp. 542–559, lists current names.

Tadasi Matsui, "Children's Books in Japan: Rapid Growth and a Promising Future," pp. 560–565, covers this growth.

Danuta Wroblewka, "Children's Book Illustration in Poland: A Landscape with a Rainbow," pp. 566–575, relates illustration to the fine arts in Poland, and notes the young artists' use of color.

Dusan Roll, "Children's Books in Czechoslovakia: A Younger Generation Takes Over," pp. 576–583, gives examples of both the old and new artists.

Anna Katharina Ulrich, "Notes on the International Picture-Book Scene," pp. 584–599, sees trends of growth and internationalization along with the rise of new themes, plus a nostalgia for old favorites. Short biographies of illustrators are in the book but not the magazine.

244. Greenlaw, M. Jean. "Books in the Classroom." *Horn Book* 67, no. 5 (September–October 1991): 636–639.

A description of how teachers have used both picture books and books about art with students to launch explorations into the arts.

245. Groff, P. "Should Picture Books and Children Be Matched?" *Language Arts* 54 (1977): 411–417.

Summarizes the previous research on children's preferences and the questions raised. Notes weaknesses. Gives valid reasons for not catering to these preferences but rather for simply selecting quality books. Useful bibliography.

246. Harrison, Barbara, and Gregory Maguire. *Innocence and Experience: Essays and Conversations on Children's Literature.* New York: Lothrop, 1987. 569pp.

Compiled from programs (unfortunately not dated); presented at Simmons College Center for the Study of Children's Literature. Part V, "Motion and Rest: The Art of Illustration," pp. 303–385, which includes an introduction by Ethel Heins, states the importance of the picture book and its fine illustrations, those currently available, and the following relevant sections:

Sonia Landes, "Picture Books as Literature," pp. 315–322, discusses the role of illustrations in telling the story, along with discussions of specific texts of picture books.

Uri Shulevitz, "How I Found 'The Treasure,'" pp. 323–325, describes the genesis and growth of his book by that name.

Robert McCloskey and Ethel Heins, "Bothering to Look: A Conversation," pp. 326–340, covers the way the author/artist has worked on various books over the years, the role of May Massee, and his feelings about a current lack of perception in children.

Tom Feelings, "A Strange Balance of Joy and Pain," pp. 341–346, discusses how he developed as an illustrator, what he sees as his role in illustrating, and the importance he feels being an African-American artist.

Ellen Raskin, "Me and Blake, Blake and Me," pp. 347–353, draws parallels between herself and William Blake as she relates some aspects of her life and how she writes.

Marcia Brown, "The Lotus Blossom—Or Whodunit?" pp. 354–361, includes comments on contemporary life along with notes on her painting and illustration technique over the years.

Maurice Sendak, "Enamoured of the Mystery," pp. 362–374, covers his work on *Outside Over There* in preparation, then answers audience questions on his work habits, inspiration, and on illustration in general. Charles Mikolaycak, "With a Jeweler's Eye: On Creating Picture Books," pp. 375–377, describes his work on *Peter and the Wolf* to show what goes into what he feels is generally underappreciated illustration. Eve Rice and Rosemary Wells also comment on picture books in this section to p. 384.

Fritz Eichenberg, "From Our Correspondent in Utopia," pp. 385–388, in describing his early life and career choice, also comments on what he feels is the decline of good taste and craftsmanship in the art of the book, which seems to go along with a nostalgia for Art Nouveau and the artists of the previous century. He describes what he sees in "the perfect book" and his hope that it will come.

Part VI, "Primacy of Mother Goose," portfolio, pp. 396–408, twelve illustrators do b & w illustrations for Mother Goose rhymes.

* Hart, Thomas L. "Delinquent Youth Write and Illustrate Their Own Books." *American Libraries*. Cited above as item 103.

247. Hearne, Betsy. *Choosing Books for Children: A Commonsense Guide*. New York: Delacorte. 1981. 150pp.

Of particular relevance is chapter IV, pp. 29–49, "The Picture Book for Younger Children—Dead or Alive?" which gives criteria for judging and some examples of successful books.

This book has been updated by a 1990 edition, with expanded and enriched introductions. Over three hundred annotated selections included.

248. ———, and Marilyn Kaye, eds. *Celebrating Children's Books*. New York: Lothrop, Lee and Shepard, 1981. 244pp.

The articles in this collection that concern picture books are: Arnold Lobel, "A Good Picture Book Should . . . ," pp. 73–80, gives his criteria for a successful picture book, and describes his motivations. David Macaulay, "How to Create a Successful Nonfiction Picture Book," pp. 97–101, is a humorous discussion of all the wrong "rules."

249. ———. "Cite the Source: Reducing Cultural Chaos in Picture Books, Part One." *School Library Journal* 39, no. 7 (July 1993): 22–27.

An attempt to analyze how to tell whether a folktale in a picture-book format is "authentic." Hearne does not deal here with illustration directly.

250. ———. "Respect the Source: Reducing Cultural Chaos in Picture Books, Part Two." *School Library Journal* 39, no. 8 (August 1993): 33–37.

Discusses, with many examples, what defines authority in picture book folklore. Specifically covers the question of "new art," to illustrate, and "artistic folklore," which is her description of what may be misappropriation or misapplication of motifs.

251. Heins, Ethel. "Storytelling Through Art: Pretense or Performance?" *Horn Book 59* (February 1983): 14–15.

Raises questions of "artistic quality" and which illustrators possess it.

252. Heller, Steven. "Kids' Books You Can Enjoy." *U & lc* 20, no. 2 (Summer–Fall 1993): 32–36.

After some comments on the requirements for successful children's book production, the author analyzes several of the current "non-traditional" artists and their picture books. Many color reproductions of illustrations.

253. Hickman, Janet, and Bernice E. Cullinan, eds. *Children's Literature in the Classroom: Weaving Charlotte's Web.* Norwood, Mass.: Christopher-Gordon, 1989. 274pp.

Chapter 7, "Picture Books for All the Ages" by Barbara Kiefer, pp. 75–88, gives a brief history of picture books, some notes on children's responses and their awareness of the artistic elements in these books, and treats them as "art objects."

Chapter 8, "Teachers Using Picture Books" by Marilyn Reed, pp. 89–98, details how several teachers of grades K–6 use picture books in different ways in their classrooms.

Chapter 9, "My Goals as an Illustrator" by Marcia Brown, pp. 99–108, is her reflection on the art of illustrating and about how she has worked on several of her books.

254. Hogarth, Grace. "A Publisher's Perspective." *Horn Book* 65, no. 4 (July–August 1989): 526–528.

In this excerpt from her autobiography, Hogarth discusses her work with artists such as Rojankovsky, Cooney, Bemelmans, and in particular Rey, with notes on color technique, etc.

255. Hollinshead, Marilyn. "Judging Art for Children." *Publishers Weekly* 229, no. 12 (March 21, 1986): 46–47.

One of fourteen members of the jury of the Biennale of Illustrations held in Bratislava in the Fall of 1985 describes the selection process for the awards, with a hope that there would be more American participation. A b & w photo and an illustration.

256. Holtze, Sally Holmes, et al., eds. *Fourth Book of Junior Authors and Illustrators.* 1978. *Fifth Book of Junior Authors and Illustrators.* 1983. *Sixth Book of Junior Authors and Illustrators.* 1989. All New York: Wilson. Pages vary.

This series has now begun to include illustrators. Each volume indexes all the previous ones. Notes and quotations on the life and work of the artists also include a brief biography or autobiography and a bibliography.

257. Horning, Kathleen T. "Are You Sure That Book Won the Caldecott Medal? Variant Printings and Editions of Three Caldecott Medal Books." *Journal of Youth Services in Libraries* 1, no. 2 (Winter 1988): 173–176.

Discusses how three books that originally won the medal have changed in subsequent editions to a greater or lesser degree: Dorothy Lathrop's *Animals of the Bible,* in absence of clarity; the Petersham's *The Rooster Crows,* where stereotyped illustrations were removed; and the d'Aulaires' *Abraham Lincoln,* where the illustrations were completely redone in a different medium for the 1957 reissue. Horning cautions to study the edition that actually won. Two small b & w illustrations.

258. Houfe, Simon. *Fin de Siecle: Illustrators of the 'Nineties.* North Pomfret, Vt.: Trafalgar Square/Barrie & Jenkins, 1992. 200pp.

Profusely illustrated on almost every page in black on pale yellow, plus an eight-page inset of reproductions of color illustrations. This analysis of the rich and varied activity in the art of the book in America and Britain in this time period, with some historic background, is primarily concerned with the artists and styles of illustrations for adult works. The chapter on "Children's Books," pp. 137–160, however, illuminates this particular area. Houfe first describes the earlier "revolution" in the style and quality of children's books, detailing the important people and events that began this period of outstanding production in the mid-1800s. Then he discusses in great detail the important illustrated children's books and magazines of the 1890s and the people responsible for them.

259. Hubbard, Ruth. *Authors of Pictures, Draughtsmen of Words.* Portsmouth, N.H.: Heinemann, 1989. 176pp.

    With a demonstration of the techniques of working with children on making illustrated books, Hubbard discusses how pictures work to help tell the story. B & w photos of children's work.

* Huck, Charlotte S., with Susan Hepler and Janet Hickman. *Children's Literature in the Elementary School.* Cited above as item 33.

260. *Human and Anti-Human Values in Children's Books.* New York: Council on Interracial Books for Children, 1976. 279pp.

    A completely different way of looking at the illustrations in picture books. Checklists rate both "art" and "words" on racist, sexist, materialist, individualist, ageist, conformist, and escapist grounds, and then rate "literary quality" and "art quality" of selected books, "pre-school and early years," pp. 27–84. The illustrators are indexed.

261. Hunt, Peter. *Criticism, Theory, and Children's Literature.* Cambridge, Mass.: Basil Blackwell, 1991. 236pp.

    This attempt at a new approach to a method of criticism of children's literature, based on the "unique conventions of shape and structure," focusses on the totality of the text and book, and the relationship of the reader. Chapter 10, "Criticism and the Picture Book," pp. 175–188, notes in particular the complexity of criticism of the simultaneous story lines of picture and text.

262. Hurlimann, Bettina. *Picture-Book World.* London: Oxford, and Cleveland, Ohio: World, 1968. 216pp.

    An international survey, stressing the art, country-by-country. An "anthology of reproductions" in b & w and color fill a good part of the book.

263. Hurt, Jeffry A. "A Preference Oriented Guide for Selecting Picture Books." *School Library Media Quarterly* (Spring 1991): 169–172.

Drawing upon some research in the field, Hurt describes some factors that seem to affect children's preferences, implying that this is a major factor in selection to insure that "a picture book collection will be used and enjoyed by the children for whom it is intended."

264. *The Illustrator as Storyteller: Caldecott Medal and Honor Books, 1938–1984.* Catalog of an exhibition drawn largely from the Kerlan Collection and organized with University Art Museum in conjunction with "The Illustrator as Storyteller," a conference held at the University of Chicago and Chicago Public Library, October 19–20, 1984. Minneapolis: University of Minnesota, 1984. 20pp.

On pp. 3–5, Ellin Greene gives some historical background on picture books and on the Caldecott Medal. Brief introductions to each type of book illustration shown are followed by details about the illustration with one b & w example for each.

* *Images a la Ppage: Une Histoire de l'image dans les livres pour l'enfants.* Cited above as item 36.

265. Inglis, Fred. "Degrees of Freedom: Narratives on the Page and the Television Screen." *Word and Image* 2, no. 2 (April–June 1986): 186–194.

An imaginative and demanding exploration of the evolution of visualization in which books play a significant role, one that television technology cannot make obsolete.

266. Ivy, Barbara. *Children's Books About Art: An Annotated Bibliography with Classroom Activities.* Palo Alto, Calif.: Dale Seymour, 1992. 96pp.

Many picture books are included, particularly in the section on classroom activities, with specific leading questions. Minimal descriptive comments listed on the art of the picture books.

267. Jacobson, Frances F. "Computerized Children's Literature: Beyond Electronic Page Turning." *Journal of Youth Services in Libraries* 5, no. 4 (Summer 1992): 411–416.

As part of her "Focus on Technology" column, Jacobson analyzes the new series of children's books on CD-ROM which offer interactive "reading." Two full-page b & w illustrations show what these illustrations are like, but there is no comment on the illustrations as such.

* Jagusch, Sybille A., ed. *Stepping Away from Tradition: Children's Books of the Twenties and Thirties.* Papers from a symposium. Cited above as item 38.

268. Jalongo, Mary Renck. *Young Children and Picture Books: Literature from Infancy to Six.* Washington, D.C.: National Association for the Education of Young Children, 1988. 119pp.

Although a strong advocate for the importance of picture books—even calling them an "art form"—Jalongo writes in the preface that she is primarily concerned about them as literature. She does, however, emphasize "artistic quality," list guidelines for selection, and give sources of reviews. Lists of top authors and illustrators and "Picture Book Classics" are included, as are b & w photos and reproductions of illustrations.

269. Jameyson, Karen. "News from Down Under." *Horn Book* 67, no. 6 (November–December 1991): 768–770.

In a discussion of Australian children's books and their literary heritage, some picture books and their illustrators are covered.

270. Johnson, Diane. "'I See Me in the Book': Visual Literacy and African-American Children's Literature." *Children's Literature Association Quarterly* 15, no. 1 (Spring 1990): 10–13.

    Explores the difficulty of defining "African-American children's literature" because of the variety of value judgments expressed. Points out the need for studies about illustrations because of their primary impact in picture books.

 * Jones, Linda Harris. "A Comparison of the Works of Walter Crane, Randolph Caldecott and Kate Greenaway and Their Contributions to Children's Literature." Cited above as item 41.

271. Judson, Bay Hallowell. "What Is in a Picture? Essay Review." *Children's Literature in Education* 20, no. 1 (March 1989): 59–68.

    An art educator reviews John Warren Stewig's *Reading Pictures* (Jenson, 1988), which includes a set of four posters and a study guide. After describing the need for help in looking at pictures and the package itself, Judson moves from noting the positive parts of the sections to the problems of "finding meanings and insights in visual arts" and "naming the parts." A detailed analysis of all sections follows.

272. Kalisa, Beryl Graham. "Africa in Picture Books: Portrait or Preconception." *School Library Journal* 36, no. 2 (February 1990): 36–37.

    The author offers observations on the strengths and weaknesses of some children's books about Africa. Very little mention of the art of the illustrations. Two small b & w illustrations.

273. Katz, Elia. *Children's Preferences for Traditional and Modern Paintings.* New York: Columbia University Press, 1944. 101 pp.

In this study of historic interest, children preferred "traditional" rather than "modern" art. The children are sorted by grade level, sex, and socioeconomic level.

274. Kiefer, Barbara. "Accent on Art." *The Reading Teacher* 44, no. 6 (February 1991): 406–418.

Analyzes over forty "recent" picture books in which the author feels that illustrators have been particularly successful in conveying meaning through their art.

275. ———. "The Artist, the Book and the Child." Paper delivered at the "Artist as Storyteller" Symposium in Chicago, October 19–20, 1984. ERIC Document ED 253868. 30pp.

Defines the elements of design used by the artist in picture books as well as paintings to convey expressive contents. Notes on how children responded to these qualities in observed classroom settings.

276. ———. "The Child and the Picture Book: Create Live Circuits." *Children's Literature Association Quarterly* 2, no. 2 (Summer 1986): 63–68.

Report of a study done in elementary classrooms observing and talking with children about their responses to a variety of picture books. She found that responses over a period of months became increasingly complex and independent of third party intervention.

277. ———. "Images and Ideas: Picture Books for All Ages." *School Library Media Quarterly* 16, no. 4 (Summer 1988): 249–250.

Briefly describes the ways the artist conveys meaning in picture books, with examples, and discusses how children respond to the illustrations.

278. ———."Looking Beyond Picture Book Preferences." *Horn Book* 61, no. 6 (November–December 1985): 705–713.

Details a study done with seven and eight-year-olds using several complex and demanding picture books, to show that given an environment that fosters inquiry and encourages introspection, young children do respond profoundly to the esthetic qualities of the books.

279. ———. "Picture Books as Contexts for Literary, Aesthetic, and Real World Understandings." *Language Arts* 65, no. 3 (March 1988): 260–271.

Kiefer uses both selected references from other scholars and many examples of children's responses, to make a strong argument for developing concepts of style to "promote the fullest communication between a child and a picture book." The focus is on Maruki's *Hiroshima No Pika*, and third and fourth graders. An imaginative list of references is included.

280. ———. "The Response of Children in a Combination First/Second Grade Classroom to Picture Books in a Variety of Artistic Styles." *Journal of Research and Development in Education* 16, no. 3 (Spring 1983): 14–20.

Report of observations over a ten-week period shows variations, and indicates the importance of where the books are placed, the teachers, and of the illustration's position in the book as a whole. Changes over time, as well as differences among students, are noted.

281. ———. "The Response of Primary Children to Picturebooks." Ph.D. diss., Ohio State University, Columbus, 1982. 268pp.

An ethnographic study of first and second graders over three months demonstrated the significance of extended periods of time needed for children to appreciate picture books, and pointed out the weaknesses of most preference studies which deal with excerpted illustrations in a very short time-span.

282. Kiefer, Monica Mary. *American Children Through Their Books, 1700–1835.* Philadelphia: University of Pennsylvania, 1948. 248pp.

Although only pp. 6–11 deal with the illustrations, the book fills in background information on children and their lives at the time. Some b & w reproductions from early books.

283. Kingman, Lee, Joanna Foster, and Ruth Giles Lontoft, comps. *Illustrators of Children's Books, 1957–1966.* Boston: Horn Book, 1968. 295pp.

Many b & w illustrations and one color spread example. Part I, "A Decade of Illustration in Children's Books," includes:

"One Wonders," by Marcia Brown, pp. 2–27, analyzes the current flood of picture books with perceptive comments on some artists and their work.

"Color Separation," by Adrienne Adams, pp. 28–35, analyzes the process in detail.

"The Artist and His Editor," by Grace Allen Hogarth, pp. 36–53, discusses many illustrators, their relationship with their editors and their texts, and the effects of new technology.

"Beatrix Potter: Centenary of an Artist-Writer," by Rumer Godden, pp. 54–64, treats her life and work.

Part II, "Biographies," pp. 66–197, and Part III, "Bibliographies," pp. 200–287, are like earlier editions.

See Bertha E. Mahony and Bertha Mahony Miller for earlier volumes in this series.

284. Kingman, Lee, Grace Allen Hogarth, and Harriet Quimby, comps. *Illustrators of Children's Books, 1967–1976.* Boston: Horn Book, 1978. 290pp.

Many b & w and some color illustrations. Part I, "A Decade of Illustration in Children's Books," includes:

"Book Illustration: The State of the Art," by Walter Lorraine, pp. 2–19, is an in-depth analysis of the works of some of the illustrators active in what he calls " a period of renaissance," and whether their art also tells a story.

"A View From the Island: European Picture Books 1967–1976," by Brian Alderson, pp. 20–43, discusses the important books and trends in criticism.

"Where the Old Meets the New: The Japanese Picture Book," by Teiji Seta and Momoko Ishii, pp. 44–57, a brief history plus the names and description of the works of important illustrators active between 1967 and 1976.

"In the Beginning Was the Word . . . The Illustrated Book 1967–1976," by Treld Pelkey Bicknell, pp. 58–80, analyzes some illustrators as their work relates to the text illustrated in realistic books, fiction and non-fiction; in illustrated books rather than picture books.

Part II, "Biographies," pp. 90–171, and Part III, "Bibliographies," pp. 174–254, are like these sections in earlier editions, but do not repeat from the earlier entries, which are listed in a cumulative index.

"Appendix" lists bibliographies for articles in part I.

285. Klemin, Diana. *The Art of Art for Children's Books.* New York: Potter, 1966. 128pp.

Identification of about fifty artists whose work exemplifies the best in book illustration. They are categorized as Storytellers, Poetic and Personal, Imaginary, Collage and Abstraction, and Specialist. Each has a b & w or color reproduction accompanied by a caption comment by Klemin.

286. ———. *The Illustrated Book.* New York: Potter, 1970. 159pp.

Seventy "fine" artists are highlighted (very few represented by illustrations for children's books). Each has an illustration reproduced with about a half page of comment by Klemin. Eighteen pages offer limited advice to would-be illustrators.

287. Krull, Kathleen, Sally Lodge, and Susan Stan. "New Textures in Children's Book Art." *Publishers Weekly* 238, no. 9 (February 15, 1991): 61–63.

Descriptions of three picture books that use innovative illustration techniques. Information is included on the artist, the technique, and the books themselves, with quotations from the artists. The works are: Faith Ringgold's *Tar Beach*, Salley Mavor's *The Way Home*, and Debra Frasier's *On the Day You Were Born*.

288. Kuskin, Karla. "How to Make a Picture Book." *New York Times Book Review* (September 24, 1987): 23.

On problems of matching author and illustrator. Examples of historic successful "marriages" and short quotations from several illustrators.

289. ———. "The Mouse in the Corner, the Fly on the Wall: What Very Young Eyes See in Picture Books." *New York Times Book Review* (November 14, 1993): 50–51.

Using many examples, Kuskin discusses how children "read" more from book illustrations than adults, if the artists have done a good job of providing the richness of detail and design she describes.

290. LaBarbera, Kathryn. "The Emotional Impact of Books by Molly Bang." *Booklinks* (July 1991): 22–26.

Analyzing four of Bang's books for content and illustrations, LaBarbera links them for style and motifs. An insert describes Bang's workshops, where she demonstrates how visual elements affect emotional response. Four color illustrations reproduced.

291. Lacy, Lyn E. *Art and Design in Children's Picture Books: An Analysis of Caldecott Award-Winning Illustration.* Chicago: American Library Association, 1986. 229pp.

   A strong case is made for the study of picture books as a significant part of all art appreciation objectives, but especially for the young child. Most of the extensive analysis of fifteen American illustrators involves line, color, light and dark, shape, and space. But some background material is also provided; and each of the sections has many suggestions for further study which include related production activities. A glossary but no illustrations (readers are requested to obtain the books discussed). Illustrators analyzed in detail: the Dillons, Virginia Lee Burton, Ed Emberly, Elmer Hader, Ezra Jack Keats, Robert McCloskey, Blair Lent, the Petershams, Uri Shulevitz, Maurice Sendak, Roger Duvoisin, and Chris Van Allsburg.

292. Lamb, Lynton. "The Way of the Book Illustrator in Britain." *The Studio,* 142, no. 701 (August 1951): 34–41, 64.

   Although mainly concerned with illustrations for books other than picture books, Lamb covers the role of the illustrator as decorative and as more than that, giving examples. He also looks toward "a revival in book illustration," which indeed has come.

293. Lamme, Linda Leonard. "Illustratorship: Key Facet of Whole Language Instruction." *Childhood Education* 66, no. 2 (Winter 1989): 83–86.

   Claiming that children should learn about illustrators as well as authors, Lamme describes ways to do this, including study of specific illustrators and their work; also treating children as authors and illustrators who display their own work and put books of their own together. A few unannotated references and a longer list of picture books.

294. Lanes, Selma. *Down the Rabbit Hole: Adventures and Misadventures in the Realm of Children's Literature.* New York: Atheneum, 1971. 239pp.

     A major work of analysis and criticism of the picture book. Chapters on the massive increase in numbers since 1945, and on individual "greats" including Sendak and Seuss. Insightful comments on Potter, Rackham, Emberly, Lionni, and many more.

295. Langford, Sondra Gordon. "A Second Look: The Real Thief." *Horn Book* 67, no. 1 (January–February 1991): 48–49.

     In a new appreciation of Steig's book, Langford discusses everything but the illustrations. One small b & w reproduction.

296. Larrick, Nancy. "The Changing Picture of Poetry Books for Children." *Wilson Library Bulletin* 55, no. 2 (October 1980): 113–117.

     Sketches descriptive history of illustrated books of poetry from Blake's *Songs of Innocence* to modern collections with photographs.

297. Laughlin, Mildred. "Visual Literacy Through Picture Books K–12: A Curriculum Approach." Paper presented at the American Association of School Librarians Conference, Louisville, Ky. September 26, 1980. ERIC Microfiche ED 198814 80. 22pp.

     Discusses using picture books to help students "see." David Macaulay's books are considered. Other illustrators mentioned include dePaola, Quackenbush, Anno, Cooney, Hyman, the D'Aulaires, and Dillons.

298. Lemieux, Louise. *Pleins fux sur la litterature de jeunesse au Canada français.* Montreal: Lemeac, 1972. 337pp.

     Lists the limited sources of information on French Canadian children's literature. Chapter V, "Illustration," pp. 107–114, gives further sources in French and other sources for discussion of the art of the picture book. The names of French-Canadian illustrators and their own works plus the other texts they have illustrated are given. There is also some discussion of children doing their own illustrations, of cost analysis of book production, some conclusions and recommendations.

299. Lent, Blair. "There's Much More to the Picture Than Meets the Eye." *Wilson Library Bulletin 52*, no. 2 (October 1977): 161–164.

His analysis of what a picture book is and how the writers and artists work.

300. Lewis, Claudia. "Searching for the Master Touch in Picture Books." *Children's Literature in Education 15*, no. 4 (Winter 1984): 198–203.

Tries to make a case for some content in picture books being outside the young child's immediate field of knowledge.

* Lewis, John. *The Twentieth Century Book.* Cited above as item 42.

301. Lewis, Marjorie. "Back to Basics: Reevaluating Picture Books." *School Library Journal 22*, no. 7 (March 1976): 82–83.

Criticism of "art experimentation" in newer picture books, as opposed to the value of the "total experience of story and illustration."

302. Lindauer, Shelley L. Knudsen. "Wordless Books: An Approach to Visual Literacy." *Children's Literature in Education 19*, no. 3 (Fall 1988): 136–142.

Maintains that "young children's exposure to wordless books can be fundamental in the development of a wide range of skills," like "reading" the pictures.

Offers suggestions and examples of how to use them.
Book list included.

303. *The Lion and the Unicorn: A Critical Journal of Children's Literature.* Special Double Issue, 7/8 (1983–1984) Picture Books. 193pp.

Many b & w illustrations. Includes:

Suzanne Rahn, "Beneath the Surface with *Fungus the Bogeyman,*" pp. 5–19, places the work with others by Briggs for some analysis of art, but mainly of content.

Stephen Roxburgh, "A Picture Equals How Many Words?: Narrative Theory and Picture Books for Children," pp. 20–33, discusses, in particular, the narrative in Sendak's *Outside Over There*, to show how current critical theory is inadequate to discuss the role of the illustrations in the narrative.

Leonard S. Marcus, "The Artist's Other Eye: The Picture Books of Mitsumasa Anno," pp. 34–46, discusses in detail the art of many of his books.

Leonard S. Marcus, "Invention and Discoveries: An Interview with Ann K. Beneduce," pp. 47–63; the editor-in-chief of Philomel Books talks about her work, the international world of children's books, and her authors Anno and Carle.

David Pritchard, "'Daddy, Talk!' Thoughts on Reading Early Picture Books," pp. 64–69, traces his daughter's relationship to books, from identification to story.

Annie Pissard, "Long Live Babar!" pp. 70–77, discusses the Brunhoffs' work in conjunction with an exhibition of original art for the books.

Jack Zipes, "A Second Gaze at Little Red Riding Hood's Trials and Tribulations," pp. 78–109, relates his radically different psychological approach and includes much analysis of different versions of the illustrations over the years as well as of the story.

John Cech, "Remembering Caldecott: *The Three Jovial Huntsmen* and the Art of the Picture Book," pp. 110–119, is a detailed analysis and appreciation.

Morton N. Cohen, "Another Wonderland: Lewis Carroll's *The Nursery Alice*," pp. 120–126, some notes on a more picture-book type version of *Alice* with color illustrations.

Leonard S. Marcus, "Picture Book Animals: How Natural a History?" pp. 127–139, analyzes the use of animal characters in picture books by types and discusses their relation to real animals.

Julie Hirsch, "Photography in Children's Books: A Generic Approach," pp. 140–155, gives examples and discusses how successfully they seem to meet the needs of the story.

Elizabeth Cleaver, "Idea to Image: The Journey of a Picture Book," pp. 156–170, covers her interest in Indian legends and details her work on *The Loon's Necklace*.

Nancy Willard, "The Birds and the Beasts were There: An Interview with Martin Provensen," pp. 171–183, gives background on the Provensens' life, how they worked, and how they came to picture books.

304. Lionni, Leo. "Before Images." *Horn Book* 60, no. 6 (November–December 1984): 727–734.

The picture book as "the door that leads into the complexities of literacy." The need for the illustrator to rediscover childhood experiences, because "every work of art contains fragments of this journey." Feelings are a basic component to work for.

305. Lipson, Eden Ross. *The New York Times Parent's Guide to the Best Books for Children*. New York: New York Times/Random House, 1988. 421pp.

Lists "Wordless Books," pp. 3–8, and "Picture Books," pp. 11–86, with very brief annotations and occasional discussion of illustrations.

306. *Lively Art of Picture Books*. 16mm film. Weston, Conn.: Weston Woods, no date (mid-1960?). 57 min.

An appreciation, including an animation of Keats' *Snowy Day;* a comparison of the works of thirty-six "outstanding artists"; interviews on their work with Robert McCloskey, Barbara Cooney, and Maurice Sendak; and an adaptation of McCloskey's *Time of Wonder.*

307. Lodge, Sally. "The Making of a Crossover: One Book, Two Markets." *Publishers Weekly* (November 23, 1992): 38–42.

Discusses some picture books, among other books published primarily for children, which have attracted readers of all ages. Perhaps, Lodge suggests, this is due to the "high quality of the art," which is also being collected as original art. The rise of such books as gift items is also covered.

308. Lorraine, Walter. "The Art of the Picture Book." *Wilson Library Bulletin* 52, no. 2 (October 1977): 144–147.

His introduction to a special issue laments the lack of content in the picture books that currently have better art than ever; defines picture books; gives some history; and looks to the future.

309. Lurie, Stephanie. "First the Word: An Editor's View of Picture Book Texts." *School Library Journal* (October 1991): 50–51.

Although she gives the "text" of the picture book (even if wordless), primary importance, as senior editor of Children's Books for Little, Brown, Lurie has comments of interest on artists and their styles and the techniques considered when choosing illustrators for stories.

310. MacCann, Donnarae. "Something Old, Something New: Children's Picture Books in Poland." *Wilson Library Bulletin* 52, no. 10 (June 1978): 776–782.

Includes some history and critical analysis of the picture book art, its relation to the "fine art" world, and its importance in the books.

311. ———. and Olga Richard. *The Child's First Books: A Critical Study of Pictures and Texts.* New York: H.W. Wilson, 1973. 135pp.

Refreshingly free from cant, this book respects the esthetic capacities of children and seeks out examples of illustrators that contain "many particular beauties of art." A very short "Historical Perspective" is followed by an even shorter section on "Stereotypes." The bulk of the book is devoted to demonstrating the graphic elements and aspects of book design as well as to pay specific attention to "Outstanding Contemporary Illustrators." The many b & w illustrations and several color reproductions are particularly well printed.

312. ———. "Children's Picture Books: Into the Second Century." *Wilson Library Bulletin* 63, no. 3 (November 1988): 92–95.

Briefly summarizes the four areas considered important by the authors in the recent history of picture books, beginning in New York City in the 1920s and 1930s. The "paradoxical unity" they find in these periods is that "the illustrators represent no unified vision or range of techniques." They examine current trends and deplore the "scarcity of books with substantial texts."

313. ———. "Internationally Derived Standards for Children's Picture Books." *Wilson Library Bulletin* 64, no. 9 (May 1990): 25–29.

The authors try to differentiate the European from the American point of view one illustration by quoting critics and artists. The connection between the "fine art" world and book art, the role of illustrations versus text, and the diversity of styles, are all noted. Specific British and European examples are analyzed.

314. ———. "Picture Books About Blacks: An Interview with Opal Moore." *Wilson Library Bulletin* 65, no. 10 (June 1991): 25–28.

In answer to questions, the teacher, writer, and critic refers to eighteen specific titles to discuss aspects such as self-esteem, universal themes, folktales, and African versus African-American subjects. Little discussion of the art of the illustrations. One b & w photo and several illustrations reproduced in b & w and color.

315. MacDonald, Eleanor. "The Illustrated Poem: An Uneasy Alliance." *School Library Journal* 36, no. 7 (July 1990): 28–29.

Probes the question of whether poetry should be illustrated. Gives examples of books where the illustrations "work" or don't work for the poetry within.

* Mahony, Bertha E., Louise Payson Latimer, and Beulah Folmsbee, comps. *Illustrators of Children's Books*, 1744–1945. Cited above as item 47.

316. Many, Joyce E. "Interactions About Text and Pictures: What Can We Learn from a Shared Reading." *Reading Research and Instruction* 28, no. 4 (Summer 1989): 48–59.

Although Nancy E. Burkert's name is never mentioned, it is her illustrated version of Jarrell's translation of *Snow White and the Seven Dwarfs* as read by a mother with two young children that is used to identify qualities of discourse. Both content and patterns of dialog were found to be different between text and pictures. No concern for the esthetic qualities of the pictures is shown.

317. Marantz, Kenneth. "The Picture Book as Art Object: A Call for Balanced Reviewing." *Wilson Library Bulletin* 52, no. 2 (October 1977): 148–151.

Deplores the lack of attention to the picture book as a "form of visual art" rather than only literature.

318. ————. "The Picture Book: Bridge from Potter to Picasso." *Prelude Tapes*, Series 7 Audiotape. New York: Children's Book Council. 1983. 30 min.

Using a broad selection of recent picture books, Marantz analyzes their components and qualities (sequence, craftsmanship, design, styles, etc.) to make the case for their classification as art objects with strong esthetic content.

319. Marantz, Sylvia S. *Picture Books for Looking and Learning: Awakening Visual Perception through the Art of Children's Books.* Phoenix, Ariz.: Oryx, 1992. 208pp.

After brief introductory chapters on the anatomy of a picture book and on media and art techniques used by illustrators, the art of over forty quality picture books is analyzed in detail, page by page, with suggestions for related books and art activities.

320. Marshall, Margaret Richardson. *An Introduction to the World of Children's Books.* 2d ed. Aldershot: Gower, 1982, 1988. 327pp.

"Illustration and Children's Books," pp. 193–211, lists some purposes of illustration, covers methods of achieving those purposes, analyzes some model picture books, gives notes on illustrated books, and discusses books with unusual features such as board books, pop-ups, books with flaps, etc.

"Evaluation," includes a note on assessing illustration, p. 238.

321. Martin, Douglas. *The Telling Line: Essays on Fifteen Contemporary Book Illustrators.* New York: Delacorte, 1989. 320pp.

Profusely illustrated in b & w and color with the work of the artists included. For each artist, Martin gives a summary of the life and training and how each came to illustration. Quotations from conversation and correspondence with them are included. His introduction places them in the context of history and in the illustration world today. All artists are English, represent the best of the current illustrators, and all except Lambourne have illustrated children's books. A chronological bibliography is included for each artist.

Included are: Charles Keeping, pp. 36–59; Faith Jacques, pp. 60–82; Victor Ambrus, pp. 83–105; Nigel Lambourne, pp. 106–125; Brian Wildsmith, pp. 126–147; Shirley Hughes, pp. 148–166; John Lawrence, pp. 167–186; Jan Pienkowski, pp. 187–201; Helen Oxenbury, pp. 202–214; John Burningham, pp. 215–227; Raymond Briggs, pp. 228–242; Quentin Blake, pp. 243–263; Janet and Allan Ahlberg, pp. 264–278; Anthony Browne, pp. 279–290; Michael Foreman, pp. 291–311.

322. McGee, Lea M., and Gail E. Tompkins. "Wordless Picture Books Are for Older Readers Too." *Journal of Reading* 27, no. 2 (November 1983): 120–123.

Of interest for its list of wordless books that appeal to older students and its list of references. The books are used only as tools for teaching reading skills here. No art criticism or analysis.

323. McMillan, Bruce. "Photographer or Photo-Illustrator: What's the Difference?" *School Library Journal* (February 1991): 38–39.

The author explains the difference in individual photographs as works of art and the way he works as a book illustrator: to make a carefully planned series the same way an illustrator in a different medium would. Uses several of his books to demonstrate his process. A few photos are reproduced in small size in b & w.

324. Miller, Bertha Mahony, Ruth Viguers, and Marcia Dalphin, comps. *Illustrators of Children's Books, 1946–1956.* Boston: Horn Book, 1958. 299pp.

Some b & w illustrations. Part I, "Eleven Years of Illustration in Children's Books," includes:
"Distinction in Picture Books," by Marcia Brown, her critical words, pp. 2–12;
"The Book Artist: Ideas and Techniques," by Lynd Ward, pp. 14–35, his analysis of the current state of the art and its development during the years covered;
"The European Picture Book," by Fritz Eichenberg, pp. 36–57, a personal observation, country-by-country.
Part II, "Biographies," pp. 60–203, lists illustrators alphabetically with brief biographical notes and quotations.
Part III, "Bibliographies," pp. 206–292, lists those active from 1946 to 1956 and their works. See Bertha E. Mahony for earlier volume and Lee Kingman for later volumes in this series.

325. Mitchell, Florence S. "Introducing Art History through Children's Literature." *Language Arts* 67, no. 8 (December 1990): 839–846.

The author demonstrates how picture books, as well as art histories written for children, may be used to enhance "cultural education" in an integrated curriculum.

326. Moebius, William. "Introduction to Picturebook Codes." *Word and Image* 2, no. 2 (April–June 1986): 141–158.

Picture-book "codes," i.e., conventions, are identified and explained, page by page, using Waber's *Ira Sleeps Over* as a case study. Other picture books are also used to point to such factors as the frame, perspective, layout, line, etc.

327. Montana, Louis. "The Expanding Market for Children's Book Illustrations." *American Artist* 54, no. 581 (December 1990): 62–67, 74–75.

Discusses the "renaissance . . . occuring in children's book illustration art, which is being showcased and creatively marketed to collectors, educators, and parents" from the artist's point of view. Many quotations from museum directors and illustrators on the phenomenon and the marketing.

328. Moran, Susan. "Creative Reading: Young Adults and Paperback Books." *Horn Book* 68, no. 4 (July–August 1992): 490–495.

In her eighth-grade class, the author has her students reexamine some favorite picture books from childhood as part of a writing project.

* Morris, Charles Henry. *The Illustration of Children's Books.* Cited above as item 52.

329. Moss, Elaine. *Picture Books for Young People, 9–13.* Rev. ed. A Signal Bookguide. Lockwood, Eng.: Thimble Press, 1985. 46pp.

An annotated bibliography with a fresh point of view of picture books challenging enough for older students.

* Moynihan, William T., and Mary E. Shaner, eds. *Masterworks of Children's Literature, Volume Eight: The Twentieth Century.* Cited above as item 53.

330. Munro, Eleanor C. "Children's Book Illustration." *Art News* 53 (December 1954): 41–48.

A pull-out "design portfolio" with many 3–inch to 4–inch b & w illustrations from the United States and abroad (a few historical but many contemporary). Munro contrasts "little adults" of the past with what she calls "Juvenile Art" of today. Examples from 1950 to 1954 by *Art News* editors show how they consider style becoming stereotyped. Examples of superficial elements borrowed from modern art since Cezanne, or from Expressionism are used to try to teach a new sensitivity, or "new patterns of thinking." Mention of study at Bank Street School on children's preferences.

331. Murphy, Stuart J. "Visual Learning Strategies." *Booklinks* (May 1992): 15–20.

    Highlights ideas from a June 1991 conference on visual learning sponsored by the Research Committee of the School Division of the Association of American Publishers, with examples of the books that use the strategies discussed. Covers research on how design and pictures help comprehension, and how words and pictures may interact. Many illustrations are reproduced from books discussed.

332. Myatt, Barbara, and Juliet Mason Carter. "Picture Preferences of Children and Young Adults." *Educational Communication and Technology* 27, no.1 (Spring 1979): 45–53.

    Reviews some previous studies; discusses difficulties of research in this area. Uses six categories from photographs and line drawings through cartoon and collage. In this study children seem to prefer color photographs and "realism."

333. Neal, Judith C. and Kay Moore. "The Very Hungry Caterpillar Meets Beowolf." *Journal of Reading* 35, no. 4 (December 1991–January 1992): 290–296.

    After providing a "rationale for incorporating picture books into the secondary school curriculum," the authors describe the selection of suitable books, noting books that illustrate story structure and genre, and offer suggestions for instructional activities, with mention of art. A list of picture books that illustrate specific art elements is included.

334. Neumeyer, Peter F. "How Picture Books Mean: The Case of Chris Van Allsburg." *Children's Literature Association Quarterly* 15, no. 1 (Spring 1990): 2–8.

The first nine of Van Allsburg's books are analyzed from the viewpoints of story, illustrations, language, and overall design. The pictures are seen as the major force driving the imaginative content as they exploit unusual perspectives and a form of surreal image construction.

335. Nodelman, Perry. "How Children Respond to Art." *School Library Journal* 31, no. 4 (December 1984): 40–41.

Nodelman's thesis is that children must be taught artistic conventions if they are to learn to value art of all kinds. He uses Burton's *Mike Milligan and his Steam Shovel* to point out thirteen conventions used in the illustrations; these conventions are ways of representing nature most adults have come to understand but where children need help.

336. ———. "How Picture Books Work." *Proceedings of the Eighth Annual Conference of the Children's Literature Association*, Minneapolis: University of Minnesota, March 1981. Pp. 57–68.

Explains, in general, the relationship between text and illustrations. Uses *Snow White* as visualized by Hyman and Burkert, as an example of the complex possibilities of illustrations, as well as to make a case for Nodelman's bias about the best kind of illustration.

337. ———. *The Pleasures of Children's Literature.* New York: Longman, 1992. 256pp.

In Chapter 10, "Picture Books," pp. 130–157, Nodelman discusses picture books, in this exploration "to provide adults with contexts and strategies of comprehension that should help them understand and, above all, enjoy children's literature." He covers in some detail (with visual examples in b & w), the means by which illustrators achieve their effects. There are sections on "mood and atmosphere," "style," "pictorial dynamics," etc. Also included are suggestions to put his ideas into practice for adults' personal explorations, or with children.

338. ———. *Touchstones: Reflections on the Best in Children's Literature. Volume 3: Picture Books.* West Lafayette, Indiana: Children's Literature Association, 1989. 187pp.

In addition to some general articles, fifteen books chosen by a committee of the Children's Literature Association as "touchstones" are analyzed with additional biographical material. Included are:
"Edward Ardizzone's *Little Tim and the Brave Sea Captain*: An Art of Contrasts," by Peter Hunt, pp. 14–21;
"L. Leslie Brooke's *Johnny Crow's Garden*: The Gentle Humor of Implied Stories," by Marilyn Apseloff, pp. 21–28;
"Virginia Burton's *The Little House*: Technological Change and Fundamental Verities," by Jon C. Stott and Teresa Krier, pp. 28–37.
"Randolph Caldecott's Picture Books: The Invention of a Genre," by Ellin Greene, pp. 38–45.
"Walter Crane's *The Baby's Opera*: A Commodious Dwelling," by Patricia Demers, pp. 46–54.
"Wanda Gag's *Millions of Cats*: Unity Through Repetition," by Mary Kissel, pp. 54–62.
"Kate Greenaway's *A Apple Pie*: An Atmosphere of Sober Joy," by Patricia Dooley, pp. 63–69.
"Ezra Jack Keats' *The Snowy Day*: The Wisdom of a Pure Heart," by Kenneth A. Marantz, pp. 70–73.
"Robert Lawson's *The Story of Ferdinand*: Death in the Afternoon or Life Under the Cork Tree?" by Jean Streufert Patrick, pp. 74–84;
"Leo Lionni's *Swimmy*: Undetailed Depth," by Mary-Agnes Taylor, pp. 85–90;

"Robert McCloskey's *Make Way for Ducklings*: The Art of Regional Storytelling," by Anthony L. Manna, pp.90–100;

"Beatrix Potter's *The Tale of Peter Rabbit*: A Small Masterpiece," by Jackie F. Eastman, pp. 100–106;

"Arthur Rackham's *Fairy Book*: A Confrontation with the Marvelous," by Gillian Adams, pp. 107–121;

"Maurice Sendak's *Where the Wild Things Are*: Picture Book Poetry," by Raymond E. Jones, pp. 122–131;

"Dr. Seuss' *The 500 Hats of Bartholomew Cubbins*: Of Hats and Kings," by Mavis Reimer, pp. 132–142;

"Contemporary Illustrators: Tomorrow's Classics?" by Patricia Dooley, pp. 153–164; plus other articles not about picture books.

339. ———. *Words about Pictures: The Narrative Art of Children's Picture Books*. Athens: University of Georgia, 1988. 318pp.

Conceiving of the picture book as a special narrative form, Nodelman exploits the speculations of estheticians, literary theorists, and psychologists to support his arguments. Chapters include: "The Implied Viewer," "Style as Meaning," "Irony," "Code, Symbol, Gesture," etc. The analysis draws on examples from the art world proper as well as from many picture books. This thorough, scholarly book written for the educated lay reader makes a very strong case for the importance of picture books for enhancing consciousness, "to think with more involvement." A sixteen-page inset of b & w illustrations, and an extensive, unannotated bibliography.

340. Packard, Myrna. "Some Second Graders' Verbal Responses to the Picturebook as Art Object." Master's thesis, Ohio State University, Columbus, 1984. 80pp.

A study that focuses on the esthetic qualities of picture books. Results suggest that these artifacts offer better vehicles to enhance esthetic development than the objects (usually reproductions of paintings) that are currently used.

341. Paley, Nicholas. "Postmodernist Impulses and the Contemporary Picture Book: Are There Any Stories to These Meanings?" *Journal of Youth Services in Libraries* 5, no. 2 (Winter 1992): 151–162.

Drawing parallels with post-modern architecture and art, Paley examines Maira Kalman's *Stay Up Late*; David Mamet's *Warm and Cold* illustrated by Donald Sultan; David Macaulay's *Black and White*; and Oscar de Mejo's *The Tiny Visitor*. He concludes that such experimentations need further analysis in light of current educational research, and require discussion beyond textual criticism to political and cultural relevance.

342. ———. "Why the Books of Harlan Quist Disappeared— Or Did They?" *Children's Literature Association Quarterly* 14, no. 3 (Fall 1989): 111–114.

The answer to the question in the title seems to be that although the ten-year (1965–1975) run of Quist picture books was strong and controversial, there is a resurgent influence in the current market. Paley highlights the Quist decade with esthetic and sociological insights.

343. Pariser, David. "The Good, the Bad and the Appropriate; or, Daddy, Will This Spoil Me for the Book?" *Canadian Review of Art Education* 15, no. 2 (1988): 17.

A discussion of the effect of versions of well-known tales, particularly Walt Disney's, on appreciation, prompting the question in the title from Pariser's daughter. Many of the issues of "translation" from book to screen and from verbal to visual that are covered here relate to picture-book illustrations.

344. Paulin, Mary Ann. *Creative Uses of Children's Literature.*
     Hamden, Conn.: Library Professional Publication/Shoe
     String, 1982. 730pp.

     Chapter One, "Introducing Books All Kinds of
     Ways," includes techniques of presenting and promoting
     picture books; for example, pp. 37–44 cover "Choosing
     Picture Books for Reading Aloud," "Hints for Reading
     Picture Books," "Picture Books About Pigs," etc.
     Chapter Two, "Experiencing Art Through Picture
     Books," is a hodgepodge collection of topics (categories)
     invented by the author which permits her to give
     annotations of several titles per topic and to offer a few
     suggestions for classroom activities. An author index
     lists 5,045 items. There are also title and subject indexes.
     She also lists 785 nonprint titles in a multimedia index.

345. ———. *More Creative Uses of Children's Literature*, Vol. 1:
     Introducing Books in All Kinds of Ways. Hamden,
     Conn.: Library Professional Publications/Shoe String,
     1992. 621pp.

     Volume 1 is like Chapter 1 of Paulin's earlier book,
     noted above in item 344. This volume updates
     "creativeness" with books published since 1982.
     Volume 2, not available at time of annotation,
     "concentrates on specific marriages of literature with
     other enrichments," and will cover experiencing art
     through picture books.

346. Peltola, Bette. "Choosing the Caldecott Medal Winners."
     Journal of Youth Services in Libraries 1, no. 2 (Winter 1988):
     153–159.

     Describes the process by which the medal winners
     are selected and announced. Includes selection criteria,
     and b & w photos of both sides of the medal.

347. *Picture Book Design Conference: From Conception to
     Consumption.* Proceedings of a conference co-sponsored
     by the Ohio Arts Council and the Art Education

Department, Ohio State University. May 18–19, 1984.
91pp.

Chaired by Kenneth Marantz. Includes: "An Editor's
Comments" by Steven Roxburgh, pp. 310, analyzing the
people, processes and some problems involved in
putting together picture books;
"A Publisher Adds to the Dialog" by David Godine,
pp. 10–21, in which he discusses some of his publishing
decisions and the design of some of his publications;
"Ava Weiss and Vera Williams," pp. 21–36, where
the author and the editor talk about their roles and how
they work together, and Williams discusses her work on
some specific books;
"Leonard Everett Fisher," pp. 36–47, discusses how
he works on both his paintings and his picture books;
"Irene Haas," pp. 47–54, covering how she develops
a book in detail, and her experience at the printer with
Little Moon Theater;
"David Macaulay," pp. 54–65, chiefly detailing his
work on the brain in *The Amazing Garden*. Also included
are questions following each presentation and a general
discussion and questions including all participants.

348. *Picture Books: Elements of Illustration and Story.*
Videocassette. Chicago: American Library Association,
1987. 25 min.

Betsy Hearne uses two editions of *The Easter Bunny
that Overslept* to compare Adrienne Adams' illustrations
and other visual aspects of the versions for the
"illustration" part of her presentation. Shows how the
differences can affect the readings of the text.

349. Pitz, Henry Clarence. *A Treasury of American Book
Illustration.* New York: Watson-Guptill, 1947. 128pp.

Chiefly illustrations, some in color. Some notes on
the nature and growth of illustration; on "Pictures for
Children," pp. 15–17; and on the design of the book and
its jacket. Pp. 27–128 are all examples.

350. Polette, Nancy J. *Brain Power Through Picture Books: Help Children Develop with Books That Stimulate Specific Parts of Their Minds.* Jefferson, N.C.: McFarland, 1992. 138pp.

The author's major concern is cognitive development, so picture books are shown here as tools for specific skills. The illustrations are treated lightly in passing, if at all. They are not as exploited as they could be for similar goals. The list of picture books referred to is, however, a fine one. Some book jackets or covers are reproduced in b & w; other b & w illustrations are of poor quality.

351. ———. *"E" Is for Everybody: A Manual for Bringing Fine Picture Books into the Hands and Hearts of Children.* Metuchen, N.J.: Scarecrow, 1976. 147pp.

An annotated bibliography of selected picture books includes little analysis of illustration in the summary, but lists related activities for each book. Part Two, pp. 87–142, describes art and craft activities for children to use to interpret literature.

352. ———. *Picture Books for Gifted Programs.* Metuchen, N.J.: Scarecrow, 1981. 220pp.

Using many examples, Polette builds from Piaget's theory of cognitive development activities and examples for selected picture books. On pp. 23–29 she gives us a taxonomy of visual communication skills for children from kindergarten through high school and then an annotated list of picture books for teaching the specific skills. Other lists are included in chapters on communication skills, productive thinking, and critical thinking. Part two moves from picture books to other books to continue the development of critical thinking. Some b & w illustrations.

353. Prince, Diana M. "Heightening the Perceptive Abilities of Middle School Art Students Through the Use of the

Picturebook." Master's thesis, Ohio State University, Columbus, 1985. 156pp.

Case studies demonstrating the use of picture books as the focus of study (both analytical and productive) in art classes of adolescents. Results were positive enough to warrant serious consideration of extending the study of picture books in art curriculums at all age levels.

354. Protheroe, Pamela. *Vexed Texts: How Children's Picture Books Promote Illiteracy.* Sussex, England: Book Guild, 1992. 174pp.

The author's thesis is that "the illustrated children's book used to teach reading is the banner at the head of the present relentless progression towards educational failure." She exploits hemispheric brain theory and research to illuminate five aspects: neurophysiological, psychological, linguistic, aesthetic, and pedagogical. She claims that using pictures in books stifles language development.

355. Purves, Alan C., and Dianne L. Monson. *Experiencing Children's Literature.* Glenview, Ill.: Scott, Foresman, 1984. 216pp.

"The role of the picture book in developing a sense of style," pp. 107–118, analyzes what a picture book is, and how the media used may convey the aim of the illustrator and the author. Influence of "fine" art discussed. "Evaluating Book Illustration," pp. 156–164, asks some questions which may help analyze and judge. Includes picture books in other discussions, especially on poetry. Some b & w illustrations are really sepia.

356. Ramsey, Inez L. "Effect of Art Style on Children's Picture Preferences." *Journal of Educational Research* 75, no. 4 (March–April 1982): 237–240.

Preferences measured and correlated by how they related to text and by sex of child. Pictures used were in "photographic," "representational," "cartoon" and "expressionistic" styles as produced by professional artists from specific photographs, as opposed to actual illustrations from picture books. These were put with selected literary passages. Then children were either shown the picture first and asked which they would most like to read about, or they listened to the passage and were then asked which illustration "went" best with the story.

357. Raymond, Chet. "Dr. Seuss and Dr. Einstein: Children's Books and Scientific Imagination." *Horn Book* 68, no. 5 (September–October 1992): 560–567.

A professor of physics draws parallels between the creativity of Dr. Seuss and that required for creative science. Other essentials offered in picture books such as those by Maurice Sendak or Graeme Base to spur scientific imagination are "curiosity," "voracious observation," "rules and variations within the rules," and "fantasy."

358. Read, Donna, and Henrietta M. Smith. "Teaching Visual Literacy Through Wordless Picture Books." *The Reading Teacher* (May 1982): 930–933.

Covers the elements of line and shape, color and symbolism with examples from the books. Discusses their use with young and older children to teach sequencing, finding the main idea, making inferences and drawing conclusions, determining cause and effect, and making judgments all from the pictures alone. Useful list of references included.

359. Rhoades, Jane. "Teaching Art" column in *Teaching K–8* from 1993 on frequently includes discussion of picture books.

360. Richard, Olga. "The Visual Language of the Picture Book." *Wilson Library Bulletin* 44, no. 4 (December 1969): 435–447.

A detailed exposition of the qualities of the illustrations that need to be evaluated in picture books. Analyzes the elements of color, line, shape, texture, composition, plus those specific to the art of the book such as binding, end papers, the type and its placement. Discusses the personal role of the artist. Gives many examples for each element, with some b & w illustrations.

361. ————, and Donnarae MacCann. "The Japanese Sensibility in Picture Books for Children." *Wilson Library Bulletin* 65, no. 2 (October 1990): 23–27.

In attempting to analyze the "sensibility" or style of Japanese picture books, the authors go back into the history of Japanese art and illustration to the scrolls, woodblock prints, and Asian art styles, and then to children's magazines of the early twentieth century. Then some specific picture book illustrations are analyzed, in general, from a Western and traditional Japanese point of view.

362. Richey, Virginia H., and Kathryn E. Puckett. *Wordless/ Almost Wordless Picture Books: A Guide.* Englewood, Colo.: Libraries Unlimited, 1992. 223pp.

The foreword by David Wiesner, pp. vii–viii, discusses the nature of a wordless picture book and its challenges for creator and reader. The book contains an alphabetical author listing, with complete bibliographic information and brief annotations. It also has a title list; a format list of books with unusual formats (like pop-ups); an "Index to Use of Print," (i.e., how wordless is the book); a series index of titles; an illustrator index (when the illustrator is not the author); and finally, a subject index. Although little attention is paid to the illustrations, this is an extremely useful tool for locating wordless books.

363. Roads, Clarice. *Exploring The Art of Picture Books.* Norman: Oklahoma State Department of Education, 1982. 53pp.

A guide for teachers which includes a list of books and illustrators, and plans of many related activities for grades K–3 and 4–8. A very useful bibliography includes sections on art techniques as well as books and media for the adult and the child.

364. Robinson, Evelyn Rose, ed. *Readings About Children's Literature.* New York: David McKay, 1966. 431pp.

Reprints include: Anne Carroll Moore, "Illustrating Books for Children," pp. 195–201, analyzing some of her favorite illustrators;

Maurice Sendak, "The Shape of Music," pp. 201–205, telling how he works with music in mind to make the art "quicken." Mentions other illustrators whose work he admires.

Madel Rudisill, "Children's Preferences for Color Versus Other Qualities in Illustration," pp. 205–214, a study of children's preferences in grades K–6 in Kentucky.

There are notes on illustration and/or art on p. 77 and p. 237, and on illustration in informational books, pp. 377–378 and pp. 390–391.

365. Rychlicki, Zbigniew. "Children's Book Illustration in Poland." *Bookbird* 27, no. 4 (November 1989): 9–12.

Analyzes several basic types of Polish illustration today and works of the successful illustrators. The use of humor, folk themes, and increasingly complex graphics are discussed, relating the latter to the visual images of film and television. Several b & w illustrations are reproduced.

366. Ryder, John. *Artists of a Certain Line: A Selection of Illustrators for Children's Books.* London: Bodley Head, 1960. 128pp.

    Brief biographies (single page plus facing page illustration) of forty artists picked for their talents in drawing. The very personal introduction discusses the qualities which are necessary for a superior illustration. Fully illustrated with b & w historic and contemporary examples.

367. Saxby, H.M. *A History of Australian Children's Literature, 1841–1941.* Sidney, Australia: Wentworth Books, 1969. 212pp.

    "Books with pictures," p. 120, gives brief mention of pictures. "The Influence in Australia of Art Nouveau," pp. 121–124, shows the style's influence on the illustrated book.

368. Schuman, Patricia. "Concerned Criticism or Casual Cop-Out?" *School Library Journal* 18 (January 1972): 21–24; and *Library Journal* 97, no. 2 (January 15, 1972): 245–248.

    Analyzes the sources of reviews and criticism of books for children available to concerned adults seeking guidance, showing the scarcity and difficulty of finding this. Calls attention to the roles of children and young adults as consumers whose input should be considered.

369. Schwarcz, Joseph H. *Ways of the Illustrator: Visual Communication in Children's Literature.* Chicago: American Library Association, 1982. 202pp.

    A thoughtful attempt to answer the two major questions set for itself: "In what ways does the illustration . . . express its contents and meanings?" and "How does the illustration relate to the verbal text?" Both themes and elements of artistic composition are employed with examples drawn from several countries as well as through many comparisons of a single story illustrated by different artists. Emphasis on current books. Illustrated books are accepted and treated as art objects.

370. ———, and Chava Schwarcz. *The Picture Book Comes of Age: Looking at Childhood through the Art of Illustration.* Chicago: American Library Assn., 1991. 217pp.

A set of essays "connected as organically as possible" by the original author's widow and by Betsy Hearne, which focus on his concern for the psychological/social content. Chapter titles include "Stress and the Picture Book," "The Emergence of Identity," "Social Action for the Disadvantaged," "The Threat of War and the Quest for Peace." Most of the analysis fixes on the visuals: how the media, style, and page design produce emotions. American as well as a range of international books are included. An unannotated bibliography also includes international sources.

371. Sendak, Maurice. *Caldecott & Co.: Notes on Books and Pictures.* Farrar, Straus, 1988. 216pp.

Some b & w illustrations are included in this collection of Sendak's essays, speeches, and reviews. Places where originally published are listed in the back. Subjects range from the historical (Mother Goose, Randolph Caldecott, Lothar Meggendorfer, Maxfield Parrish, Beatrix Potter) to Walt Disney.

372. Sheppard, Valerie. "Give All Ages a Look at a Mother Goose Book." Paper presented at the Texas State Council Conference of the International Reading Association, El Paso, Texas. March 11–13, 1982. ERIC Microfiche ED 218604 82. 9pp.

The different illustrators and their styles include Rojankovsky, Wildsmith, Jeffers, Spier, Galdone, Lobel, and the Provensens. Bibliography.

373. Short, Kathy G. "Visual Literacy: Exploring Art and Illustration in Children's Books." *Reading Teacher* 46, no. 6 (March 1993): 506–516.

   Because children need to be able to "read" pictures along with text, art and illustration are the focus of a series of brief reviews of new books, including a section on those "featuring illustrators, illustration and bookmaking," and one on picture books that "explore various elements of art, illustration styles and bookmaking formats." List appended.

374. Shulevitz, Uri. "What Is a Picture Book?" *Wilson Library Bulletin* 55, no. 2 (October 1980): 99–101.

   ". . . A picture book is unclear or incomplete without the pictures," says the artist, and gives examples.

375. ———. "What Is a Picture Book?" *The Five Owls* II, no. 4 (March–April 1988): 49–53.

   Shulevitz tries to distinguish between picture books, where pictures primarily tell the story, and "storybooks," where the words are of primary importance. There are also "Picture book and storybook concepts combined," where the words tell the story but the pictures extend it. A few b & w illustrations and lists of examples of each type.

 * ———. *Writing with Pictures: How to Write and Illustrate Children's Books.* Cited above as item 130.

376. Slapin, Beverly, and Doris Seale, eds. *Through Indian Eyes; Books without Bias.* Rev. ed. Berkeley, Calif.: Oyate, 1989. 452pp.

   Poems, stories, and articles on recommended reading materials for Native American children. Also includes a criteria checklist, lists of publishers and additional resources, controversial opinions on cultural copyright, and a different slant on analysis of illustrations.

377. Smith, Irene. *A History of the Newbery and Caldecott Medals.* New York: Viking, 1957. 140pp.

    Details the people involved and the events that led to the establishment of the awards. Also some discussion of the award events. The chapter on award-winning books and their continual popularity, pp. 93–101, discusses the Caldecott winners, giving brief descriptions and possible reasons for their popularity. No illustration except of medals.

378. Smith, James A., and Dorothy M. Park. *Word Music and Word Magic: Children's Literature Methods.* Boston: Allyn and Bacon, 1977. 564pp.

    "Picture Books, Picture-Story Books and Illustrated Books" are briefly treated in pp. 28–30. In chapters on "Classical Illustrators," pp. 219–235, and "Modern Illustrators," pp. 236–267, many articles about illustrators and the use of their works with children are excerpted and commented upon, as are several illustrators in the chapter, "New Models, New Faces," pp. 192–218. Some b & w photos and illustrations.

379. Smith, James Steel. *A Critical Approach to Children's Literature.* New York: McGraw-Hill, 1967. 442pp.

    Chapter 12, "To read, to Look," pp. 305–342, discusses the importance of the visual image for the child. Gives a brief history of illustration. Covers effects of Modern Art, Representational Art, Disney School, Seuss and other comics; abstraction and trends in layout; printing; and relating illustration to text. Gives many examples plus a long list of illustrators and their work. B & w illustrated examples.

380. Smith, Nicole Gnezda. "Aesthetic Literacy: Teaching Preschool Children to Respond to Book Illustrations."

Master's thesis, Ohio State University, Columbus, 1981. 76pp.

The author defines "aesthetic literacy" as the ability to "read" pictures, to become sensitive to the visual qualities of colors, textures, shapes, etc. Based on her research findings, she points to the need for preschool education. At this age children do respond aesthetically to pictures, and this capacity can be enhanced through education.

381. Soriano, Marc. *Guide de litterature pour la jeunesse: courants, problemes, choix, d'auteurs.* Paris: Flammarion, 1975. 568pp.

This general dictionary of children's literature has a discussion of illustration on pp. 326–336 with the psychological role of image in education. A general history ends with the role of the mass media and the improvement in the technical process of reproduction. "Research and criticism in the field of children's literature," pp. 439–453, discusses the problem of approaching and appreciating art destined for children, and the inadequacy of most criticism. Some French illustrators are included in the dictionary section.

382. Spaid, Elizabeth Levitan. "Children's Book Art Attracts Collectors." *Christian Science Monitor* (February 4, 1993): 12–13.

Describes the growing market for both children's picture books themselves and for the illustrators' original artwork. Names the galleries currently selling the art and the collections, and includes notes on the growing number of shows and museum exhibitions.

383. Spitz, Ellen Handler. "Primary Art Objects: Psychoanalytic Reflections on Picturebooks for Children." *Psychoanalytic Study of the Child* 44 (1989): 351–368.

Uses psychological analytic developmental theory to analyze several picture books briefly, and Sendak's *Nutshell Library* in depth, in an effort to explain their impact on youngsters and their function in the acculturation process, where they transmit ethical and esthetic values.

384. St. John, Judith. "The Osborne Collection of Early Children's Books: Highlights in Retrospect." *Horn Book* 60 (September–October 1984): 652–660.

The retiring head of the Osborne Collection describes the collection and its growth, including key acquisitions and publications.

385. Stephens, Catherine. "Peepo Ergo Sum? Anxiety and Pastiche in the Ahlberg Picture Books." *Children's Literature in Education* 21, no. 3 (September 1990): 165–177.

An analysis of seven titles by the Ahlbergs from the late 1980s; points out ways that the illustrations reflect current social concerns through a child's eye, but with underlying adult perceptions.

386. Stephens, John. "Language, Discourse, and Picture Books." *Children's Literature Association Quarterly* 14, no. 3 (Fall 1989): 106–110.

Linguistic analyses of texts in picture books showing ranges of complexity. Mention of pictures only when they support words.

387. Stewig, John Warren. "Alphabet Books: A Neglected Genre." *Language Arts* (January 1978): 6–11.

Shows how to use these books to help develop visual and verbal skills with children. Gives many examples.

388. ———. "Book Illustration: Key to Visual and Verbal Literacy." Paper presented at the Annual Meeting of the International Reading Association, New York City. May 13–16, 1975. ERIC Document ED 112352. 11pp.

Discusses the subskills of visual and verbal literacy: describing, comparing, and oral valuing (i.e., "prefer or like"). Uses versions of "Red Riding Hood," "Cinderella," "Mother Goose," and the "Owl and the Pussycat."

389. ———. *Children and Literature.* Chicago: Rand McNally, 1980. 562pp.

Space devoted shows the attention to picture books. Chapter two, "Studying Book Illustration," pp. 38–73, emphasizes the importance of illustration and the artist, with a discussion of related art movements. Chapter three, pp. 74–95, covers "The Alphabet Book," purposes, types and evaluation. Chapter four, "Picture Books," pp. 96–129, analyzes, evaluates and discusses children's responses. Chapter five, pp. 130–158, is a discussion and analysis of wordless picture books. Bibliographies of examples and sources for further information. Many b & w and a few color illustrations.

390. ———. "Children's Preference in Picture Book Illustration." *Educational Leadership* 30, no. 3 (December 1972): 273–277.

Stewig reviewed sixteen studies designed to assess children's preferences in pictures and found them all to be erroneous or inconclusive. He concludes that picture books are chosen primarily by means of "simple intuition" and asks if better research methods might provide less idiosyncratic bases for choice.

391. ———. "Choosing the Caldecott Winner: Fifth Graders Give Their Reasons." *Journal of Youth Services in Libraries* 3 no. 2 (Winter 1990): 128–133.

The author describes a program designed to be part of a possible visual literacy program, trying to determine if children's responses to pictures change in quality or quantity after being in such a program. Students talked and wrote about the illustrations in Caldecott-winning books before and after being introduced to visual elements like line, shape, color, etc.

392. ———. "The Emperor's New Clothes." *Booklinks* (May 1993): 35–38.

Analyzes and gives discussion points for four versions of the Andersen tale, adding information on five more.

393. ———. *An Experimental Visual Literacy Program in Schools.* 1989. ERIC Microfiche ED311470. 16pp.

Describes a one-year program in grades one and five in two schools, urban and suburban, during which children looked at, discussed, wrote about, and made art about both picture books and art reproductions, organized to introduce visual elements like line, shape, color, etc. Discusses responses.

394. ———. "Picture Books: What Do Reviews Really Review?" *Top of the News* 37 (Fall 1980): 83–84.

Briefly examines reviews of picture books in four "widely respected" sources during 1979 to tally percentage of words describing visual aspects. Deplores low percentage as indicator of lack of attention to this most important aspect.

395. ———. *Reading Pictures: Exploring Illustrations with Children. Ezra Jack Keats; Marcia Brown; Gerald McDermott; Nonny Hogrogian.* New Berlin, Wisc.: Jenson, 1988. 4 sets.

Each set includes four color posters, 17½" × 22", one of each of four books, and a study guide, with reviews, ways to study, and a bibliography.

396. ———. "Ten from the Decade: Visually Significant Picture Books and Why." Paper presented at the 36th IRA Conference, Las Vegas, Nevada. May 6–10, 1991. ERIC Microfilm ED 33358. 24pp.

Analyses of the art and design of ten picture storybooks with pictures in a wide range of styles and media considered personally "significant," although no criteria for this are given. Many other works are referred to, including reprints of historic texts, concept books such as ABC's, and textless works. Several notions are offered for educational uses of picture books.

397. ———. "Trends in Caldecott Award Winners." *Elementary English* 45 (February 1968): 218–223, 260.

A careful analysis of both winners and honor books over thirty years as to "realism quotient": to see if, in these books at least, there was a trend toward, or away from, realism; and any trends to or from certain media. There seems to be "an increasing willingness . . . to depart from the traditional. . . ."

398. ———. "Visual and Verbal Literacy." Paper presented at the Annual Meeting of the NCTA, San Antonio, Texas. November 21–26, 1986. ERIC Microfiche ED 278028. 13pp.

In search of "seeing with insight," or the educated eye, Stewig shows how children can examine components of pictures, draw relationships, extract meaning, and respond by talking or writing. Examples are the use of picture books.

* *Story of a Book* Sound filmstrip. Cited above as item 133.

399. Stott, Jon C. *Children's Literature from A to Z: A Guide for Parents and Teachers.* New York: McGraw-Hill, 1984. 318pp.

Dictionary format reference covering general terms, themes, and important people in children's literature. Entries run from less than one page to more than two in the case of "Picture Books and Illustration." Biographical and critical information on over fifty picture-book artists are included under their individual names; "Tips for parents and teachers" follows each entry. Thirty-four small b & w page-spread illustrations.

400. Sullivan, Peggy. "A Tale of Callie Kott." *Journal of Youth Services in Libraries* 1, no. 2 (Winter 1989): 183–186.

Using a fictional composite, Sullivan reviews the experience of being on the Newbery-Caldecott Committee, mainly from the 1940s to the 1970s.

401. Sutherland, Zena, and May Hill Arbuthnot. *Children and Books* 7th ed. Glenview, Ill.: Scott, Foresman, 1986. 768pp.

Chapter 5, pp. 80–129, "Books for the Very Young," discusses picture books with critical comments. Chapter 6, pp. 132–162, "Artists and Children's Books," also has critical comments as it discusses particular artists.

The eighth edition was published in 1991. More color art is included, and material on illustration is included. Illustrated in b & w and color.

402. ———, and Betsy Hearne. "In Search of the Perfect Picture Book Definition." *Wilson Library Bulletin* 52, no. 2 (October 1977): 158–160.

Many examples are given to support a range of picture books that show how the pictures should "either dominate the text or are as important."

403. Szekely, George. "An Introduction to Art: Children's Books." *Childhood Education* (Spring 1990): 132–138.

An enthusiastic account, with b & w photos and illustrations, of how picture books play a significant role in the life of this artist/teacher. Over a dozen specific ideas for classroom activities and many more general comments on helping children value picture books as art objects.

404. Townsend, John Rowe. *Written for Children: An Outline of English-Language Children's Literature.* Rev. ed. Philadelphia: Lippincott, 1965, 1974. 368pp.

A history and analysis of the types of literature, including picture books. Some b & w illustrations. "Picture Books in Bloom," pp. 308–320, discusses the United States scene. Pages 321–330 cover picture books in Britain. The author is concerned that the reviewers don't have the qualifications to review picture books, while art critics have generally not become involved, leading to less satisfactory reviewing. See item 73 above for newer edition.

405. Vandergrift, Kay E. *Children's Literature: Theory, Research, and Teaching.* Englewood, Colo.: Libraries Unlimited, 1990. 277pp.

Includes a discussion of multiple versions of a single traditional tale using both Trina Schart Hyman's and Nancy Burkert's versions of *Snow White*, p. 7. In suggestions for research, she notes the questions for inner-textual studies presented by picture books, p. 37, and some in intratextual studies pp. 37–39. A worksheet for analyzing elements of a "picture-story book" is on p. 153. An extensive bibliography is included.

406. Warthman, John Burns. "A Study of Picture Preferences of Caldecott Award Winners and Runners-up by Fourth, Fifth, and Sixth Grade Children of Selected Schools." University of Southern Mississippi, 1970. University Microfilm No. 71-1 589.

Five hundred eighty-two children in grades four, five, and six made choices from twenty-eight Caldecott

Award and honor books, and selected the Award book for only two of the seven years sampled.

407. Watanabe, Shigeo. "Japanese and American Picture Books . . . Similarities and Differences." *Michigan Librarian* 37 (Winter 1971) 11–14.

After a brief history, discusses several modern Japanese illustrators, including Nakatani, Akaba, Segawa; and the problem in Japan of well-educated children having quality books and poorer children having the gaudy. Watanabe feels that American books have more humor and fantasy, Japanese parents' views have more importance, and that values differ in the two cultures.

408. Watts, Lynne, and John Nisbet. *Legibility in Children's Books: A Review of Research.* New York: Humanities, 1972. Windsor, England: NFER Publishing Co. Ltd., 1974. 104pp.

Discusses the effect on the young reader of various aspects of book design, such as type, margins, and paper. Section 4, "Color and Illustration," pp. 70–86, treats size, position, and nature of pictures. Includes examples and illustrations.

409. Weller, Joan. "Picture Books for Older Children." *The Five Owls* VII, no. 2 (November–December 1992): 25–30.

Notes the increasing number of picture books for more mature readers aged eight to thirteen. Discusses how to promote these. Includes some small b & w illustrations and an extensive annotated bibliography of good examples of such books.

410. ———. "Sophisticated Picturebooks." *Canadian Library Journal* 41, no. 1 (February 1984): 21–24.

Comments on the quality of recent picture books. Higher quality of color is made possible by new technology and has produced a "New Breed" for an older child, reflecting a variety of art movements.

411. Whalen-Levitt, Peggy. "Picture Play in Children's Books: A Celebration of Visual Awareness." *Wilson Library Bulletin* 55, no. 2 (October 1980): 102–107.

Gives examples of images in picture books that challenge our expectations or offer allusions or parodies beyond the story.

412. White, Mary Lou. *Children's Literature: Criticism and Response.* Columbus, Ohio: Charles E. Merrill, 1976. 252pp.

Reprints of works appearing elsewhere. Uses a framework of four theories of criticism: psychological, sociological, archetypical, and structural. Includes activities for children. Patricia Cianciolo, "Use Wordless Picture Books . . . ," and Rose Agree, "Lionni's Artichokes: An Interview," are the only selections dealing with picture books. These articles appear in separate annotations further in this document.

413. White, Maureen. "Children's Books in Other Languages: A Study of Succesful Translations." *Journal of Youth Services in Libraries* 5, no. 3 (Spring 1992): 261–275.

Gives statistics and characteristics common to successful translated children's books, including genre, major subject areas, authors and illustrators, publishers, and translators. Very little specifically about picture books. Extensive appendix-bibliography of successful translated children's books, including picture books.

414. Williams, Clarence M., and John L. Debes, eds. *Proceedings of the First National Conference on Visual Literacy.* New York: Pitman, 1970. 295pp.

Since "Visual Literacy" is a term used by some critics of picture books, this volume is helpful in clarifying the many meanings of the term, although it does not deal anywhere with picture books directly. Almost fifty pages cover concepts, research, and programs in the schools, including teacher preparation. Of particular interest is "Design in Communication," pp. 36–41, by Donis A. Dondis, which tries to show that we receive messages from our visual associations with basic shapes.

415. Williams, Helen E. *Books by African-American Authors and Illustrators for Children and Young Adults.* Chicago: American Library Assn., 1991. 270pp.

Very brief annotations in age-grouped sections do not discuss the illustrations. Chapter 4, "Black Illustrators and Their Works," pp. 195–219, lists the illustrators alphabetically with extremely brief descriptions of "their illustrative style, technique, use of color language, and composition" followed by a list of their publications. Description of art is generalized, mostly formalistic, and often confusing. A glossary of art terms is in the appendix.

416. Wilson, Trudy G. "The Medium of Wordless Picture Books: An Overview of Classroom Applications." *Visible and Viable: The Role of Images in Instruction and Communication.* Readings from the Annual Conference of the International Visual Literacy Assn., 1987. Pp. 5–19.

Summarizes the research on uses of wordless books by teachers for teaching "visual literacy"; for literary style, with older children or those with special needs, for art appreciation, and for "creativity." Specific books for each purpose are suggested, along with an extensive list.

417. Yeager, Allan. *Using Picture Books with Children: A Guide to Owlet Books.* New York: Holt, Rinehart and Winston, 1973. 203pp.

For each of sixty-one Owlet books, Yeager summarizes the story, discusses the illustrations very briefly and relates them to the text. He also gives other information and suggestions for the teacher working with students and the book. The illustrators included are listed in the index.

418. Zerfoss, Charlotte. "The Picture Book: Art for Children." *Drexel Library Quarterly* 12, no. 4 (October 1976): 12–19.

Brief paragraphs point out a string of qualities that illustrations should possess including that freedom from stereotype, skilled draftsmanship, style, adaptation to the narrative, etc. Uses a score of examples as models of qualities.

PART IV

Artists Anthologized

* Alderman, Belle, and Lauren Harman, eds. *The Imagineers: Writing and Illustrating Children's Books*. Cited above as item 142.

419. *The Artist and the Child: Exhibition of Children's Books and Original Illustration from the John D. Merriam Collection*. Boston: Public Library, 1980. 96pp.

    Chiefly b & w illustrations from the exhibition. Brief biographical sketches of the sixty-two illustrators are included.

420. *Author Profile Collection*. Compiled by the editors of *The Book Report* and *Library Talk*. Worthington, Ohio: Linworth Publishing, 1992. 106pp.

    These profiles, originally published in the magazines, with b & w illustrations and photos, cover the life and the work of the artists with extensive quotations. Includes the following illustrators:
    Carole Byard by Sylvia Marantz, pp. 14–17;
    Lois Ehlert by Sylvia Marantz, pp. 33–36;
    Gail E. Haley by Susan R. Austin, pp. 41–44;
    John Steptoe by Cheryl Abdullah, pp. 81–83;
    David Wiesner by Cheryl Abdullah, pp. 85–88.

421. *Authors & Artists for Young Adults*. Approx. 2 vols. pub'd each year. Agnes Garrett and Helga P. McCue, editors of early volumes. Detroit, Mich.: Gale, 1989.

    Occasionally includes a picture book artist.

*   Bader, Barbara. *American Picture Books from Noah's Ark to the Beast Within.* Cited above as item 4.

*   *Beginning with Excellence: An Adult Guide to Great Children's Reading.* Cited above as item 153.

422. *Biennale of Illustrations Bratislava.* Catalog. Bratislava: Mlade leta, publ. after the two biennales 1967 and 1969; 1971 and 1973.

These profusely illustrated color catalogs contain prize-winning illustrations and brief information on the illustrators in several languages including English. More recent catalogs cover single biennales and are not in English.

*   Bingham, Jane M., ed. *Writers for Children: Critical Studies of Major Authors Since the Seventeenth Century.* Cited above as item 158.

423. Bolton, Theodore. *American Book Illustrators: Bibliographic Checklists of 123 Artists.* New York: Bowker, 1938. 290pp.

Some earlier American illustrators of children's books (e.g., Lynd Ward, N. C. Wyeth, Kurt Wiese, Helen Sewell, Howard Pyle, the Petershams, Robert Lawson, Wanda Gag, James Daugherty, Gelett Burgess, Boris Artzybasheff, and Valenti Angelo) are included in this alphabetical listing along with places where the illustrations are published.

424. Brown, Muriel W., and Rita Schuch Foudray. *Newbery and Caldecott Medalists and Honor Book Winners: Bibliographies and Resource Material through 1991.* Edited by Jim Roginski. 2d ed. New York: Neal-Schuman, 1992. 511pp.

Includes for each entry: awards received, a bibliography of their work, the collections where original materials are housed, plus a bibliography of sources.

425. Bunanta, Murti. "They Never Give Up: Indonesian Writers and Illustrators." *Bookbird* 29, no. 4 (December 1991): 11–13.

Introduces five of Indonesia's top artists and writers for children, including Hardiyono, the first winner of the INABBY Illustration competition. B & w photos and illustrations.

426. Butler, Francelia, and Richard Rotert, eds. *Reflections on Literature for Children.* Hamden, Conn.: Library Professional Publications, 1984. 281pp.

Roger Sale, "Child Reading and Man Reading; Oz, Babar and Pooh," pp. 19–31, includes discussion of the relationship between De Brunhoff's words and pictures.

Seth Sicroff, "Prickles Under the Frock: The Art of Beatrix Potter," pp. 39–44, includes relation of illustrations to text.

Michael Patrick Hearn, "Mr. Ruskin and Miss Greenaway," pp. 182–190, briefly analyzes his relationship with her as well as her life and work.

Jennifer R. Waller, "Maurice Sendak and the Blakean Vision of Childhood," pp. 260–268, compares the two and shows Blake's influence on Sendak. Analyzes both art and language of Sendak's books in this light.

427. Carpenter, Humphrey, and Mari Richard. *The Oxford Companion to Children's Literature.* New York: Oxford University Press, 1984. 586pp.

Occasional small b & w reproductions and twenty-six photos. Uneven treatment, though very comprehensive, with British emphasis, of the entire field. In dictionary format with extensive cross-references. Includes important subjects and characters from books and other media in English, plus those from other countries which have become part of our culture. Greenaway and Potter are given several pages, while E.J. Keats rates only one paragraph.

428. Cech, John, ed. *American Writers for Children, 1900–1960,* vol. 22. Dictionary of Literary Biography. Detroit, Mich.: Gale, 1983. 412pp.

    Photographic portraits and b & w reproductions of works. Contains multi-page essays with biographical and critical comments, lists of works and further references, interviews and locations of papers. The picture book illustrators included are: Bemelmans, M.W. Brown, Burton, the D'Aulaires, de Angeli, Ets, Gag, Gramatky, Lawson, Lenski, McCloskey, the Petershams, Rey, Thurber, Ward, and Garth Williams.

 * Chevalier, Tracy, ed. See Kirkpatrick, D. L., ed. *Twentieth-Century Children's Writers.* Cited below as item 463.

429. *Children's Book Showcase.* Catalogs of traveling exhibits sponsored yearly by the Children's Book Council, 1970s, 67 Irving Place, New York.

    The books were selected by a committee. Each catalog lists the title with a small b & w reproduction, gives technical production details, and a summary of each book included in the "showcase."

430. "Coming Attractions." *Publishers Weekly* 236, no. 4 (July 28, 1989): 132–135.

    Brief interviews concerning new books allow artists to discuss their work. Included are Richard Egielski on *The Tub People*, Thomas Locker on *The Young Artist*, Catherine Brighton on *Nijinsky*, and Chris Van Allsburg on *Swan Lake*.

431. Commire, Anne et al., eds. *Something About the Author: Facts and Pictures About Authors and Illustrators of Books for Young People.* Cont. publ. Detroit, Mich.: Gale.

    Volumes 1–74 (1993) all include illustrations. Donna Olendorf became editor in 1991 for volumes 66–69, with

Diane Telgrin for volumes 70–74 in 1993. Includes illustrators and major writers for children. Biographical and critical information is included, plus a list of works. A cumulative "Illustrations Index" precedes the author index. Before volume 15, only authors and illustrators alive in 1961 were included. Beginning with volume 15, "the time scope was broadened" to include some major authors who died before 1961, formerly in the editor's *Yesterday's Authors of Books for Children.*

432. ———. *Yesterday's Authors of Books for Children: Facts and Pictures about Authors and Illustrators of Books for Young People from Early Times to 1960.* 2 vols. Detroit, Mich.: Gale, 1976 and 1978. Varying pages.

Illustrations are from books or from motion pictures of books. Includes biographies, criticism, quotations from diaries, and illustrations listed by illustrator; for example, Kate Greenaway, pp. 129–141, volume 1, and Robert Lawson, pp. 222–241, volume 2.

433. *Contemporary American Illustrators of Children's Books.* Catalog of an exhibition. New Brunswick, N.J.: Rutgers University Press, 1974. 72pp.

Full b & w illustrations on each page facing artist's information. Catalog of an exhibition that travelled from Rutgers to four other museums during 1974 and 1975. Following a two-page essay by A. Hyatt Mayor, there is a page of biographical information, a quotation, and a list of illustrations for each artist. Contributing are: Adrienne Adams, Erik Blegvad, Marcia Brown, Jean Charlot, Tony Chen, Barbara Cooney, James Daugherty, Harry Devlin, William Pene du Bois, Roger Duvoisin, Fritz Eichenberg, Antonio Frasconi, Don Freeman, Edward Gorey, Lorenzo Homar, Ezra Jack Keats, Blair Lent, Leo Lionni, Arnold Lobel, Joseph Low, Robert McCloskey, Evaline Ness, Peter Parnall, Leona Pierce, Ellen Raskin, John Schoenherr, Maurice Sendak, Marc

Simont, Lynd Ward, Garth Williams, Taro Yashima, and Margot Zemach.

* Cott, Jonathan. *Pipers at the Gates of Dawn: The Wisdom of Children's Literature.* Cited above as item 194.

434. Crouch, Marcus. *Treasure Seekers and Borrowers: Children's Books in Britain, 1900–1960.* London: Library Assn., 1962. 162pp.

Generally a chronological survey of all children's literature. Index is only of authors and titles, so his views on picture books and illustrators must be searched out in the text. Pages 134–138 discuss some contemporary illustrators.

435. Cummings, Pat, comp. and ed. *Talking with Artists: Conversations with Victoria Chess, Pat Cummings, Leo and Diane Dillon, Richard Egielski, Lois Ehlert, Lisa Campbell Ernst, Tom Feelings, Steven Kellogg, Jerry Pinkney, Amy Schwartz, Lane Smith, Chris Van Allsburg, and David Wiesner.* New York: Bradbury, 1992. 96pp.

Illustrated with b & w and color photographs of the artists as children and adults, and with examples of their illustrations. Aiming at a young audience, Cummings has asked illustrators to summarize their early life, art training, and other significant life events. Then each illustrator answers the eight frequently asked questions about areas like where their ideas come from, how and where they work, and how their first book came about. A glossary of terms used for picture books and illustrations is included.

436. Cummins, Julie, ed. *Children's Book Illustration and Design.* New York: PBC International/Rizzoli, 1992. 240pp.

Sumptuously illustrated with full-color reproductions of the book illustrations and b & w photographs of the artists. Basic facts on each illustrator are included. Quotations from most artists tell something about how they work or about a particular book. Artists are: Thomas B. Allen, Mitsumasa Anno, Jim Arnosky, Graeme Base, Nicola Bayley, Quentin Blake, Jan Brett, Patience Brewster, Eric Carle, Peter Catalanotto, Chris Conover, Barbara Cooney, Donald Crews, Pat Cummings, Tomie dePaola, Henrik Drescher, Richard Egielski, Lois Ehlert, Leonard Everett Fisher, Paul Galdone, Arthur Geisert, Roy Gerrard, Diane Goode, Ann Grifalconi, Helme Heine, Kevin Henkes, Ronald Himler, Pat Hutchins, Warwick Hutton, Trina Schart Hyman, Erick Ingraham, Susan Jeffers, Ann Jonas, William Joyce, Ezra Jack Keats, Bert Kitchen, Leo Lionni, Anita Lobel, Arnold Lobel, Suse MacDonald, James Marshall, Petra Mathers, Gerald McDermott, Charles Mikolaycak, Wendell Minor, Beni Montresor, Barry Moser, Roxie Munro, Keiko Narahashi, Bill Oakes, Jan Ormerod, Nancy Winslow Parker, Robert Andrew Parker, Brian Pinkney, Jerry Pinkney, Patricia Polacco, Alice and Martin Provensen, Ted Rand, Robert Rayevsky, Barbara Reid, Glen Rounds, Marisabina Russo, Allen Say, John Schoenherr, Amy Schwartz, Marcia Sewell, Uri Shulevitz, Peter Sis, Lane Smith, Diane Stanley, John Steptoe, Nancy Tafuri, Julie Vivas, Ellen Stoll Walsh, Richard Jesse Watson, David Wiesner, Ashley Wolff, Don Wood, Ed Young, Paul O. Zelinsky, and Margot Zemach.

* Dalby, Richard. *The Golden Age of Children's Book Illustration.* Cited above as item 19.

437. Entry deleted.

438. Darling, Richard, L. *The Rise of Children's Book Reviewing in America, 1865–1881.* New York: Bowker, 1968. 452pp.

Describes the publishing at the time, types of children's books, general criticism, and some notes on reviewing. Then surveys *Literary Monthly* and other periodicals, including a chapter on children's periodicals. Includes bibliography of reviews and sample reviews. Finding criticism of picture books requires searching. There is no analysis of picture books. Greenaway and Caldecott are mentioned. Some b & w illustrations.

* Egoff, Sheila A., ed. *One Ocean Touching: Papers from the First Pacific Rim Conference on Children's Literature.* Cited above as item 213.

439. ———, et al. *Only Connect: Readings on Children's Literature.* 2d ed. New York: Oxford University Press, 1980. 457pp.

Contains: Edward Ardizzone, "Creation of a Picture Book," from *Top of the News,* Dec. 1959; Roger Duvoisin, Children's Book Illustration: The Pleasures and Problems," from *Top of the News,* Nov. 1965; Frederick Laws, "Randolph Caldecott," from *The Saturday Book,* no. 16 (Cupid Press); Walter Lorraine, "An Interview with Maurice Sendak," from *Wilson Library Bulletin,* Oct. 1977.

* Estes, Glen E., ed. *American Writers for Children since 1960: Poets, Illustrators, and Nonfiction Authors.* Cited above as item 221.

440. Evans, Dilys. "Four African American Illustrators." *Booklinks* (January 1993): 26–29.

After giving some brief background information, Evans quotes from and analyzes some of the illustrations of Carole Byard, Brian Pinkney, Donald Crews, and Pat Cummings.

441. Field, Elinor Whitney, ed. *Horn Book Reflections on Children's Books and Readings: Selected from Eighteen Years of the Horn Book Magazine, 1949–1966.* Boston: Horn Book, 1969. 367pp.

Includes: Warren Chappell, "Benchmarks for Illustrators of Children's Books," pp. 73–77. "There

should be no such category as children's illustration"—
good artist illustrators don't change hats for children,
from Rembrandt, Daumier, Goya, etc., to Tenniel and
Shepard (Oct. 1957).
Henry C. Pitz, "The Art of Illustration," pp. 78–81.
Summary of his impressions of foreign illustrations of
the time (Oct. 1962). Includes the editors in the United
States and the quality of the field in general.
Barbara Cooney, "An Illustrator's Viewpoint," pp.
82–85 (Feb. 1961). Includes impressions of the history,
current production in the United States and abroad, and
the importance of good design.
Bettina Ehrlich, "Story and Picture in Children's
Books," pp. 86–93. On illustration: how the child "reads"
pictures and how to illustrate for them (Oct. 1952).

442. Freedman, Russell. *Holiday House: The First Fifty Years.*
New York: Holiday House, 1985. 152pp.

The history includes anecdotes about the illustrators
who worked with the firm, from Glen Rounds to Janet
Stevens. Also includes Tomie dePaola, Donna Diamond,
Fritz Eichenberg, Leonard Everett Fisher, Gail Gibbons,
Trina Schart Hyman, Steven Kroll, and Charles
Mikolaycak among others. Complete, year-by-year, list
of their publications with illustrators. The hundreds of b
& w illustrations add to the carefully designed pages to
produce a book both handsome and easy to read. Several
b & w illustrations on most pages.

* Gagnon, Andre. "French Canadian Picture Books in
Translation." Cited above as item 229.

443. Gankina, E. *Khudozhnik v Sovremennoi Detskoi Knige.*
Moscow: Sovietski Khudozhnik, 1977. 215pp.

Includes b & w and color illustrations, and
bibliography. Covers the 1920s to the present with many
illustrations as examples on every page. Worthwhile
even if you can't read the language.

444. Harms, Jeanne McLain, and Lucille J. Lettow. *Emerging Authors and Illustrators in the '80s: Noteworthy Contributions to Children's Literature.* ERIC Microfiche EJ367946.

     Brief discussions of work include illustrators Steven Gammell, Charles Mikolaycak, and Chris Van Allsburg.

  * Harrison, Barbara, and Gregory Maguire. *Innocence and Experience: Essays and Conversations on Children's Literature.* Cited above as item 246.

445. Haviland, Virginia. *Children and Literature: Views and Reviews.* Glenview, Ill.: Scott Foresman, 1973. 461pp.

     A few b & w illustrations. "A selection of essays, criticism, and statements of trends in the world of children's books. . . ." Chapters 1–5 discuss the history of children's books, with some mention of illustrations. Chapter 5, pp. 169–201, is "Illustrators and illustrations." Pages 169–172 are an introduction. Then it includes:
     Louise Seaman Bechtel, "The Art of Illustrating Books for the Younger Reader," pp. 173–176, reprinted from her book, *Books in Search of Children.* Summarizes history and mentions some noteworthy names.
     Roger Duvoisin, "Children's Book Illustration: The Pleasures and Problems," pp. 177–187, from *Top of the News* (Nov. 1965): 22–33. Discusses the role of illustrator; a painting as opposed to an illustration (including art history discussion); comparisons of illustrations (Dore versus Derain of Rabelais' *Gargantua*); and child's awareness.
     Maurice Sendak, "Mother Goose's Garnishings," pp. 188–195, from *Book Week*, Fall Children's Issue (Oct. 31, 1965). Discusses verse and illustration, historically, including Crane, Caldecott, Greenaway, Brooke, Tudor, and, more contemporary, Reed, Wildsmith and Cooney, Low, Briggs. Page 196 has other reviews by Viguers and Heins.

Crispin Fisher, "A Load of Old Nonsense, Edward Lear Resurrected by Four Publishers," pp. 198–201, from *Growing Point* (Nov. 1969). Criticism of versions of Lear with illustrations by Helen Oxenbury, Gerald Rose, Dale Maxey, and Edward Gorey.

Chapter 10, "The International Scene," pp. 326–390, includes mention of the H.C. Andersen Award, p. 329; a list, p. 449; Australian picture books, p. 343; German picture books, pp. 345–347, 354; French, p. 355; Czech and Slovak, pp. 368–369.

Chapter 12, "Awards," includes criteria for Caldecott medals and winners, pp. 416–431; Greenaway, pp. 447–448.

446. ——, ed. *The Openhearted Audience: Ten Authors Talk About Writing for Children.* Washington, D.C.: Library of Congress, 1980. 198pp.

Includes "Questions to an Artist Who Is also an Author," pp. 25–45, Maurice Sendak with Virginia Haviland. Biographical and bibliographic information, many b & w illustrations, and answers to a series of questions.

447. Heller, Steven, ed. *Innovators of American Illustration.* New York: Van Nostrand Reinhold, 1986. 224pp.

Discusses the work of Robert Andrew Parker, Seymour Chwast, Milton Glaser, Edward Sorel, Maurice Sendak and Guy Billout, among others. No discussion of picture books. B & w and color illustrations.

448. Hoffman, Miriam, and Eva Samuels. *Authors and Illustrators of Children's Books: Writings on Their Lives and Works.* New York: Bowker, 1972. 471pp.

Appendix lists English-language works of each author and illustrator. The book includes a chapter on fifty of them, almost half of whom are illustrators; all have some critical comments. All articles are reprinted from periodicals, newspapers, and journals with publication dates from 1950 to 1971 and have editor's notes. Illustrators include:

Ardizzone, Edward: "An Autobiographical Note," pp. 1–5.

Bemelmans, Ludwig: "The Children's World of Ludwig Bemelmans," pp. 6–18.

Burton, Virginia Lee: "Virginia Lee Burton's Dynamic Sense of Design," pp. 41–55.

de Angeli, Marguerite L.: "Marguerite L. de Angeli: Faith in the Human Spirit," pp. 108–114.

Duvoisin, Roger: "Roger Duvoisin—Distinguished Contributor to the World of Children's Literature," pp. 125–134.

Emberly, Ed: "The Meteoric Career of Ed Emberly," pp. 135–140.

Ets, Marie Hall: "Marie Hall Ets—Her Picture Storybooks," pp. 141–148.

Geisel, Theodor Seuss: "Who Thunk You Up Dr. Seuss?" pp. 165–171.

Gramatky, Hardie: "Little Toot—Hero," pp. 172–179.

Hader, Berta, and Elmer Hader: "Berta and Elmer Hader," pp. 180–185.

Holling, Holling C.: "Holling C. Holling: Author and Illustrator," pp. 209–216.

Keats, Ezra Jack: "Ezra Jack Keats, Author and Illustrator," pp. 231–242.

Lawson, Robert: "Robert Lawson: Author and Illustrator," pp. 256–267.

Lenski, Lois: "Lois Lenski: Children's Interpreter," pp. 268–274.

Lionni, Leo: "My Books for Children," pp. 302–307.

McCloskey, Robert: "Robert McCloskey: Master of Humorous Realism," pp. 308–326.

Milhous, Katherine: "Enjoying Festivals with Katherine Milhous," pp. 327–339.

Politi, Leo: "To the Children with Love, from Leo Politi," pp. 348–352.

Rey, Margaret & H.A. Rey: "Margaret & H.A. Rey," pp. 359–363.

Sendak, Maurice: "Questions to an Artist Who Is also an Author," pp. 364–377.
Ward, Lynd: "Mary McNeer Ward and Lynd Ward," pp. 403–406.
Wildsmith, Brian: "Antic Disposition," pp. 412–416.

* Holtze, Sally Holmes et al., eds. *Fourth Book of Junior Authors and Illustrators*. Cited above as item 256.

449. Homes, A. M. "Flying Starts: New Faces of 1989." *Publishers Weekly* 236, no. 25 (December 22, 1989): 26–32.

Brief summaries of careers with photos and quotes from the artists for Brian Pinkney, Jonathan Hunt, Lisa Desimini, Vladimir Radunsky, Mark Teague, and Marjorie Priceman.

450. Hopkins, Lee Bennett. *Books Are by People: Interviews with 104 Authors and Illustrators of Books for Young Children*. New York: Citation. 1969. 349pp.

Several pages on each entry include some biographical information, a discussion of the persons and how they live, and some information on their work. Small b & w photos of the people.

451. *Horn Book Sampler on Children's Books and Reading: Selected from Twenty-Five Years of The Horn Book Magazine, 1924–1948*. Boston: Horn Book, 1959. 261pp.

Part I, "How the Story Happened," includes "About Lucy and Tom" by Edward Ardizzone from the March 1938 issue.
Part II, "Let Us Now Praise Artists!" includes: "Flowers for a Birthday—Kate Greenaway, Mar. 17, 1846" by Anne Parish, with notes on life and work, from March 1946.
"Arthur Rackham and *The Wind in the Willows*" by George Macy, with notes on life and art, from the May 1940 issue.

"The Genius of Arthur Rackham" by Robert Lawson, an appreciation of his art from the May 1940 issue.

"Leslie Brooke: Pied Piper of English Picture Books" by Anne Carroll Moore, who met him. From the March 1925 issue.

"Leslie Brooke" by Anne Carroll Moore, with comments on other books, from the May 1941 issue.

"A Publisher's Odyssey" by Esther Averill; her experiences with Rojankovsky, from the Sept. and Dec. 1938, and the Feb. 1939 issues.

"Illustrations Today in Children's Books" by Warren Chappell, discussing the art and technology involved, from the Nov. 1941 issue.

Part VII, "Small Children and Books," includes: "A Canadian Tribute to Leslie Brooke," by Lillian H. Smith from the May 1941 issue.

"Beatrix Potter and Her Nursery Classics," by Bertha Mahoney Miller from the May 1941 issue.

Alice Dalgliesh on children's choices from the August 1933 issue, updated in 1959.

* Houfe, Simon. *Fin de Siecle: Illustrators of the 'Nineties.* Cited above as item 258.

452. Hyland, Douglas. *Howard Pyle and the Wyeths: Four Generations of American Imagination.* Memphis, Tenn.: Memphis Brooks Museum of Art, 1983. 104pp.

Published in conjunction with the exhibition held at the Memphis Brooks Museum of Art, Sept. 1 to Oct. 23, 1983; Montgomery Museum of Fine Arts, Nov. 12, 1983 to Jan. 2, 1984; North Carolina Museum of Art, Feb. 4 to April 1, 1984. Introductory essays cover the lives of the artists and give some criticism of their work. Their illustrations for children are included but not treated separately. Many b & w and a few color illustrations.

453. *Illustrating in the Third Dimension: The Artist Turned Craftsman,* vol. 1. Society of Illustrators, Library of

American Illustration. Edited by Howard Munce, designed by Robert Geissman. New York: Hastings House, 1978. 112pp.

Two or three pages on each illustrator include examples of work plus biographical information and comments by the artist. Artists include Leo and Diane Dillon and Caldecott winners. Chiefly b & w and color photos of 3–D work.

* *Illustrators of Children's Books.* Cited above as item 35.

* Jacques, Robin. *Illustrators at Work.* Cited above as item 108.

454. Entry deleted.

455. Jan, Isabelle. *On Children's Literature.* Translated from the French. Edited by Catherine Storr. London: Allen Lane, 1973. 189pp.

Only a brief mention of Maurice Sendak, and of Beatrix Potter's animal pictures.

456. Jones, Cornelia. *British Children's Authors: Interviews at Home.* Chicago: American Language Assn. 1976. 176pp.

Includes some biographical information, some quotations (which are mainly answers to questions), and bibliographies, some annotated. Illustrators are Victor G. Ambrus, pp. 11–19; Edward Ardizzone, pp. 21–29; Charles Keeping, pp. 101–113; and Brian Wildsmith, pp. 155–166. Illustrated.

457. Jones, Dolores Blythe, ed. *Children's Literature Awards and Winners: A Directory of Prizes, Authors, and Illustrators.* Detroit, Mich.: Gale, 1983. 495pp.

Part I, "Directory of awards," gives full information on awards, criteria, history, etc., plus bibliographical information on winners and runners-up.

Part II, "Award-Winning Authors and Illustrators," lists all recipients alphabetically with awards won.

Part III, "Selected Bibliography," lists relevant books, chapters, journal articles, dissertations, and reports. First edition supplement, 1984, updates all awards through May 31, 1984 and includes thirty-two new awards.

"Subject List of Awards" includes "Illustration."

The second edition, 1988, 671pp., lists more awards, titles, authors, and illustrators. The format is the same. Three new indexes have been added.

* Jones, Linda Harris. *A Comparison of the Works of Walter Crane, Randolph Caldecott and Kate Greenaway and Their Contributions to Children's Literature.* Cited above as item 41.

458. Kanerva, Arja, Kaisa Lange, and Maria Laukka, eds. *Meilikuvia/Images: Finnish Illustrators of Children's Books.* Helsinki, Finland: Lasten Keskus, 1989. 103pp.

Finnish and English text. Thirty-two Finnish illustrators are showcased, with a b & w photo or drawing of the artist, a full-page color reproduction of one of their illustrations, and information about the life and work of each.

459. Kingman, Lee. *The Illustrator's Notebook.* Boston: Horn Book, 1978. 153pp.

Profusely illustrated in b & w and color. All articles are excerpted from *Horn Book* magazine or another of their publications. They cover many aspects of the field, but especially for children. Part I, "Notes on the History and Philosophy of Illustration, Its Standards, and Its Place in the Arts," pp. 1–28, includes the views of Fritz Eichenberg, Lynd Ward, Warren Chappell, Hilda van Stockum, Barbara Cooney, Marcia Brown, Leonard Weisgard and Lee Kingman.

Part II, "Notes about Artists and by Artists about Their Work," pp. 29–78, includes Marcia Brown, Ernest H. Shepard, Dahlov Ipcar and editor Grace Allen Hogarth talking about their own work; Dudley Lunt on N.C. Wyeth; Hilda Van Stockum on Randolph Caldecott; Rose Dobbs on Wanda Gag; and a series of "Artists' Choice" pages where artists choose the work of another for comment.

Part III, "Notes about Illustration and Techniques," pp. 79–122, has general notes by Lynd Ward and Walter Lorraine and specific descriptions of techniques by Leonard Weisgard, Ezra Jack Keats, Evaline Ness, Blair Lent, Adrienne Adams, Juliet Kepes, Dahlov Ipcar, Lynd Ward, Barbara Cooney, Ed Emberly and Edwin Tunis.

Part IV, "Notes about Illustration as Communication," pp. 123–142, contains articles by Lynd Ward, Joseph Low, Bettina Ehrlich, Uri Shulevitz, Blair Lent, and Gerald McDermott.

460. ———. *Newbery and Caldecott Medal Books: 1956–1965.* With acceptance papers, biographies and related materials chiefly from the *Horn Book* magazine. Boston: Horn Book, 1965. 300pp.

Caldecott award information from page 163. Artists covered include:

Feodor Rojankovsky, speech, pp. 166–170; "Unfinished Portrait of an Artist," by Esther Averill, pp. 171–175.

Marc Simont, speech, pp. 177–179; "Marc Simont," by Elizabeth Lansing, pp. 180–186.

Robert McCloskey, speech, pp. 194–195; "Bob McCloskey, Inventor," by Marc Simont, pp. 196–197.

Barbara Cooney, speech, pp. 199–202; "Barbara Cooney," by Anna Newton Porter, pp. 203–207.

Marie Hall Ets, speech, pp. 209–211; "Marie Hall Ets," by May Massee, pp. 212–216.

Nicolas Sidjakov, speech, pp. 218–220; "Nicolas Sidjakov," pp. 221–224.

Marcia Brown, speech, pp. 226–231; "From Caldecott to Caldecott," pp. 232–237.

Ezra Jack Keats, speech, pp. 239–240; "Ezra Jack Keats," by Esther Hautzig, pp. 241–245.

Maurice Sendak, speech, pp. 247–253; "Maurice Sendak," by Leo Wolfe, pp. 254–257.

Beni Montresor, speech, pp. 259–265; "Beni Montresor," pp. 266–269.

"Picture Books Today," by Norma R. Fryett, pp. 270–280, a description and appreciation of the winners; and a list of honor books and a b & w insert with illustrations from each winner, are also included.

461. ———. *Newbery and Caldecott Medal Books: 1966–1975.* With acceptance papers, biographies and related materials chiefly from the *Horn Book* magazine. Boston: Horn Book, 1975. 321pp.

Caldecott information from p. 155, with color illustrations from the medal books and b & w portrait photographs. Artists are:

Nonny Hogrogian, speech, pp. 179–180; "Nonny Hogrogian," by John Paul Itta, pp. 181–185.

Evaline Ness, speech, pp. 186–191; "Evaline Ness," by Ann Durell, pp. 192–198.

Ed Emberly, speech, pp. 199–204; "Ed Emberly," by Barbara Emberly, pp. 205–207.

Uri Shulevitz, speech, pp. 209–213; "Uri Shulevitz," by Marjorie Zaum, pp. 214–216.

William Steig, speech, pp. 218–219; "William Steig," by Robert Kraus, pp. 220–222.

Gail E. Haley, speech, pp. 223–228, note, pp. 229–231; "Gail E. Haley," by Arnold Arnold, pp. 232–235.

Nonny Hogrogian, speech, "How the Caldecott Changed My Life—Twice," pp. 237–239; "Nonny Hogrogian," by David Kherdian, pp. 240–242.

Blair Lent, speech, pp. 244–249; "Blair Lent," by William Sleator, pp. 250–255.

Margot Zemach, speech, pp. 257–259; "Margot Zemach," by A.L. Lloyd, pp. 260–264.

Gerald McDermott, speech, pp. 266–271; "Gerald McDermott," by Priscilla Moulton, pp. 272–275.

Also includes "Picture Books, Art and Illustration," by Barbara Bader, pp. 276–290, which describes the winners with appreciation, a list of the honor books and a discussion of honor books by Elizabeth Johnson, pp. 297–302, mentioning illustration in particular.

462. ———. *Newbery and Caldecott Medal Books: 1976–1985.* With acceptance papers, biographies and related materials chiefly from the *Horn Book* magazine. Boston: Horn Book, 1986. 358pp.

Caldecott information begins on p. 167. Artists are:

Leo and Diane Dillon, speech, pp. 170–174; "Leo and Diane Dillon," by Phyllis J. Fogelman, pp. 175–180, and speech, pp. 181–187;

"Diane Dillon," by Leo Dillon, pp. 188–189; "Leo Dillon," by Diane Dillon, pp. 190–191; "Leo and Diane Dillon," by Leo Dillon, pp. 191–192.

Peter Spier, speech, pp. 193–200; "Peter Spier," by Janet D. Chenery, pp. 201–203.

Paul Goble, speech, pp. 205–207; "Paul Goble," by Joseph Epes Brown, pp. 208–209.

Barbara Cooney, speech, pp. 211–215; "Barbara Cooney," by Constance Reed McClellan, pp. 216–219.

Arnold Lobel, speech, pp. 220–225; "Arnold Lobel," by Elizabeth Gordon, pp. 226–228.

Chris Van Allsburg, speech, pp. 230–233; "Chris Van Allsburg," by David Macaulay, pp. 234–237.

Marcia Brown, speech, pp. 239–249; "Marcia Brown," by Janet Loranger, pp. 250–253.

Alice and Martin Provensen, speech, pp. 255–258; "Alice and Martin Provensen," by Nancy Willard, pp. 259–262.

Trina Schart Hyman, speech, pp. 264–274; "Trina Schart Hyman," by Katrin Hyman, pp. 275–278.

Also includes "The Caldecott Spectrum," by Barbara Bader, pp. 279–314; critical analysis with illustrations from the books; and "A Decade of Books: A Critic's

Response," by Ethel L. Heins, pp. 323–342; includes critical comments on picture books, pp. 325–333.

* Kingman, Lee, Joanna Foster, and Ruth Giles Lontoft, comps. *Illustrators of Children's Books, 1957–1966*. Cited above as item 283.

* Kingman, Lee, Grace Allen Hogarth, and Harriet Quimby, comps. *Illustrators of Children's Books, 1967–1976*. Cited above as item 284.

463. Kirkpatrick, D.L., ed. *Twentieth-Century Children's Writers*. New York: St. Martin's, 1978. 1507pp. 3d ed. Consulting editor, Tracy Chevalier, 1989. 1288pp.

No illustrations. The scope is those writers published after 1900. Appendix includes some from the late nineteenth century. Includes some illustrators (e.g., Anglund, Ardizzone, Bemelmans, Brooke, D'Aulaire, etc.). Gives basic biographical facts, a list of their publications, sometimes a quotation from the artist about the work, and one or two paragraphs of criticism. Section on books in translation. The second edition (1983) is basically the same book with some names added and others omitted, as is the third edition (1989). Information on specific people seems the same, but all three editions need to be checked for particular persons.

* Klemin, Diana. *The Art of Art for Children's Books*. Cited above as item 285.

* Krull, Kathleen et al. "New Textures in Children's Book Art." Cited above as item 287.

464. Kujoth, Jean Spealman. *Best-Selling Children's Books*. Metuchen, N.J.: Scarecrow, 1973. 305pp.

Sixty-eight publishers were surveyed to find the names of children's books that had sold more than 100,000 copies. The list by authors includes a brief description. Chapter four, pp. 192–220, lists best-sellers by illustrator. In Chapter seven, the books are grouped by "type of book, subject category and age level." Those for preschool through grade three are considered picture books and can be located this way.

465. Kuskin, Karla. "Two Illustrators Can Be Better than One." *New York Times Book Review* (January 6, 1985): 24.

Descriptions of the works of five married couples (Provensens, Dillons, Berenstains, Lobels, Deweys, and Aruegos), highlighting working styles.

* Lamme, Linda Leonard. "Illustratorship: Key Facet of Whole Language Instruction." Cited above as item 293.

* Lanes, Selma. *Down the Rabbit Hole: Adventures and Misadventures in the Realm of Children's Literature.* Cited above as item 294.

466. Lechner, Judith V. "Picture Books as Portable Art Galleries." *Art Education* 46, no. 2 (March, 1993): 34–40.

Quoting from illustrators, Lechner describes the art of the picture book in general, and that of some specific books, analyzing how the artists have achieved their results. She notes the relevance to "fine art," and suggests ways to enhance children's appreciation of this art. B & w reproductions of illustrations and an extensive list of references.

* Lemieux, Louise. *Pleins feux sur la litterature de jeunesse au Canada français.* Cited above as item 298.

* Lewis, John. The *Twentieth Century Book.* Cited above as item 42.

* *Lively Art of Picture Books.* Cited above as item 306.

467. Lloyd, Pamela. *How Writers Write.* Portsmouth, N.H.: Heinemann, 1987. 149pp.

     Divided into sections by the activity, i.e. "Research," "The First Draft," this collection of lengthy quotations by authors on each subject includes a paragraph on each writer. The illustrators whose words occur throughout the book are Michael Foreman, Steven Kellogg, and Arnold Lobel.

 *   "A Look at the Creative Process." Cited above as item 116.

 *   Mahony, Bertha E., and Elinor Whitney. *Contemporary Illustrators of Children's Books.* Cited above as item 48.

 *   Mahony, Bertha E., et al. *Illustrators of Children's Books, 1744–1945.* Cited above as item 47.

468. *Major Authors and Illustrators for Children and Young Adults: A Selection of Sketches from "Something about the Author."* 6 vols. Selected by Laurie Collier and Joyce Nakamura. Detroit, Mich.: Gale, 1993.

     Eight hundred biographical sketches have been updated and rewritten.

469. *Making Picture Books: Shirley Hughes, Babette Cole, Pat Hutchins with Heather O'Neill.* Videocassette. Northbrook, Ill.: Roland Collection, undated. 42 min.

     The three author-illustrators discuss how they conceive of, design, and write their books, covering the qualities they seek in a picture book, their sources of inspiration, and their influences.

470. Marantz, Sylvia and Kenneth Marantz. *Artists of the Page: Interviews with Children's Book Illustrators.* Jefferson, N.C.: McFarland, 1992. 255pp.

B & w photos or self-portraits. The artists who talk about their life and work include: Allan and Janet Ahlberg, pp. 1–12; Molly Bang, pp. 13–20; Nicola Bayley, pp. 21–27; Gavin Bishop, pp. 28–34; Quentin Blake, pp. 35–43; Anthony Browne, pp. 44–51; Ashley Bryan, pp. 52–58; John Burningham and Helen Oxenbury, pp. 59–67; Carole Byard, pp. 68–78; Babette Cole, pp. 79–88; Peter Collington, pp. 89–95; Roy Gerrard, pp. 96–101; M. B. Goffstein, pp. 102–107; Diane Goode, pp. 108–115; Shirley Hughes, pp. 116–127; Pat Hutchins, pp. 128–135; Ann Jonas, pp. 136–142; Errol Lloyd, pp. 143–152; Deborah Niland, pp. 153–160; Graham Oakley, pp. 161–168; Jan Ormerod, pp. 169–175; Ken Robbins, pp. 176–183; Tony Ross, pp. 184–194; Amy Schwartz, pp. 195–201; Posy Simmonds, pp. 202–208; Peter Sis, pp. 209–217; Ralph Steadman, pp. 218–226; Ed Young, pp. 227–240; Paul Zelinsky, pp. 241–249. Interviews which appeared earlier in the *Horn Book* have been updated.

* Martin, Douglas. *The Telling Line: Essays on Fifteen Contemporary Book Illustrators.* Cited above as item 321.

471. McCormick, Edith. "Educating the Eye." *American Libraries* 21, no. 8 (September 1990): 804–806.

A report on the A.L.A Preconference "The Educated Eye II," held June 21–22, 1990. George Nicholson keynoted with a historic survey of illustrated books for children in America. Margaret McElderry discussed how her "eye" developed. Nancy Ekholm Burkert, Ashley Bryan, and Alice Provensen talked about their work in one session. Barry Moser, Dilys Evans, and Ed Young covered practical bookmaking. Tomi Ungerer responded to questions from his editor, Nicholson. David Macaulay showed his work in progress. Some color photos of participants.

472. McElmeel, Sharon M. *Bookpeople: A First Album.* Englewood, Colo.: Teacher Ideas/Libraries Unlimited, 1990. 176pp.

A brief biography and bibliography plus suggested questions for students are given for forty-one illustrators and authors. B & w photos.

473. ⸺. *Bookpeople: A Multicultural Album.* Drawings by Deborah L. McElmeel. Englewood, Colo.: Teacher Ideas/Libraries Unlimited, 1992. 170pp.

For each person listed, there is biographical background and some critical comments on their work. Suggestions for related activities and further reading follow. B & w photos and drawings. Illustrators include: Mitsumasa Anno, pp. 1–8; Ashley Bryan, pp. 9–19; Donald Crews, pp. 29–40; Pat Cummings, pp. 41–51; Paul Goble, pp. 63–73; Brian Pinkney, pp. 107–115.

474. Meyer, Susan E. *America's Great Illustrators.* New York: Abrams, 1978. 311pp.

Introduction, pp. 8–37, presents historic background and technical processes. Among the illustrators whose lives and art are discussed are Howard Pyle, pp. 40–63, and N.C. Wyeth, pp. 64–87. Profusely illustrated in b & w and color.

*   ⸺. *A Treasury of the Great Children's Book Illustrators.* Cited above as item 51.

475. Miller, Bertha Mahony, and Elinor Whitney Field, eds. *Caldecott Medal Books: 1938–1957.* With acceptance papers, biographies and related materials chiefly from the *Horn Book* magazine. Boston: Horn Book, 1957. 329pp.

A year-by-year compilation with both acceptance and biographical papers. Some b & w illustrations. See Kingman, Lee, ed. *Newbery and Caldecott Medal Books: 1956–1965, 1965–1975* for subsequent years.

*   Miller, Bertha Mahony, et al., comps. *Illustrators of Children's Books, 1946–1956.* Cited above as item 324.

* Nakamura, Joyce, ed. *Something about the Author Autobiography Series.* See item 487 below.

* Nodelman, Perry. *Touchstones: Reflections on the Best in Children's Literature.* Cited above as item 338.

* Olendorf, Donna, ed. *Something about the Author: Facts and Pictures About Authors and Illustrators of Books for Young People.* See item 431 above.

476. Entry deleted.

477. Ovenden, Graham, ed. *The Illustrators of Alice in Wonderland and Through the Looking Glass.* New York: St. Martin's, 1972. 88pp.

Introduction by John Davis, pp. 7–14, discusses Carroll and Tenniel. Lists many of the artists who have illustrated *Alice* since, with brief comments on their work. Pp. 8–98 are mainly b & w illustrations, chapter-by-chapter.

478. Peppin, Brigid, and Lucy Micklethwait. *Dictionary of British Illustrators: The Twentieth Century.* London: John Murray, 1983. 336pp.

Neatly organized, concise biographies of almost 1,000 illustrators published between 1900 and 1975 in Britain. Includes many titles of illustrated books, periodicals in which work appears, sources of information, and, in about a third of the cases, a b & w reproduction.

* *Picture Book Design Conference: From Conception to Consumption.* Cited above as item 347.

479. Pitz, Henry C. *The Brandywine Tradition.* Boston: Houghton Mifflin, 1968. 252pp.

Sixteen color and thirty-two b & w plates, some of which are children's book illustrations. A description of the Brandywine area and its history and of the artists who have worked or currently work there. Those who illustrated children's books include Howard Pyle, pp. 33–162; Jesse Willcox Smith, pp. 98 and 179; and N.C. Wyeth, pp. 188–208.

* Poltarnees, Welleran. *All Mirrors Are Magic Mirrors: Relections on Pictures Found in Children's Books.* Cited above as item 62.

* Prentice, Jeffrey, and Bettina Bird. *Dromkeen: A Journey into Children's Literature.* Cited above as item 63.

480. *Profiles in Literature.* Videotape. Norristown, Penn.: Dr. Jaqueline Weiss, dates vary. Three-quarter inch U-Matic, half inch VHS, 30 min. each.

Interviews with authors, illustrators, and editors of children's books. Those concerned with picture books include #4, Stan, Jan, and Michael Berenstain (color) 1979; #10, Marguerite de Angeli (color) 1976; #11, Tomie dePaola (color) 1984; #13, Tom and Muriel Feelings (b & w) 1971; #21, Tana Hoban and Susan Hirschman (b & w) 1975; #24, Ezra Jack Keats (b & w) 1970; #27, Joe and Beth Krush (b & w) 1972; #32, Arnold Lobel (b & w) 1973; #33, Robert McCloskey (b & w) 1977; #43, Maurice Sendak (color) 1977; #45, John Steptoe (b & w) 1975; #50, Lynd Ward and May McNeer (b & w) 1974.

* Reed, Walt, and Roger Reed. *The Illustrator in America, 1880–1980: A Century of Illustration.* Cited above as item 65.

481. Roback, Diane, and Elizabeth Devereaux. "Flying Starts." *Publishers Weekly* 238, no. 29 (July 5, 1991): 38–39.

Notes on the lives and works, and quotes from new artists of picture books cover Gary Blythe, Kevin Hawkes, Will Hillenbrand, and Leslie Tryon.

482. Robinson, Moira, ed. *Readings in Children's Literature: Proceeding of the National Seminar on Children's Literature.* Victoria, Australia: Frankston State College, 1975. 293pp.

Includes "A Dialogue on Illustrating," pp. 104–123, in which John Burningham and Helen Oxenbury both talk about their books and illustrations.

483. Roginski, James W. *Behind the Covers: Interviews with Authors and Illustrators of Books for Children and Young Adults.* Littleton, Colo.: Libraries Unlimited, 1985. 249pp.

Includes Martha Alexander, pp. 1–7; Donald Crews, pp. 42–50; Demi (Charlotte Dumaresq Hunt), pp. 59–72; Charles Mikolaycak, pp. 138–153; Rolf Myller, pp. 154–160; Elise Primavera, pp. 161–166; Ellen Raskin, pp. 167–176. Roginski includes a biographical note and a prelude, in which he describes the subject and his impressions of how and where he or she works. A bibliography of the subjects' works, a list of awards won, and possessers of further information follow.

Appendices include the library collections where original art and/or manuscripts are retained, an explanation of the awards and honors won, and bibliographies of sources.

484. ———. *Behind the Covers: Interviews with Authors and Illustrators of Books for Children and Young Adults, Volume II.* Englewood, Colo.: Libraries Unlimited, 1989. 261pp.

All sections include a prelude, the interview with dialog, a bibliography including awards won, and further information. Illustrators are: Pat Cummings, pp. 81–92; Ann Jonas, pp. 120–131; Steven Kellogg, pp. 144–160; Leonard Lubin, pp. 191–201; Margot Tomes, pp. 224–237; Chris Van Allsburg, pp. 238–249; and a piece on Arnold L. Shapiro, a "packager," who does pop-ups, pp. 202–209; with information on the preparation of pop-ups on pp. 205–207.

485. ———. *Newbery and Caldecott Medalists and Honor Book Winners: Bibliographies and Resource Materials through 1977.* Littleton, Colo.: Libraries Unlimited, 1982. 339pp.

Each entry lists awards won; books written and/or illustrated; what media presentations have been made; the location of original manuscripts, artwork and non-book materials; what exhibitions of artwork have been held; and a list of books for background reading.

486. Rollock, Barbara. *Black Authors and Illustrators of Children's Books: A Biographical Dictionary.* New York: Garland, 1992. 234pp.

Each entry has brief biographical information, some quotations, and a bibliography of works. An insert has b & w photos and illustrations from some of the artists. Appendices of publishers, bookstores, and awards won.

* Ryder, John. *Artists of a Certain Line: A Selection of Illustrators for Children's Books.* Cited above as item 366.

487. Sarkissian, Adele, ed. *Something About the Author Autobiography Series.* Detroit, Mich.: Gale, continuing series begun 1986. Joyce Nakamura became editor with vol. 6, 1988. Vol. 16, 1993.

Authors relate varying amounts of information on their life and work. A complete listing of each author's works, and an index to publishers, geographic references, personal names and titles are included. The number of authors who are also illustrators to be included is not clear. Volume one contains Leonard Everett Fisher, Nonny Hogrogian, Evaline Ness, and Rosemary Wells. Several b & w photos illustrate each article.

488. Selden, Rebecca, and Sarah Smedman. "The Art of the Contemporary Picture Book." *Proceedings of the Seventh Annual Conference of the Children's Literature Association.* Baylor University (Waco, Tex.) (March 1980): 152–165.

Examines artists who illustrate in a wide variety of styles, including Sendak, Steig, Lent, Lionni, Ward, McDermott, Lawrence, Grifalconi, Wildsmith, Macaulay and Burkert, with a bit about each and their art. References are made to page numbers of examples shown in slides but not pictured.

489. Senick, Gerard J., ed. *Children's Literature Review: Excerpts from Reviews, Criticism and Commentary on Books for Children and Young People.* Cont. publ. Detroit, Mich.: Gale, 1976.

Each volume includes numerous b & w illustrations from books; portraits of the authors and author-illustrators covered. These are listed alphabetically, followed by a biocritical introduction; comments by the subject if available; chronological list of works with excerpts from several reviews; and bibliographic citation. Illustrators are not listed in a separate index, but each volume has a cumulative author, title, and, since volume six, a nationality index. Volume 30 (1993) includes many illustrators in its cumulative author index. Since volume five, guest essays cover special topics.

490. Smaridge, Norah. *Famous Author-Illustrators for Young People.* New York: Dodd, Mead, 1973. 159pp.

Illustrated with b & w photographs or drawings of the illustrators. Includes biographical information and some criticism of: Edward Lear, pp. 11–18; Kate Greenaway, pp. 19–28; Beatrix Potter, pp. 29–36; Robert Lawson, pp. 37–43; Wanda Gag, pp. 44–53; Lois Lenski, pp. 54–61; Marie Hall Ets, pp. 62–69; Ludwig Bemelmans, pp. 70–77; H.A. Rey, pp. 78–84; Roger Duvoisin, pp. 85–92; Theodor Geisel (Dr. Seuss), pp. 93–100; Leo Lionni, pp. 101–106; Robert McCloskey, pp. 106–112; Brinton Turkel, pp. 113–117; Marcia Brown, pp. 118–123; Richard Scarry, pp. 124–129; Joan Walsh

Anglund, pp. 130–137; Maurice Sendak, pp. 138–145; Tomi Ungerer, pp. 146–152.

* Targ, William, ed. *Bibliophile in the Nursery: A Bookman's Treasury of Collectors' Lore on Old and Rare Children's Books.* Cited above as item 70.

* Telgen, Diane. *Something about the Author: Facts and Pictures About Authors and Illustrators of Books for Young People.* See item 431 above.

* Townsend, John Rowe. *Written for Children.* Cited above as item 73.

491. Ward, Martha Eads. *Illustrators of Books for Young People.* New Yolk: Scarecrow, 1970. 166pp.

Contains 370 brief, one-paragraph biographies.

492. ———. *Illustrators of Books for Young People.* 2d ed. New York: Scarecrow, 1975. 223pp.

Contains 750 brief paragraphs of biographies. Both the first and second editions include Caldecott winners, title index, and references to other sources.

* Williams, Helen E. *Books by African-American Authors and Illustrators for Children and Young Adults.* Cited above as item 415.

493. Wintle, Justin, and Emma Fisher. *The Pied Pipers: Interviews with the Influential Creators of Children's Literature.* New York: Paddington Press Ltd., Two Continents Publishing Group, 1974. 320pp.

The introduction, pp. 11–19, gives the history of children's book publishing, including a current assessment, followed by individual interviews with brief biographical and critical comments, then a question-and-answer format on life and work. Artists include Maurice Sendak, pp. 20–23; Edward Ardizzone, pp. 35–48;

Charles Keeping, pp. 49–63; Richard Scarry, pp. 64–76; Laurent de Brunhoff, pp. 77–86: Dr. Seuss (letter, answers) pp. 113–123. Some b & w illustrations and photographs of subjects.

494. Woolman, Bertha. *The Caldecott Award: The Winners and the Honor Books.* Rev. ed. Minneapolis, Minn.: T.S. Denison, 1981. 96pp.

An explanation of the award, questions and answers about the winners, and honor books for children of various ages. List of the illustrators with some information about them, pp. 29–50. Award winners listed, pp. 51–56. General sources for further information, pp. 57–58. Sources on each individual artist, pp. 59–94.

495. Zinsser, William, ed. *Worlds of Childhood: The Art and Craft of Writing for Children.* Boston: Houghton Mifflin, 1990. 213pp.

From a series of talks conceived by the Book-of-the-Month Club, Inc. held at the New York Public Library and given by writers including Jean Fritz, Jill Krementz, Jack Prelutsky, and Katherine Paterson. Authors who are also illustrators include: Maurice Sendak, "Visitors from My Boyhood," pp. 47–69, describing sources of his inspiration, how *Where the Wild Things Are* evolved, some background on *Dear Mili* and *Higglety Pigglety Pop*, plus childhood experiences behind *Outside Over There* and *The Sign on Rosie's Door.*
Rosemary Wells, "The Well-Tempered Children's Book," pp. 121–143, discussing the origins of her Ruby and Max stories, plus other sources of her tales.

PART V

Books, Articles, and Audiovisual Materials on Individual Picture Book Artists

496. Abdullah, Cheryl. "Artist Profile: David Wiesner." *Library Talk* (September–October 1989): 15–18.

In answer to questions, Wiesner describes his early life and devotion to his artwork despite his lack of a "fine art" background, his training at Rhode Island School of Design, his start in illustration, and his method of working. Includes photos and small reproductions of his illustrations and a description of some of his work.

497. Abrahamson, Richard F., and Marilyn Colvin. "Tomie dePaola: Children's Choice." *Reading Teacher* 33 (December 1979): 264–269.

Includes discussion of his treatment of costumes and borders in *Clown of God*, comparisons with works by others, illustrations from *When Everyone Was Fast Asleep* and follow-up activities for children.

498. Agosta, Lucien L. *Howard Pyle.* Boston: Twayne, 1987. 162pp.

The biographical chapter covers Pyle's childhood, when his mother immersed him in literature and art (he was always drawing pictures). His brief art training, his start at publishing words and drawings, his career as illustrator for publishers, especially *Harper's*, are covered, as well as his influences on others. Analysis of the books includes some discussion of the illustrations and design, with a few b & w illustrations.

499. Agree, Rose. "Lionni's Artichokes: An Interview." *Wilson Library Bulletin* 44. no. 9 (May 1970): 947–950.

His books as his "autobiography," and his illustrations as stage sets, are among the ideas expressed as Lionni answers questions about his work.

Also in Mary Lou White, *Children's Literature: Criticism and Response*, cited above as item 412.

500. Alderson, Brian. "Margot Zemach: A European Perspective." *Horn Book* 67, no. 5 (September–October 1991): 573–579.

While discussing many of her books, Alderson pays particular attention to the European influences that are evident in her work, including those from contemporary art. An appreciation of her art, with a list of her "most important books."

501. ———. "Maurice before Max: The Yonder Side of the See-Saw." *Horn Book* 69, no. 3 (May–June 1993): 291–295.

A search back to the early Sendak illustrations to examine the development of the skill and craft of illustrating to match the words of an author. Sendak's comments on his illustrations for *I Saw Esau* as perhaps a return to an earlier style before *Where the Wild Things Are* brings Alderson to this re-examination.

   * ———. *Sing a Song for Sixpence: The English Picture Book Tradition and Randolph Caldecott*. Cited above as item 2.

502. Allender, David. "William Steig at 80." *Publishers Weekly* 232, no. 29 (July 24, 1987): 116–118.

The artist is quoted extensively as his life and work, illustrations and picture books are discussed. One photo, several b & w, one color illustration.

503. Ammon, Richard. "Profile: David Macaulay." *Language Arts* 59 (April 1982): 374–378.

An appreciative description of Macaulay, his life and where he lives and works, with quotations. Notes on some of his books and the art within them. B & w portrait photos and small illustrations.

504. Andersen, Hans Christian, and Kate Greenaway. *Kate Greenaway's Original Drawings for the Snow Queen.* New York: Schocken. 1981. 58pp.

Studies from an unpublished edition. "Afterword," pp. 53–58, has comments on the author and the artist by Michael Patrick Hearn.

505. Anderson, Dennis. "Tomie dePaola, Tough and Tender Storyteller." *Instructor* 89, no. 8 (March 1980): 32–34, 38.

Interview includes his feelings about children and the children's book world. Nothing about his illustrations.

506. Anderson, William. "Garth Williams after Eighty." *Horn Book* 69, no. 2 (March–April 1993): 181–189.

The author discusses Williams' background, early years, art training, major illustration projects, and current life. Includes many quotes.

507. Andryszczak, Maria Ewa. "Marian Murawski, Winner of the BIB '89 Grand Prix. Portrait of a Polish Illustrator." *Bookbird* 27, no. 4 (November 1989): 7–8.

Traces the artist's development, covers important work, and includes notes on ethical as well as aesthetic considerations. B & w portrait and illustrations.

508. Aoki, Hisako. "A Conversation with Mitsumasa Anno." *Horn Book* 59, no. 2 (April 1983): 137–145.

Anno's views on art from his perspective as a former art teacher. Background on some of his works; notes on how he works.

509. Ardizzone, Edward. "Creation of a Picture Book." *Top of the News* 16, no. 2 (December 1959): 289–298.

Discusses his problems with text and illustrations in creating *Little Tim and the Brave Sea Captain*. Gives examples of how he progressed and the choices made.

510. *Arnold Lobel.* Sound Filmstrip. Rev. ed. New York: Random House, 1986. 11 min. Videocassette. Chicago: American School Publishers/SRA, 1991. 12 min.

Lobel introduces himself and tells about his life and work.

* *Art and Man.* Cited above as item 147.

511. Bailey, Diane. "The Illustrated Sendak." *USAir Magazine* (February 1992): 39–48.

Intersperses quotations from the artist with a discussion of his career, life, and books. Small b & w illustrations.

512. Bassett, Lisa. *Very Truly Yours, Charles L. Dodgson, Alias Lewis Carroll: A Biography.* New York: Lothrop, 1987. 118pp.

Bassett tries to make Dodgson more understandable by examining his life and his writings through his relations with children. Chapter VI, "Art and Photography," is about his drawings and sketches, but chiefly about his photography; an insightful note on Tenniel's troubled relationship with Dodgson and its effect on his illustrations. B & w photos, some drawings by Dodgson, and reproductions of Tenniel's work.

513. *Beatrix Potter: A Private World.* Videocassette. Princeton: Films for the Humanities, 1991. 42 min.

    Covers her childhood and youth, with examples of artwork and interviews with those who knew her as an adult.

514. *Beatrix Potter Had a Pet Named Peter.* Sound Filmstrip. Westminster, Md. Random House/Miller Brody/ American School Publishers/SRA, 1985. 1 filmstrip, 1 cassette. Videocassette, 14 mins.

    The story of her life and her creation of Peter Rabbit.

515. Bechtel, Louise S. "Boris Artzybasheff." *Horn Book* 42 (April 1966): 176–180.

    An appreciation, including information on his life and discussion of the art of his illustration in many of his books.

516. *Bill Peet in His Studio.* Videotape. Boston: Houghton Mifflin, no date. ¾ inch, ½ inch Beta, ½ inch VHS. 13 min.

    Peet tells of his early days and his work with Disney studios. He demonstrates how his characters and stories develop as he sketches. Finally, he talks about his appearances in schools and the many letters and pictures he gets from children.

517. Blake, Quentin. "Wild Washerwomen, Hired Sportsmen, and Enormous Crocodiles." *Horn Book* 57 (October 1981): 505–513.

    His account of how he works to "act the story" when he collaborates, plus how he draws. His own books start as pictures or series of pictures. Discusses some individual books. B & w examples.

518. Blegvad, Erik. "N.M. Bodecker: A Reminiscence." *The Five Owls* (September–October 1988): 13–14.

Blegvad tells how he first met Bodecker in art class, fills in his family background, and tells a bit about his life. A photo and some small drawings reproduced.

519. ———. *Self-Portrait: Erik Blegvad.* Reading, Mass.: Addison-Wesley, 1979. 32pp.

Beginning with other members of his family with drawing talent, Blegvad tells of his childhood in Denmark, his study of art, and the start of his career; with examples. Profusely illustrated in color by the author and others.

520. Brainard, Dulcy. "Ed Young." *Publishers Weekly* 235, no. 8 (February 24, 1989): 208–209.

The interview summarizes Young's early life and start in children's books. His working method and several of his titles are analyzed. Includes many quotes; photo.

521. Brown, Marc. "The Artist at Work: The Importance of Humor." *Horn Book* 66, no. 5 (September–October 1990): 563–570.

Brown begins with his childhood and school experiences leading to his start in teaching and illustration. He discusses where his story ideas come from and how he produces his illustrations. Several small illustrations.

  * Brown, Marcia. *Lotus Seeds: Children, Pictures and Books.* Cited above as item 168.

522. Burkert, Nancy Ekholm. *The Art of Nancy Ekholm Burkert.* Edited by David Larkin and introduced by Michael Danoff. New York: Harper & Row, 1977. Unpaginated.

A few pages on her life, some personal quotations, some analysis of her art plus examples of the children's book illustrations and a few other paintings. Forty illustrations in color; others in b & w.

523. ———. "A Second Look: *Lion.*" *Horn Book* 56 (December 1980): 671–676.

An affectionate appreciation of this classic by William Pene du Bois, with analysis of the design and the artwork of the illustrator, including details of his technique using Dinobase for the effect of a lithograph. Comparison of the original with the smaller, less effective paperback.

524. ———. "Valentine and Orson." *Horn Book* 67, no. 1 (January–February 1991): 45–47.

The Boston Globe–Horn Book Special Award acceptance speech describes the background and creation of the award-winning book, along with all the people who helped to put it together.

525. Burton, Virginia Lee. "Making Picture Books." *Horn Book* 19 (July–August 1943): 228–229.

Her brief discussion of how she works, particularly on *The Little House.*

526. Butler, Francelia. "Seuss as a Creator of Folklore." *Children's Literature in Education* 20, no. 3 (September 1989): 175–181.

In a "reassessment" of Seuss's work, Butler treats some of his illustrations along with extensive discussion of his words.

527. Cart, Michael. "Ben, Mr. Popper and the Rabbits: Remembering Robert Lawson." *New York Times Book Review* 93 (November 13, 1988): 59.

Some notes and observations on the life and work of Lawson, with personal quotations on the 50th

anniversary of the publication of *Mr. Popper's Penguins.*
Comments on his art and a small b & w illustration.

528. Carus, Marianne. "Randolph Caldecott, Father of the
     Modern Picture Book." *Journal of Youth Services in
     Libraries* 1, no. 1 (Winter 1988): 143–151.

     Summarizes Caldecott's early life, beginning career
     sketching and illustrating, his agreement to work with
     engraver Edmund Evans on color picture books for
     children, and his life and work thereafter. Many b & w
     illustrations and sketches are reproduced.

529. Cech, John. "Maurice Sendak: Off the Page." *Horn Book*
     62, no. 3 (May–June 1986): 305–313.

     Describes some of the processes involved in creating
     operas of several of Sendak's books; mainly, *Where the
     Wild Things Are,* as well as his setting of *The Nutcracker,*
     the ballet.

530. Chambers, Aidan. "Fungus Encore." *Horn Book* 56, no. 1
     (January–February 1980): 99–103.

     An examination of Briggs's talent and of this "comic
     strip" book in light of the criticism it has evoked.

531. *Children of the Northern Lights.* 16mm color film.
     Videocassette. Weston, Conn.: Weston Woods, no date.
     20 min.

     Ingri and Edgar Parin D'Aulaire discuss their work
     and describe their lithographic process of illustrating.
     Includes scenes from animations made from their books.

532. Clemons, Walter. "The Grimm Reaper." *Newsweek*
     (December 19, 1988): 50–52.

     In conjunction with the publication of *Dear Mili* and
     the 25th anniversary of *Where the Wild Things Are,*
     Clemons describes Maurice Sendak's life and activities

today, with some discussion of his earlier life and work. Color photo and illustrations.

533. Climo, Shirley. "Creating a Picture Book." *Writer* 96 (July 1983): 18–20, 44.

The author-illustrator describes the steps necessary to create a picture book, concentrating chiefly on the words. Two small b & w illustrations.

534. Cobb, Nathan. "The Show-and-Tell Tale(s) of the Great Explainer." *Smithsonian* 23, no. 2 (May 1992): 70–81.

An extensive treatment of David Macaulay's studio, work habits, childhood, and books. Profusely illustrated with color photos and reproductions of his illustrations.

535. Conant, Jennet. "Dream Weaver." *Harper's Bazaar* 3363 (March 1992): 179, 191–192.

Tells just a bit about Maira Kalman's work in picture books and painting, with quotes from the artist. Color illustrations.

536. Conrad, Barnaby III. "Maurice Sendak." *Horizon* 24, no. 5 (May 1981): 24–33.

A lush, colorful tribute.

537. Cooper, Ilene. "The Booklist Interview: Leo Lionni." *Booklist* (January 1, 1991): 930–931.

Answering questions, Lionni briefly describes his childhood, how he came to do children's books, how children react to some books, and the message he hopes to convey to them. Photo and two book jackets.

538. Cornell, Robert W. "Robert Lawson: For All Children." *Elementary English* 50 (May 1973): 718–725, 738.

An appreciation detailing his life and each book he did, with some quotes. Little analysis of his art.

539. Cott, Jonathan. "Maurice Sendak, King of All Wild Things." *Rolling Stone* no. 229 (Dec. 30, 1976): 48–59.

An extensive and lively interview at the artist's house. Wide-ranging in subject matter and uninhibited in its conversation.

*   *Creating Jack and the Bean Tree: Tradition and Technique.* Cited above as item 89.

540. Crichton, Jennifer. "Dr. Seuss Turns 80." *Publishers Weekly* (February 10, 1984): 22–23.

Summary of other works, plus longer discussion of *The Butter Battle Book.* Interview with quotes.

541. ———. "Picture Books That Explain." *Publishers Weekly* 226, no. 4 (July 27, 1984): 88–89.

Gail Gibbons describes to the interviewer how she came to do children's books, how she researches, the difficult choices of what to include, the making of the dummy, and something about her style. Two b & w illustrations.

542. Cummings, Pat. "Talking with Artists." *Horn Book* 69, no. 1 (January–February 1993): 54–56.

After some personal background, Cummings describes how her book *Talking with Artists* came together.

543. Cutts, Alida von Krogh. "An Interview with IRA Book Award Winner Marisabina Russo." *Reading Teacher* 41, no. 6 (February 1988): 540–543.

Russo answers questions about her youth, her writing, and her own reading, with little on her art.

*   Darling, Harold, and Peter Neumeyer, eds. *Image and Maker: An Annual Dedicated to the Consideration of Book Illustration.* Cited above as item 200.

544. *David Macaulay in His Studio.* Videotape. Boston: Houghton Mifflin, no date. ¾ inch, ½ inch Beta, ½ inch VHS. 25 min.

After telling something about how he became an illustrator, Macaulay shows us where and how he works, describing in particular the gathering of background information and progression from first drawing to the finished and printed volume of his book, *Pyramid.*

545. Davis, Mary Gould. *Randolph Caldecott, 1846–1886: An Appreciation.* Philadelphia: Lippincott, 1946. 47pp.

Part I, pp. 1–22, "The Picture Books," has a description and some children's reactions. Part II, pp. 25–44, "The Artist," discusses his life and art. Bibliography includes his books and books about him.

546. de Angeli, Marguerite. *Butter at the Old Price: The Autobiography of Marguerite de Angeli.* New York: Doubleday, 1971. 258pp.

Along with the details of her life, de Angeli gives us her first memories of her father and his artwork. But it was not until after her brief singing career, marriage, and the birth of three children that she followed an inclination and went to art school. After fourteen years of illustrating, she began to write her own books. Brief discussion of her technique, but many details on her life and family. Illustrated with b & w photos, drawings, and a seven-page insert that includes color reproductions.

547. Delessert, Etienne. *Etienne Delessert.* New York: Stewart Tabori & Chang, 1992. 160pp.

Chiefly color illustrations. This sampling of 140 of the artist's works includes some from his picture books. Brief essay comments on his work are by Bortil Galland, Yves Beccarin, Judy Garlan, Janine Despinette, David Macaulay, and Antonio Faeti.

548. "Demi: Drawing and Writing." *School Library Media Activities Monthly* VIII, no. 9 (May 1992): 30–31.

    In answer to the interviewer's questions, Demi reviews her childhood interest in art, her education, her change from large artwork to illustration, and her current involvement with Chinese and Oriental art.

549. dePaola, Tomie. "The Artist at Work." *Horn Book* 69, no. 5 (September–October 1993): 573–576.

    The author-illustrator sums up his art training and early influences, discusses personal "style," then analyzes the way he works, his technique, and research. Two small b & w reproductions.

550. Despinette, Janine. "The French Illustrators Bernard Jannemin and Mach Eveno." *Bookbird* 29, no. 1 (March 1991): 23.

    Brief notes on the work of two illustrators who have been instrumental in beginning a new international biennial of illustrations in the small medieval French town of Lannion. B & w illustrations.

551. Dillon, Leo and Diane Dillon. "The Tale of the Mandarin Ducks." *Horn Book* 68, no. 1 (January–February 1992): 35–37.

    In their speech accepting the Boston Globe–Horn Book award, the Dillons describe how they studied and selected the Japanese "ukiyo-e" style to use for illustrations, how they actually painted them, and the problems that come from the scanning process that reproduces the illustrations. B & w illustrations.

552. Entry deleted.

553. *Dr. Seuss from Then to Now.* Catalog. New York: Random House, 1987. 96pp.

Over 250 illustrations in b & w and color fill this catalog compiled by the San Diego Museum of Art to accompany the exhibit celebrating sixty years of Dr. Seuss.

554. Durrell, Ann. "Nonny Hogrogian." *Library Journal* 91 (March 15, 1966); and *School Library Journal* 13 (March 1966): 128–129.

Some notes on how Hogrogian works.

555. *Edward Ardizzone.* 16mm color film. Videocassette. Weston, Conn.: Weston Woods, no date. 13 min.

The artist live, discussing his life and work in his studio in Kent, England, and talking with children. Includes some of his sketches.

556. Edwards, James P. *Randolph Caldecott.* ERIC Document ED 196020, 1980. 18pp.

Summary of his life with a description of his work and changes in style.

557. Ehlert, Lois. "The Artist at Work: Card Tables and Collage." *Horn Book* 67, no. 6 (November–December 1991): 695–704.

The artist describes how she grew up creating, studied art, became a graphic designer, then came to do books. She discusses how she creates her illustrations, where some of her ideas come from, then provides details about making specific books. Some b & w illustrations.

558. Elleman, Barbara. "The Booklist Interview: Graeme Base." *Booklist* (January 1, 1990): 914–915.

The author-illustrator talks about how he came to do picture books, how he contracts his pictures, his audience, how his books are received by the public, and his future plans. Photo.

559. ———. "The Booklist Interview: Steven Kellogg." *Booklist* (May 15, 1989): 1640–1641.

After filling in some background information on the artist and some of his books, Elleman asks about Kellogg's feelings concerning the Regina medal he is receiving, how he began in the field, how he works, his opinion on the field of children's books, and his current projects. Photo and one illustration.

560. Elliot, Ian. "Bruce Degen: Doing What He Likes Best." *Teaching K–8* (October 1991): 44–47.

After tracing his interest in art through school and into art-related jobs, Elliot quotes Degen on his becoming an illustrator, because "that was the kind of art I always loved to draw." Elliot tells a bit about Degen's works. Color photo and several illustrations.

561. ———. "Meet Kevin Henkes: Young Man on a Roll." *Teaching K–8* (January 1989): 43–45.

Henkes talks about how he got started with art and picture books. He discusses how he works, and what he hopes to accomplish. Photo and sketch.

562. Ellis, Sarah. "News from the North." *Horn Book* 67, no. 5 (September–October 1991): 631–633.

In a discussion of new Canadian books for children, the author covers the books and illustrations of Stephane Poulin. Small b & w illustrations.

563. Elzea, Rowland. *Howard Pyle*. New York: Peacock/Bantam, 1975. Unpaginated.

Chiefly a portfolio of forty-three of Pyle's color illustrations. Rowland's five-page introduction to the illustrations covers Pyle's life and the milieu in which he worked. Some critical comments included.

564. Engen, Rodney. *Kate Greenaway: A Biography.* New York: Schocken Books, 1981. 240pp.

   Covers her childhood, education, and art school training; her start as a greeting card illustrator; her meetings with Caldecott and Ruskin; her success, fall from favor, and the revival of her work. Some analysis of the influences on her work and a little about her style. Lists all her illustrated books. Many b & w and color illustrations, including photos.

565. *Eric Carle: Picture Writer.* Videocassette. New York: Philomel, 1993. Approx. 30 min.

   The artist talks about his childhood and experiences that influenced him. He reads from, and talks about the making of *Draw Me a Star*, *The Very Busy Spider*, and *The Very Quiet Cricket*, with a demonstration of how he paints his own colored paper for his collages and designs the pages. He concludes with pictures from *The Very Hungry Caterpillar* and *Will You Be My Friend?*

* *Evolution of a Graphic Concept: The Stonecutter.* Cited above as item 91.

566. *Ezra Jack Keats.* 16 mm film. Weston, Conn.: Weston Woods, no date. 17min.

   In his studio, the late artist talks about his life and work. Includes adaptation of *A Letter to Amy* to show how he works.

567. *Faith Ringgold: The Last Story Quilt.* Videocassette. Chappaqua, New York: L & S Video Enterprises/ Pleasantville, New York: Educational Audio Visual, 1992. 30 min.

   This autobiographical film for adults covers her life and art, with mention of the *Tar Beach* quilt as the subject of the picture book.

568. Fakih, Kimberly Olson. "Keith Baker" in "Flying Starts: New Faces of 1988." *Publishers Weekly* 234, no. 26 (December 23, 1988): 28–29.

     Mainly quotes from Baker on his life and work. Photo.

569. Feelings, Tom. "The Artist at Work: Technique and the Artist's Vision." *Horn Book* 61, no. 6 (November–December 1985): 685–695.

     Relates his life experiences as they have influenced his work as a Black American artist. Details how he works in general and on particular books. Five b & w examples.

570. Ferguson, Jesseca. "Interview with Henrik Drescher." *Horn Book* 67, no. 5 (September–October 1991): 556–561.

     In answer to questions, the artist describes his education, his objectives when illustrating, how he works, and other artists he finds of interest. Some b & w illustrations.

571. Field, Michele. "John Burningham and Helen Oxenbury." *Publishers Weekly* 232, no. 29 (July 24, 1987): 168–169.

     A brief summary of the lives of the two illustrators and of the different ways they work. Some quotes included. Photo.

572. Fisher, Leonard Everett. "The Artist at Work: Creating Nonfiction." *Horn Book* 64, no. 3 (May–June 1988): 315–323.

     After a brief summary of his youth and early art training, Fisher tells of his entry into children's books. He then describes the creation of some of his nonfiction works as artistic statements. Three b & w illustrations.

* Ford, Elizabeth A. "Resurrection Twins: Visual Implications in *Two Bad Ants*." Cited above as item 226.

573. "Frasconi's Brio with a Book." *Horizon* 3 (March 1961): 122–128.

Brief introduction to his life and work, with description and photo of his one-of-a-kind books. Several b & w and color prints reproduced.

574. Frederick, Heather. "A Talk with Lisbeth Zwerger." *Publishers Weekly* 237, no. 43 (October 1990): 42.

A brief summary of Zwerger's background and current work, including many quotations from the artist. Photo.

575. Frith, Margaret. "Interview with Eric Hill." *Horn Book* 63, no. 5 (September/October 1987): 577–585.

His background, how he came to do the books about Spot for his young son, where he gets his ideas, and how he does his art work and works out his stories. Two b & w illustrations.

576. ———, Linda Zuckerman, and Dorothy Briley. "Margot Tomes: Three Editors' Perspectives." *Horn Book* 68, no. 4 (July–August 1992): 486–489.

Each editor briefly recalls working with Tomes, with anecdotes, for a celebration in her memory.

577. Gag, Wanda. *Growing Pains: Diaries and Drawings for the Years 1908–1917.* New York: Coward–McCann, 1940. 479pp.

Gives a first-person account of her time in school studying art. Sixty b & w reproductions of her "fine art" work as well as her illustrations.

* *Gail E. Haley: Wood and Linoleum Illustration.* Cited above as item 94.

578. Glistrup, Eva. "Two Danish Illustrators." *Bookbird* 29, no. 4 (December 1991): 3–8.

    Covers the early life and training of Ib Spang Olsen and Svend Otto S., then comments on their books on the occasion of their 70th and 75th birthdays, respectively. Photos and several b & w illustrations of each artist's work.

579. Goddard, Connie. "Alive with Color." *Publishers Weekly* 239, no. 9 (February 12, 1992): 18–19.

    Discusses Lois Ehlert's background and several of her recent books. Details her methods and includes many personal quotes. B & w photo and illustrations.

580. Goldstein, William. "Jacket IS Overture." *Publishers Weekly* 233, no. 20 (May 20, 1988): 48–50.

    Some comments by Goldstein, but this is chiefly Maurice Sendak's reflections on *Dear Mili*, with some notes on his other books. He discusses the symbolism, his feelings about the illustrations, and the parallels to music. Photo and color illustration.

581. Golynets, Sergei. *Ivan Bilibin*. New York: Harry N. Abrams, 1981. 226pp.

    One hundred ninety-five illustrations with ninety-eight full color plates and some b & w photographs. A critical summary of his artwork and his place in the Art Nouveau movement, pp. 5–22; his life, with chronology and quotes from his letters, pp. 181–208. His book illustrations are not separated from his work in general.

582. Gordon, Lucy Latane. "An Interview with Leo Lionni." *Wilson Library Bulletin* 66, no. 10 (June 1992): 56–58.

    After briefly summarizing the artist's life, Gordon asks about his early life and influences, his relationship with the "fine art" world, and how he came to do children's books. B & w photo.

583. Gormsen, J. "Interview with Svend Otto S. The Famous Danish Illustrator." *Bookbird* 17, no. 1 (1979): 6–12.

He briefly describes his life and early training and discusses his current work, influences and goals.

584. Gough, John. "May Gibbs—Australia's Greatest Children's Writer." *Bookbird* 30, no. 4 (November 1992): 13–16.

Along with notes on her writing, Gough gives comments on Gibbs's illustrations, their quality and effectiveness. B & w photo and sketch.

585. Green, Roger Lancelyn, ed. *Lewis Carroll by Roger Lancelyn Green; E. Nesbit by Anthea Bell; Howard Pyle by Elizabeth Nesbit.* London: Bodley Head, 1968. 219pp.

The section on Pyle, pp. 163–219, discusses his life and "theories of illustration," pp. 178–188. Notes on his technique and the effect of new photo-engraving methods on it. Stresses the results of his teaching and how he inspired and challenged his students.

586. Greenaway, Kate. *Kate Greenaway.* New York: Rizzoli, 1977. 49pp.

Mainly color illustrations. A short text about Greenaway accompanies reproductions of her work from the Victoria and Albert Museum, originally printed by woodblock process by Evans.

587. Greene, Ellin. *Roger Duvoisin (1904–1980) The Art of Children's Books.* Catalog of an exhibition. New Brunswick, N.J.: Rutgers University Press, 1989. 38pp.

Catalog of an exhibition at the Jane Voorhees Zimmerli Art Museum at Rutgers includes annotated entries by Dorothy Hoogland Verkerk. Greene discusses the artist's life and work, including quotations from his own writings about his books. Profusely illustrated with a b & w photo and many b & w and color illustrations by the artist.

588. Grozdanov, Dimiter. "Alexander Alexov: Illustration as an Art." *Bookbird* 29, no. 1 (March 1991): 25–26.

A brief description of the life and work of this Bulgarian illustrator. B & w illustrations.

589. Hale, Robert D. "Musings." *Horn Book* 67 no. 1 (January–February 1991): 106–107.

Brief comments on the work of Barbara Cooney.

590. Hamilton, James. *Arthur Rackham*. Boston: Arcade/Little, Brown, 1990. 199pp.

A detailed biography, drawing on primary sources, with considerable material on Rackham's "traditional" art as well as his illustrations.

591. Hamilton, Lawrie. "The Art in Lois Lenski's Book, *The Little Auto*." *The Barnes Foundation Journal of the Art Department* 4, no. 2 (Autumn 1973): 53–63.

Discusses the words of the story and the illustrations, as they relate to design and other theories of art and "fine" artists, espoused by the Barnes Foundation.

592. Hancher, Michael. *The Tenniel Illustrations to the Alice Books*. Columbus: Ohio State University Press, 1985. 152pp.

Brief notes on Tenniel's life and training. Focus is "mainly on Tenniel's *Alice* illustrations and on the contexts and conditions that most affected them." Particularly insightful b & w illustrations showing the many and varied sources for some of the characters as well as illustrations he made for other publications.

593. Harris, Muriel. "Impressions of Sendak." *Elementary English* 48, no. 7 (November 1971): 825–832.

   An interview with the artist when he still lived in a "fortress against any of today's distractions" in New York City. Includes his comments on his family and early years and notes on some sources of inspiration. Some brief pictorial analysis of *In the Night Kitchen*.

594. Hearn, Michael Patrick. "Arnold Lobel: An Appreciation." *Washington Post Book World* (January 10, 1988): 7, 12.

   Along with a brief summary of Lobel's life, Hearn analyzes the style and quality of the artist's work, noting the loss to children's books that Lobel's death has caused. Photo and illustration.

595. ———. "Drawing Out William Steig." *Bookbird* 3–4 (1982): 61–65.

   Steig talks briefly about his background, how he came to do children's books, and how he works, including why he uses animal characters.

596. ———. "Maurice Boutet de Monvel: Master of the French Picture Book." *Horn Book* 55 (April 1979): 170–181.

   Covers his life, training, and how he came to illustrate for children, plus possible influences on his work. Some of his own comments are quoted. Includes an analysis of some of his books and suggestions of his influence on picture book artists today.

597. ———. "The 'Ubiquitous' Trina Schart Hyman." *American Artist* 43 (May 1979): 36–43, 96–97.

   Describes her life, art training, and early illustrations, including those provoking controversy. Notes on her work with *Cricket* magazine, a detailed analysis of her techniques and method of character development, and an appreciation of her "drama." Many b & w and color examples of her illustrations.

598.   ———. "W.W. Denslow: The Forgotten Illustrator." *American Artist* 37 (May 1973): 40–45, 71–73.

Summary of Denslow's career and work. Description of techniques used. Some quotations from his writing about himself. B & w and color illustrations.

599.   Hedderwick, Mairi. "The Artist at Work: A Sense of Place." *Horn Book* 66, no. 2 (March–April 1990): 171–177.

The artist begins with her childhood and art training, then tells how she began to do children's books. She analyzes her art technique and the way she puts a book together, along with the aims of her stories. Three b & w illustrations.

600.   Heins, Ethel L. "From Mallards to Maine: A Conversation with Robert McCloskey." *Journal of Youth Services in Libraries* 1, no. 2 (Winter 1988): 187–196.

The author-illustrator, replying to questions, discusses the importance of the Caldecott medal for him, how he feels about the relationship of text to illustration, and the influence of his youthful experiences and his Maine home on his work. Three b & w photos of the artist and of his sculptured ducklings in the Boston Public Gardens.

601.   Henderson, Darwin, and Anthony L. Manna. "An Interview with Jerry Pinkney." *Children's Literature in Education* 21, no. 3 (September 1990): 135–144.

After a brief introduction to the artist and his art, the authors interview him by telephone. Their questions cover his start in illustrating, the way he works, and his aims as an illustrator.

602. Henkes, Kevin. "The Artist at Work." *Horn Book* 68 no. 1 (January–February 1992): 38–47.

Henkes covers how he worked on picture books while still in college, after growing up wanting to be an artist. He describes his method of working, on both words and pictures, then with his editor and designer. He relates some books to personal experiences as he tells how they came to be. Some small b & w illustrations.

603. Hepler, Susan Ingrid. "Profile: Tomie dePaola: A Gift to Children." *Language Arts* 56 (March 1979): 296–301.

Summary of his life; some quotations on life and work. Notes on story and artwork from many books. B & w photo portrait.

604. Higgins, James. "William Steig: Champion for Romance." *Children's Literature in Education* 9, no. 1 (Spring 1978): 3–16.

An appreciation of Steig's fiction, not his illustrations. Pp. 10–15 are from a "conversation" between Higgins and Steig which covers how he came to write for children, his feelings about it, and a few sentences on his illustrations. One b & w illustration.

605. Hirschman, Susan. "Arnold Lobel." *Horn Book* 64, no. 3 (May–June 1988): 324–325.

In this commemorative piece, Hirschman reminisces about her years of working with Lobel, how he presented his books, and how he will be missed. Two b & w illustrations.

606. Hoare, Geoffrey. "The Work of David Macaulay." *Children's Literature in Education* 8, no. 1 (Spring 1977): 12–20.

Notes on children's changing preferences in illustration, perhaps because of media exposure, as Hoare analyzes Macaulay's art. Criticism of his inability to draw believable figures, his "vaguenesses," other lacks of connections between illustrations and missing specifics. Provocative discussion. Many b & w illustrations.

607. Holme, Bryan. *The Kate Greenaway Book.* New York: Studio Viking, 1976. 144pp.; Penguin, 1977.

Profusely illustrated in alternating b & w and color two-page spreads. "Success," pp. 7–11, comments on her impact in her time. "Background," pp. 13–32, gives introductory biographical information. Selections from her works follow, each preceded by background information and contemporary criticism. Their arrangement is more or less chronological.

608. Holmes, Joseph O. "The Way David Macaulay Works." *Publishers Weekly* 234, no. 18 (October 28, 1988): 30–31.

An interview allows Macaulay to describe the lengthy and difficult project of producing *The Way Things Work.* B & w photo and illustration.

* *How a Picture Book Is Made: The Making of the Island of the Skog from Conception to Finished Book.* Cited above as item 105.

609. Hoyle, Karen Nelson. "Gustav Tenggren's Golden Anniversary." *The Five Owls* 1, no. 3 (January–February 1987): 43–44.

The curator of the Kerlan Collection, in conjunction with an exhibit of Tenggren's work donated to the collection, talks about the illustrator's books as well as the acquisition of his work for the Kerlan. Three b & w illustrations.

610. ———. "Three Scandinavian Contributions to American Children's Literature." *Journal of Youth Services in Libraries* 2, no. 3 (Spring 1990): 219–225.

Hoyle feels that the work of James Fenimore Cooper had a great influence abroad and may have also impacted on the three Scandinavian author-illustrators who came to America, and whom she discusses here. She summarizes the life and work of Gustaf Tenggren from Sweden, Robert Hofsinde from Denmark, and Ingri Maartenson D'Aulaire from Norway. Ingri D'Aulaire is best known for her work with her husband Edgar. All three artists arrived in the United States in the 1920s and dealt with American themes from the Scandinavian perspective.

611. Hudson, Derek. *Arthur Rackham: His Life and Work.* New York: Scribner, 1960. 180pp.

A chronological review of his life and work, with critical comments by the author. Some quotations from Rackham and from his contemporaries about his art. Appendices include the author's sources and a checklist of Rackham's printed work. Some b & w illustrations and many tipped-in color plates.

612. Huntoon, Elizabeth. "A Caldecott Album." *Journal of Youth Services in Libraries* 1, no. 2 (Winter 1988): 177–182.

B & w photos and captions of some Caldecott award winners and others involved in the awards over the years.

613. Hurley, Beatrice J. "Wanda Gag—Artist, Author." *Elementary English* 32 (October 1955): 347–354.

Summary of the illustrator's early family life and growth, and quotations from her biography, *Growing Pains* (New York: Coward-McCann, 1940). Notes on some books, but no analysis of pictures.

614. Hurwitz, Laurie S. "Chris Van Allsburg." *American Artist* 54, no. 574 (May 1990): 58–66.

Summarizes the illustrator's life and training, plus how he began to do picture books. Describes and analyzes some of his books, with many b & w and color illustrations.

615. Hutton, Warwick. "How Jonah and the Great Fish Began." *Horn Book* 61, no. 1 (January–February 1985): 35–37.

In this speech written upon receipt of the Boston Globe-Horn Book Award for illustration, Hutton describes how he decided to do the book and his technique for the illustrations.

616. Hyman, Trina Schart. "Illustrating *The Water of Life.*" *Proceedings of the Thirteenth Annual Conference of the Children's Literature Association,* University of Missouri-Kansas City. May 16–18, 1986. Pp. 5–13.

The artist describes her task of illustrating. B & w illustration.

617. ———. *Self-Portrait: Trina Schart Hyman.* Reading, Mass.: Addison-Wesley, 1981. 32pp.

The simple story of how she grew up and became an illustrator, rich with details of her friends and life.

618. "An Interview with David Wiesner." *Clarion News* no. 5 (Spring 1992): 1–4.

After filling in background, an interviewer asks, and Wiesner answers, questions about how he works. Photo and small b & w illustration.

619. Irvine, Ruth R. "Marie Hall Ets—Her Picture Story Books." *Elementary English* 33 (May 1956): 259–265.

Summary of some of her books as to story, with only brief comments on the illustrations. B & w photo portrait, few b & w illustrations.

620. Jaaksoo, Andres. "Jaan Tamsaar: An Illustrator from Estonia." *Bookbird* 29, no. 3 (September 1991): 22.

    Notes on the artist and style of illustration, with quotations.

621. Jakobsen, Gunnar. "Svend Otto S., Winner of the Nordic Prize." *Bookbird* 27, no. 4 (November 1989): 13–16, 21–22.

    After briefly summarizing his training, Jakobsen describes the artist's method from sketches and beyond, including a discussion of several of his works, with quotes from the artist and from some of his writing. B & w portrait and full-page illustration.

622. *James Daugherty.* 16mm color film. Videocassette. Weston, Conn.: Weston Woods, no date. 19 min.

    Interview at his home and studio where he discusses his work as illustrator as well as author and historian.

623. *James Marshall in His Studio.* Videocassette. Boston: Houghton Mifflin, 1987. 10 min.

    A visit with the illustrator, while he talks about his life and work.

624. "James Warhola: Science Fiction to Pumpkinville." *School Library Media Activities Monthly* VIII, no. 10 (June 1992): 32–33, 47.

    Warhola gives lengthy, detailed answers to questions such as how he came to be an illustrator, how he prepares to illustrate a particular book, and his future plans.

625. "John Steptoe." *Publishers Weekly* 236, no. 12 (September 29, 1989): 38.

    A brief summary of his career and a eulogy. Photo.

626. Jones, Helen L. *Robert Lawson, Illustrator: A Selection of His Characteristic Illustrations.* Boston: Little Brown, 1972. 121pp.

    The illustrations are divided into types and briefly introduced. "Vital statistics and techniques" fill pp. 109–114. A list of books illustrated by Robert Lawson is on pp. 119–120.

627. Keeping, Charles. "My Work as a Children's Illustrator." *Children's Literature Association Quarterly* 8, no. 4 (Winter 1983): 14–19.

    His background, childhood memories, art school training and start as an illustrator. He tells how he began to write for children and the background of some of his other books, including discussion of his controversial titles.

628. Kellogg, Steven. "Colleagues and Co-Conspirators." *Horn Book* 46, no. 6 (November–December 1990): 704–707.

    After discussing the two voices—verbal and visual—with which the picture book communicates, Kellogg talks about how these are balanced and blended; the role of the editor; and finally, the "creative role" of those who bring the books to children: teachers, librarians, and parents.

629. Kingman, Lee. "Virginia Lee Burton's Dynamic Sense of Design." *Horn Book* 46 (October–December 1970): 449–460, 593–602.

    A detailed analysis of her illustrations and technique in *Calico the Wonder Horse* is included in this appreciation of Burton, along with some information on her life, background, and training. Five b & w illustrations.

630. Klingberg, Delores R. "Profile: Eric Carle." *Language Arts* 54 (April 1977): 445–452.

Facts about his life, training, and his concerns, plus personal notes on his collage technique. A description of his works, book-by-book, by Klingberg. B & w photo portrait and examples of his original art.

631. Knox, Rawle. *The Work of E.H. Shepard.* New York: Schocken, 1979. 256pp.

The story of Shepard's life, his start as an artist, and his many illustrations for children and others are detailed. Chapter eight, "A Master of Line" by Bevis Hillier, pp. 246–251, is an appreciation of his skill. Profusely illustrated in b & w and color.

632. Kroll, Steven. "Steig: Nobody Is Grown-up." *New York Times Book Review* (June 28, 1987): 26.

In this interview, Steig talks briefly about how he illustrates, along with comments on his work and life.

* LaBarbera, Kathryn. "The Emotional Impact of Books by Molly Bang." Cited above as item 290.

633. Lacy, Lyn. *Randolph Caldecott, The Man Behind the Medal.* Sound filmstrip. Weston, Conn.: Weston Woods, 1983. 1 filmstrip, 1 cassette. 57 frames. 15 min.

Covers his life and art, including his drawings, and illustrations for picture books. Includes some information on the medal.

634. Lahr, John. "The Playful Art of Maurice Sendak." *New York Times Magazine* (October 12, 1980): 44–48, 52–60.

A perceptive exploration of the artist's development, and the interrelationship of his books and his theatrical designs.

635. Landes, Sonia. *A Closer Look at Peter Rabbit.* Sound filmstrip. Weston, Conn.: Weston Woods, 1984. 1 filmstrip, 1 cassette. 49 frames, 17 min.

Analysis of words and pictures and how they work together. Comparison with another, less effective illustrator.

636. Lanes, Selma G. *The Art of Maurice Sendak*. New York: Harry N. Abrams, 1980. 278pp.

Biography, discussion of works, and conversations with the artist. Profusely illustrated with b & w and ninety-four full-color illustrations. Includes photographs.

637. ———. "Ezra Jack Keats: In Memoriam." *Horn Book* 40 (September/October 1984): 551–558.

Includes personal reminiscences, quotations about his life and work from those who knew him, and an appreciation of his art.

638. ———. "A Second Look: Joan of Arc." *Horn Book* 58 (February 1982): 79–83.

A short background introduction and brief criticism of text, but mainly a detailed analysis of the Boutet de Monvel illustrations and their art, with consideration of the overall design.

 * Larkin, David, ed. *The Art of Nancy Ekholm Burkert*. Cited above as item 523.

639. ———. *The Fantastic Paintings of Charles and William Heath Robinson*. New York: Bantam, 1976. Unpaginated.

Chiefly forty full-page color plates of the illustrators' works. A brief introduction covers their life, some discussion of their art, and a few quotations from the artists.

640. *Laurent de Brunhoff, Daydreamer*. Sound filmstrip. Westminster, Md.: Random House, 1982. 1 filmstrip, 1 cassette.

Interview in which he tells how he works.

641. Lent, Blair. "Artist at Work: Cardboard Cuts." *Horn Book* 41 (August 1965): 408–412.

A factual, step-by-step account of how he makes cardboard cuts, including specifics on the art in some of his books; with b & w examples.

642. Levine, Arthur. "Emily Arnold McCully." *Horn Book* 69, no. 4 (July–August 1993): 430–432.

A brief appreciation of the artist and of some of her outstanding picture books.

643. Linder, Leslie. *History of the Tale of Peter Rabbit.* New York: Warne, 1977. 64pp.

From its origin in an illustrated letter through writing, editing and publication, with related correspondence.

644. ———, and Enid Linder. *The Art of Beatrix Potter.* New York: Warne, 1955. 406pp.

Detailed analysis of development of art through her life. Profusely illustrated.

645. Lionni, Leo. *Leo Lionni at the Library of Congress.* Lecture. Washington, D.C.: Government Printing Office, 1993. 28pp.

In a lecture given as part of the International Children's Book Day 1988 at the Children's Literature Center of the Library of Congress, Lionni tells how *Little Blue and Little Yellow* was born, and tells of other sources of inspiration for other characters in his books.

646. Lobel, Arnold. "Birthdays and Beginnings." *Theory Into Practice* 21, no. 4 (Fall 1982): 322–324.

Remarks at the Children's Literature Conference at Ohio State University in January 1982, on a day that happened to also be his birthday. Some remarks on his childhood and how his distance from it makes it harder to write for children. With inspiration from Lear and Grandville, he tells how he began to write *Pigericks*, and a bit on how he does his drawing: "the dessert after the spinach of writing."

647. ———. "Show Me the Way to Go Home." *Horn Book* 65, no. 1 (January–February 1989): 26–29.

A very personal reminiscence of the street on which Lobel lives, on his life and troubles as a child in 1938, and how this relates to what he tries to do for each child in his writing and illustrating.

648. Lodge, Sally. "Dancing to a Different Tune." *Publishers Weekly* (April 20, 1992): 21.

Briefly summarizes Rachel Isadora's life, her entry into the children's book field, and current work.

649. Logan, Claudia. "The Fresh Vision of Lucy Cousins." *Publishers Weekly* 238, no. 11 (March 1, 1991): 44–45.

A brief summary of Cousins's life and career includes quotations and notes on how she works with her editors, particularly on her "action books." Color illustrations.

650. Loranger, Janet A. "Marcia Brown." *Horn Book* 68, no. 4 (July–August 1992): 440–443.

This introduction, with Brown's acceptance speech for the Laura Ingalls Wilder Award, describes Brown's studio, her work, and a bit of her life.

651. Lorraine, Walter. "An Interview with Maurice Sendak." *Wilson Library Bulletin* 52 (October 1977): 326–336.

Sendak discusses his techniques, his interpretive illustrations of Grimm's and other tales, and gives his definitions of "picture book." Mentions that he is not happy with the conservatism of publishers nor with contemporary criticism.

652. "A Lost Art." *New Yorker* (November 2, 1992): 40.

A brief appreciation of the work of James Marshall after his death.

653. Lundin, Anne H. "Kate Greenaway's Vision of Childhood." *The Five Owls* 3, no. 2 (November–December 1988): 29–30.

Discusses Greenaway in the context of her time. Describes how she came to do children's books; the role of her printer, Edmund Evans; the reception of her work; and her lasting appeal. Two illustrations.

654. Lystad, Mary. "Taming the Wild Things." *Children Today* 18, no. 2 (March–April 1989): 16–19.

A commemorative reexamination of Maurice Sendak's *Where the Wild Things Are* on the 25th anniversary of its reception of the Caldecott medal. Sendak is quoted extensively, as are other writers, including Bruno Bettelheim. Some other works of Sendak are also discussed, but little is said about his art. Two b & w illustrations.

655. Macaulay, David. "David Wiesner." *Horn Book* 68, no. 4 (July–August 1992): 423–428.

Macaulay describes Wiesner's youth, his early artistic and creative activities and education, and his eventual evolution into illustrator, in this introduction to Wiesner's Caldecott acceptance speech.

656. MacCann, Donnarae, and Olga Richard. "Picture Books for Children." *Wilson Library Bulletin* 65, no. 8 (April 1991): 98–99, 129.

   This particular review column discusses the work of James Stevenson, analyzes the story content of several books, and the style of his artwork. Includes small b & w illustrations and a list of his books.

657. ———. "Picture Books for Children." *Wilson Library Bulletin* 66, no. 5 (January 1992): 105–107, 137.

   This column is a detailed appreciation of both the text and the illustrations of many books by Rosemary Wells, with an extensive list of recommended titles. Four small b & w illustrations.

658. MacDonald, Ruth K. *Beatrix Potter.* Boston: Twayne, 1986. 148pp.

   Potter's text is the main focus, although the preface states, "I have also sought to evaluate the pictures as part of a series designed to tell a story and as commentary on the text that accompanies them." Covers her life including her study of art and influences. Some comments on illustration in the discussion of each book. How her animal illustrations have influenced other illustrators' attempts at her stories is noted.

659. ———. *Dr. Seuss.* Boston: Twayne, 1988. 185pp.

   After an initial chapter summarizing Seuss's life up to the date of publication, MacDonald analyzes each of his books in detail. Although her primary focus is on "the language" because of the series' emphasis, MacDonald comments on the illustrations as well, but in far less detail, and then more descriptively than analytically. B & w photo and b & w illustrations of the pages of many books.

660. Mahne, Sabine. "The German Illustrator Christa Unzer-Fischer." *Bookbird* 29, no. 2 (May 1991): 16.

    Brief summary of the artist's life with some description of her illustration technique. B & w photo.

661. *The Man Who Invented Snoopy.* Sound filmstrip. Westminster, Md.: Random House, 1982. 1 filmstrip, 1 cassette.

    Charles Schulz discusses his life and work.

662. Marantz, Sylvia, and Kenneth Marantz. "Interview with Ann Jonas." *Horn Book* 63, no. 3 (May–June 1987): 308–313.

    How she works, with details on some particular books. B & w illustrations.

663. ———. "An Interview with Anthony Browne." *Horn Book* 61, no. 6 (November–December 1985): 696–704.

    How he became an illustrator, how he works, and thoughts on some of his books. B & w examples from *Gorilla* and *Hansel and Gretel.*

664. ———. "Interview with Paul O. Zelinsky." *Horn Book* 62, no. 3 (May–June 1986): 295–304.

    Discusses how he came to illustration and how he attacks each book, with some details on *Hansel and Gretel.* B & w examples.

665. ———. "M.B. Goffstein: An Interview." *Horn Book* 62, no. 6 (November–December 1986): 688–694.

    How the artist works, with some details on individual books. Three b & w examples.

666. ———. "Patricia Polacco." *Library Talk* 5, no. 5 (November–December 1992): 11–14.

With extensive quotations from the artist, her
background, life, and family are covered, along with
information on the genesis of many of her books and her
own description of how she works. B & w illustrations.

667. ———. "Will Hillenbrand." *Library Talk* 6, no. 2 (March–
      April, 1993): 18–21.

In the interview, the artist talks about his life, his art
training and career, the start of his picture book
illustrating, and how he has worked on several books.
Photo. The b & w illustrations include a storyboard
layout.

668. Marcus, Leonard. "Garth Williams." *Publishers Weekly*
      237, no. 8 (February 23, 1990): 201–202.

Including many quotes from the artist, Marcus
summarizes Williams's early life, beginning career,
collaborations with famous authors like E.B. White and
Laura Ingalls Wilder, and his interest in the possibilities
offered by new printing technology. Photo.

669. ———. "An Interview with Amy Schwartz." *Horn Book*
      66, no. 1 (January–February 1990): 36–45.

In answer to questions, Schwartz describes her early
interest in books and art, her art training, and how she
came to children's picture book illustration. She talks
about how she works on her books, details her aims in
some, and discusses her characters. Five b & w
illustrations.

670. ———. "James Marshall." *Publishers Weekly* 236, no. 4
      (July 28, 1989): 202–203.

After a summary of his early life and career, the
interview describes how Marshall came to do some of
his books. Marshall is quoted on his work and style,
which is also discussed by Marcus. Photo.

671. ————. "Rearrangement of Memory: An Interview with Allen Say." *Horn Book* 67, no. 3 (May–June 1991): 295–303.

   In answering questions, Say tells about his growing up, beginning interest in and study of art, and how he has worked on several of his picture books. B & w illustrations.

672. Marshall, James. "Arnold Lobel." *Horn Book* 64, no. 3 (May–June 1988): 326–328.

   This tribute to Lobel notes his courage, his craftsmanship, and his hard work and discusses many of his works, including his fine watercolor painting, and the gifts he leaves us. Three small b & w illustrations.

673. Mathers, Petra. "The Artist at Work." *Horn Book* 68, no. 2 (March–April 1992): 171–177.

   Mathers describes her book-loving childhood in post-war Germany, how she and her husband came to America, and how she began to paint. She discusses her work on several of her books. B & w illustration.

674. *Maurice Sendak—1965.* 16mm color film. Video-cassette.Weston, Conn.: Weston Woods, 1965. 14 min.

   Interview in his New York apartment. He discusses his early books, influence of painters and composers, and *Where the Wild Things Are.*

675. *Maurice Sendak with Paul Vaughn.* Videocassette. Northbrook, Ill.: Roland Collection, undated. 45 min.

   Sendak talks about his life and work, including his writing and illustrating for children, and how he got published.

676. May, Jill P., ed. "Howard Pyle Commemorative." *Children's Literature Association Quarterly* 8, no. 2 (Summer 1983): 9–34.

Includes Patricia Dooley's "Romance and Realism: Pyle's Book Illustrations for Children," pp. 17–19: a discussion of his "decoration" style appearing in many of his books; and discusses both the design and the individual details of the illustrations.

677. ———. "Illustration as Interpretation: Trina Hyman's Folk Tales." *Children's Literature Association Quarterly* 10 (Fall 1985): 127–131.

Discusses Hyman's version of *Snow White, Rapunzel,* and *Little Red Riding Hood* in great detail, including influences, models for the characters, symbolism, book and page design, clothing of characters, and parallels with Hyman's life; quoting Hyman as well.

678. ———. "Trina S. Hyman." *Children's Literature Association Quarterly* 11, no. 1 (Spring 1986): 44.

Interview that emphasizes the artist "with a strong understanding of art, of psychology, and of people— including children." Illustration as interpretation.

679. McDermott, Gerald. "Sky Father, Earth Mother: An Artist Interprets Myth." *The New Advocate* 1, no. 1 (1988): 1–7.

The artist describes his quest "to give contemporary voice form to traditional tales," in books he has done in the past and one he is currently doing. Several small b & w illustrations.

680. McKee, Barbara. "Van Allsburg: From a Different Perspective." *Horn Book* 65, no. 5 (September–October 1986): 566–571.

A detailed analysis of the artwork in each of Van Allsburg's first six books, showing how his figure drawings evolved with the development of his addition of color. Also discusses his increasing psychological depth of character. B & w examples.

681. McPherson, William. "Maurice Sendak in Profile." *Washington Post Book World* (May 10, 1981): 1, 8–9, 12.

     A thoughtful interview and appreciation of a variety of the artist's works.

682. McQuade, Molly. "Wendy Watson." *Publishers Weekly* (July 28, 1989): 30.

     Watson is quoted as she discusses her illustrated version of *Mother Goose.*

683. McWhorter, George. "Arthur Rackham: The Search Goes On." *Horn Book* 48 (February 1972): 82–87.

     A brief appreciation of his development as an illustrator as part of a discussion of the growing value of his original works and the consequent search for more.

684. Meek, Margaret, Aidan Warlow, and Griselda Barton, eds. *The Cool Web: The Pattern of Children's Reading.* London: Bodley Head, 1977. 427pp.

     Relevant to illustration, includes "The Artist as Author: The Strength of the Double Vision: Questions to an Artist Who Is also an Author," pp. 241–256, based on the transcript of a discussion at the Library of Congress between Virginia Haviland and Maurice Sendak, in which Sendak covers his childhood, where his ideas come from, other influences, his favorites, his style, and what he sees as the difference between books for children and those for adults.

685. *Meet Ashley Bryan: Storyteller, Artist, Writer.* Videocassette. Chicago: American School Publishers/ SRA, 1992. 23 min.

     Viewers can see Bryan in his home as he works on art and other projects, and can hear him tell stories.

686. *Meet Leo Lionni.* Videocassette. Chicago: American School Publishers/SRA, 1992. 19 min.

Includes Lionni's comments on his life and interests as it shows him working with children in a New York City school, and then on his farm in Italy. Scenes from his books are shown.

687. *Meet Marc Brown.* Videocassette. Chicago: American School Publishers/SRA, 1991. 20 min.

Brown talks about his life, his characters, and what inspired them. Live action and animation, but little about his art.

688. *Meet Stan and Jan Berenstain.* Sound filmstrip. Videocassette. Chicago: American School Publishers/ SRA, before 1986. 13 min.

The Berenstains tell how they work together and both write and illustrate their books.

689. *Meet the Artist: Barbara Reid.* Videocassette. Mead Educational Ltd./EAV, 1988. approx. 20 min.

The illustrator describes how she prepares to make her color Plasticine creations for a particular book, then demonstrates the process. She also discusses her childhood, art education, and her influences.

690. *Meet the Caldecott Illustrator: Jerry Pinkney.* Videocassette. Chicago: American School Publishers/SRA, 1991. 21 min.

An opportunity to watch the artist in his studio develop the dummy of a picture book from a manuscript. He also talks about his life and work.

* *Meet the Newbery Author: Arnold Lobel.* Alternate title. Cited above as item 510.

691. Mehren, Elizabeth. "Babar, Reborn in the U.S.A." *The Washington Post* (December 25, 1989): 10–11.

Describing Laurent de Brunhoff and his current home, Mehren also relates how he came to pick up and continue the Babar books first begun by his father Jean. Many quotes from the artist illuminate a discussion of the psychology of Babar. Photo.

692. Mercier, Jean F. "Sendak on Sendak." *Publishers Weekly* (April 10, 1981): 45–46.

A detailed description by the author of the development of *Outside Over There*, including the relevance to his own childhood. Some small b & w illustrations.

* Mestrovich, Marta. "Perestroika and Picture Books." Cited above as item 121.

693. Meyer, S. "N.C. Wyeth." *American Artist* 39 (February 1975): 38–45, 94–100.

His life and work, quotations from his writing, description of how he painted, and his influence on his children and other artists. B & w and color examples of his illustrations; portrait.

694. Michel, Joan Hess. "A Visit with Tomi Ungerer." *American Artist* 33 (May 1969): 40–45, 78–79.

Many illustrations. Informal description of the artist, his work place, his life and some of his books for both children and adults. Some analysis of his art.

695. Mikolaycak, Charles. "The Artist at Work: The Challenge of the Picture Book." *Horn Book* 62 (March 1986): 167–173.

A detailed description of how this artist works and his ideas about how picture books should be illustrated.

696. Monin, Yevgeny. "I Immerse Myself in This Fairy-Tale World." *Horn Book* 67, no. 5 (September–October 1991): 569–572.

The Russian artist-illustrator describes his early art interest, his education, his beginnings as a picture-book illustrator, and how he works today. B & w photo.

697. Morsberger, Robert E. *James Thurber.* New York: Twayne, 1964. 224pp.

This study of Thurber's life and work deals only peripherally with his picture books, and hardly at all with their illustrations. Chapter 8, "Thurber's Drawings," pp. 160–173, mentions only *Last Flower* briefly.

698. Mortensen, Heddi. "Dorte Karrebaek, the Danish Illustrator." *Bookbird* 30, no. 2 (May 1992): 22–24.

Discusses the technique and some individual works of the artist. B & w illustration.

699. Moser, Barry. "Artist at Work: Illustrating the Classics." *Horn Book* 63, no. 6 (November–December 1987): 703–709.

The artist discusses his role as illustrator as he sees it: as a servant to the story. He begins with typography before images and describes his work on *Alice in Wonderland* and *Jump!*

700. *Mr. Shepard and Mr. Milne.* 16mm color film. Videocassette. Weston, Conn.: Weston Woods, no date. 29 min.

The original Christopher Robin discusses the collaboration of the author and illustrator. Includes visits to original locales.

701. Nazarevskaia, Nadezhda. "Nikita Charuschin: A Leningrad Artist." *Horn Book* 67, no. 3 (May–June 1991): 307–311.

Describes the life of this artist and illustrator and his method of working. Four b & w illustrations.

702. Ness, Evaline. "The Artist at Work: Woodcut Illustration." *Horn Book* 40 (October 1964): 520–522.

A detailed and loving account of how she makes woodcuts.

* Neumeyer, Peter F. "How Picture Books Mean: The Case of Chris Van Allsburg." Cited above as item 334.

703. Nikola-Lisa, W. "Scribbles, Scrawls, and Scratches: Graphic Play as Subtext in the Picture Books of Ezra Jack Keats." *Work and Play in Children's Literature:* Selected Papers from the 1990 International Conference of the Children's Literature Association. Sponsored by the College of Education and the College of Arts and Letters, San Diego State University. May 31–June 3, 1990. Edited by Susan R. Gannon and Ruth Anne Thompson. Pp. 45–49.

Discusses Keats's illustrations and "style" in general, but more specifically, the "superimposition of pictographic-like images on his already solid painting and/or collage foundation." These images are discussed, as they appear in several books, as pivotal additions to the "text" of Keats's stories.

704. Nudelman, Edward D. *Jessie Willcox Smith: American Illustrator*. Gretna, La.: Pelican, 1990. 144pp.

A comprehensive study covering her life, art training, and comments on her art. Traces all her books. Divided by themes. Many illustrations and photos in color and b & w.

705. ———. *Jessie Willcox Smith: A Bibliography*. Gretna, La.: Pelican, 1989. 184pp.

This chronological bibliography contains all of her illustrations in color plus technical information.

706. O'Connell, Diane. "A Conversation with Tomie dePaola." *Sesame Street Magazine and Parents' Guide* (October 1989): 40–43.

DePaola tells stories of his childhood and school experiences, how he came to illustrate children's books after teaching, and his work as editor of Whitebird Books. Photo and book jacket.

707. Olson, Marilynn Strasser. *Ellen Raskin.* Boston: Twayne, 1991. 120pp.

A biographical chapter says little about Raskin's art, except her education and advertising work. "Illustrations for Others," pp. 11–30, describes some of her 1,000 book jackets, her "decorated" poetry and non-poetry books, and her illustrated poetry and non-poetry books, including some on the illustrations. Special attention is given to the woodcuts. Chapter 3, "Picture Books," pp. 31–34, describes the change to cartoon-style drawings for *Nothing Ever Happens on My Block* and subsequent books, analyzing stories and illustrations. Since Raskin did not like to see illustrations in a novel, the subsequent chapters on the novels hold no further relevant information.

708. Oxenbury, Helen. "The Artist at Work: Books for the Very Young." *Horn Book* 68, no. 5 (September–October 1992): 555–559.

The illustrator covers how her art evolved, how she began to work with Sebastian Walker of Walker Books on the books for younger children, and how she works currently.

709. Painter, Helen W. "Leonard Weisgard: Exponent of Beauty." *Elementary English* 47 (November 1970): 922–935.

Covers details of his life, with quotations, and his training in the arts. Discusses many of his books, how they happened to be done, and gives an analysis of the art in many of them plus some criticism of the quality of his work in general. A very useful discussion in more depth than most. Small b & w illustrations.

710.   ————. "Little Toot—Hero." *Elementary English* 37 (October 1960): 363–367.

Brief summary of Gramatky's life; sketchy attempt to analyze the illustrations in a few paragraphs. B & w photo portrait, one illustration.

711.   ————. "Lynd Ward: Artist, Writer, and Scholar." *Elementary English* 39 (November 1962): 663–671.

Brief summary of his life and success as an artist. Discussion of the relationship between his research and his illustration, and analysis of the emotional impact of some of the illustrations in a few of his books. B & w photo portrait and some b & w illustrations.

712.   ————, and Ulla Hyde Parker. *Cousin Beatie: A Memory of Beatrix Potter.* London: Warne, 1981. 40pp.

Personal reminiscences of what Beatrix Potter was like, with mention of the relationship of her art and her picture books. B & w and color illustrations and photos.

713.   Peet, Bill. *Bill Peet: An Autobiography.* Boston: Houghton Mifflin, 1989. 190 pp.

Peet tells the story of his life with humor, for young readers, beginning with his childhood when he was always drawing and involved with many other adventures. His art talent earned him a scholarship to an Art Institute, and his career was launched. He describes his time at Walt Disney Studios, from Mickey Mouse and Snow White to Cinderella, Peter Pan and Sleeping Beauty. He then discusses the beginnings of his picture books. Peet worked on many other Disney productions as he continued to create books (which he describes), with parallels to his experiences with Disney. There is more about life with Disney than picture books. Profusely illustrated in b & w.

714. Perry, Erma. "The Gentle World of Ezra Jack Keats." *American Artist* 35 (September 1971): 48–53, 71–73.

Many quotes from Keats help describe the technique and materials used, how he works, and where he finds ideas. Notes on his life and hard times before attaining success. Illustrated in b & w and color, also a photo portrait.

715. *Picture Books: The Symposium.* Videocassette. Scarborough, New York: Tim Podell Productions, 1989. Approx. 30 min.

Lee Bennett Hopkins chairs a discussion with picture book authors Charlotte Zolotow, Bernard Waber, and Alice Lowe. Because Waber is the only one who both writes and illustrates all his books, the discussion has little to say about the art.

716. Pinkney, Jerry. "The Artist at Work: Characters Interacting with the Viewer." *Horn Book* 67, no. 2 (March–April 1992): 171–179.

The artist describes how he came to study art, then began creating books. He covers the way he works now, his influences, the importance of careful book production, typography, and design. He then covers how he finds models for people and settings, always keeping in mind that this is not a "museum painting" but a series of book illustrations. Some b & w illustrations.

717. ———. "Personal Visions." *What Is Art For?* Keynote addresses, 1991 National Art Education Association (NAEA) Convention, Reston, Va., 1991. Pp. 51–61.

The artist begins by describing his early life and start as an illustrator. He details his working method, some of his projects, his teaching, and his current challenges. B & w photo and six full-page illustrations.

718. Porte, Barbara Ann. "The Picture Books of M.B. Goffstein." *Children's Literature in Education* 11, no. 1 (Spring 1980): 3–9.

   Mainly about the "story"; paragraph on p. 5 describes illustrations.

719. Preiss, Byron, ed. *The Art of Leo and Diane Dillon*. New York: Ballantine, 1981. Unpaginated.

   The introductory essay, about a third of which is devoted to picture books, is a romantic tracing of the couple's training and twenty-three years of marriage. It describes in text and b & w illustrations their development of a unique working pattern where both create each picture together. Most of the book is devoted to a collection of thirty-five full-page, full-color examples of illustrations, only two from picture books. Facing pages contain comments by the artists most of which present valuable information describing the media and techniques of production. No table of contents, index, or bibliography.

720. *Quentin Blake with Heather Neill*. Videocassette. Northbrook, Ill.: Roland Collection, undated. 24 min.

   The artist covers aspects of his work, including the humor, the preparation, the interpretation, and illustrating versus writing.

721. *Ralph Steadman with Peter Fuller*. Videocassette. Northbrook, Ill.: Roland Collection, undated. 50 min.

   In his discussion of his art and writing in general, Steadman also covers drawing, cartooning and caricature, but says little about his picture books for children.

722. Ramseger, Ingeborg. "An Exhibition in Memory of Bettina Hurlimann." *Bookbird* 1 (1986): 25–28.

    After describing the memorial exhibition and Hurlimann's collection, Ramseger briefly discusses Hurlimann's life and work. Photo.

723. Raymond, Allen. "Anita Lobel: Up From the Crossroad." *Teaching K–8* (November–December 1989): 52–55.

    With many quotes from the artist, the interviewer notes Lobel's almost miraculous escape from death in a concentration camp in World War II, the family's arrival in the United States via Sweden, and finally comes to Lobel's start in picture books and her method of working on a book. Many color photos.

724. ———. "Beni Montresor: Carmen, Cannes, and Caldecott." *Teaching K–8* (April 1990): 31–33.

    In an interview, Montresor discusses his work on operatic stage sets, in the theater, and his picture books. Color photos and illustrations.

725. ———. "Douglas Florian: Keeping a Balance Between Simplicity and Reality." *Teaching K–8* (March 1991): 36–38.

    An interview during which Florian describes how he works, what his aims are, how he got started doing children's books, and a bit about his life and his family. Color photo.

726. ———. "It Adds Up to Magic: Jeanne and Bill Steig." *Teaching K–8* (August–September 1991): 52–54.

    An appreciaton of the work of the Steigs, with quotes on how Bill Steig works. Color photos.

727. ———. "Jan Brett: Making It Look Easy." *Teaching K–8* (April 1992): 38–40.

Brett and her husband are quoted about their life at their Massachusetts home. Her training and the start of her career are summarized. Her artwork and methods are covered. Color photo and two illustrations.

728. ———. "Jose Aruego: From Law Books to Kids' Books." *Teaching K–8* (August–September 1987): 46–49.

An interview covers the artist's home, his childhood, his art training and beginning as an illustrator, with many quotations. Color photo and illustrations.

729. ———. "Meet Dennis Kyte: A Modern-Day Aesop." *Teaching K–8* (February 1989): 50–52.

Details Kyte's career in advertising art, how he happened to move to picture books, and his future plans. Photo.

730. ———. "Nancy Winslow Parker: 'I Knew It Would Happen.'" *Teaching K–8* (May 1990): 34–36.

After describing her childhood, education, and family background, Raymond describes Parker's current residences. Personal quotes relate how she left her position as art director to become an author and illustrator. Some of her books are described. Color photos.

731. ———. "Uri Shulevitz: For Children of All Ages." *Teaching K–8* (January 1992): 38–40.

The artist recalls his childhood in Europe in World War II, his early art studies, and his entry into the children's picture book field. Color photo and illustrations.

732. ———. "Vera B. Williams: Postcards and Peace Vigils." *Teaching K–8* (October 1988): 40–42.

A summary of Williams's active life, plus a description of *Stringbean's Trip to the Shining Sea.* Color photo and illustrations.

733. *Raymond Briggs with Barry Took.* Videocassette. Northbrook, Ill.: Roland Collection, undated. 45 min.

Briggs covers how he became a cartoonist, how he gets his inspirations and develops characters; then discusses his illustrations and the role of the drawing and the writing in telling the story.

734. Reef, Pat Davidson. *Dahlov Ipcar/Artist.* Maine Art Series for Young Readers. Falmouth, Mass.: Kennebec River Press, 1987. 45pp.

Reef's text is simple enough for elementary readers. Beginning with the artist's childhood, the author describes Ipcar's life and her start in painting. Some changes in painting style, her cloth sculptures, hooked rugs and tapestries, murals, and lithographs are shown and noted. Her books for children are described on pp. 28–32; her "creative process" in a series of questions and answers on pp. 35–45; many illustrations in b & w and color, including photos of the artist at work.

735. Roback, Diane. "Arnold Lobel's Three Years with Mother Goose." *Publishers Weekly* 230, no. 8 (August 22, 1986): 32–33.

Including extensive quotes from Lobel, Roback describes his three years of work on his *Random House Book of Mother Goose*, noting the importance of the art director and support of the publisher. Photo and two b & w illustrations.

736. ———. "Eric Hill and His Dog Spot." *Publishers Weekly* 230, no. 4 (July 25, 1986): 116–117.

Summarizes how Hill came to create the books about Spot, how the success of the character continues in many countries and languages, and what he plans to do next. Some quotes from Hill included. Photo and several b & w illustrations.

737. *Robert McCloskey.* 16mm color film. Videocassette. Weston, Conn.: Weston Woods, no date. 18 min.

The artist discusses the influences on his work, from his Maine studio and in the other places that have inspired him.

738. Rochman, Hazel. "The Booklist Interview: Maurice Sendak." *Booklist* (June 15, 1992): 1848–1849.

The questions Sendak answers are mainly concerned with his work illustrating *I Saw Esau:* how he decided to do it, what he feels about it, how he worked out the illustrations. Also includes his reflections on current picture books, and on his "scary" illustrations. B & w photo and illustration.

739. Rollin, Lucy. "The Astonished Witness Disclosed: An Interview with Arnold Lobel." *Children's Literature in Education* 15, no. 4 (Winter 1984): 191–197.

Includes his reasons for drawing animals as main characters rather than people. Covers his early development and mentions current work.

740. Roop, Peter. "Conversations: Robert McCloskey." *The Five Owls* II, no. 4 (March–April 1988): 63–64.

Extensive quotations about McCloskey's life and on some of his books, with a description of the island he immortalized and where he now lives. Two small b & w illustrations.

741. Sadowski, Eloise. "Glimpses of an Artist: Adrienne Adams." *Elementary English* 51 (October 1974): 933–939.

Facts of her life plus a detailed description of how she works on a book from start to finish, including mention of her techniques for different books, details of her color separation work, and use of the Dinobase process. List of her books and awards; photo portrait.

742. Saul, Wendy. "Once-Upon-a-Time Artist in the Land of Now: An Interview with Trina Schart Hyman." *The New Advocate* 1, no. 1 (1988): 8–17.

The artist answers questions frankly and openly about her working methods, how she thinks the field has changed, some of her books and their problems, and in particular the questions and criticisms raised by her portrayal of African-Americans in *Big Sixteen*. Several small b & w illustrations.

743. Say, Allen. "Musings of a Walking Stereotype." *School Library Journal* 32, no. 12 (December 1991): 45–46.

Say summarizes his fight against stereotyping as an artist and as an Asian. Then he discusses a few of his current books. Photo; three small b & w illustrations.

744. Schiff, Stephen. "Edward Gorey and the Tao of Nonsense." *New Yorker* (November 9, 1992): 84–94.

Describes the artist, his education and growth, and his current home, with many quotes, including calling his "chosen form [of art] a kind of subversive imitation of the children's book." Descriptions and quotes from some of his books. Includes a color "cartoon" story and a b & w photo.

745. Schmidt, Gary D. *Robert McCloskey*. Boston: Twayne, 1990. 163pp.

The first chapter summarizes McCloskey's life, with a chronology of his work in the area of art and children's books. He created only eight picture books. Subsequent chapters analyze his books in detail, describing technical processes as well as esthetic considerations relating to media and page designs. Emphasis is on the integration of pictures and text. B & w photo and illustration.

746. See, Lisa. "Audrey and Don Wood." *Publishers Weekly* 234, no. 5 (July 29, 1988): 211–212.

An interview includes a description of the Woods' home and many quotations from both of them. Their early lives are summarized. Their entry into children's books is described, as well as the unusual way they collaborate. Photo.

747. *Sendak.* 16mm color film. Videocassette. Weston, Conn.: Weston Woods, 1987. 27 min.

The artist describes some events in his life and how they have influenced his work.

748. Sendak, Maurice. "The Aliveness of Peter Rabbit." *Wilson Library Bulletin* 40 (December 1965): 345–348.

In a speech answering critics of Potter's *Peter Rabbit* and other such works for children, Sendak gives an enthusiastic and detailed analysis of Potter's illustrations and technique along with an appreciation of the story.

749. ———. "Picture Book Genesis: A Conversation with Maurice Sendak." *Proceedings of the Fifth Annual Conference of the Children's Literature Association,* Harvard University. March 1978. Pp. 29–40.

Discusses the background and influences upon several of his works, including *Outside Over There, Some Swell Pup, Animal Family, Really Rosie.* His disgust with television for children, and the influence of music on his work are also touched upon.

750. Shannon, George. *Arnold Lobel.* Boston: Twayne, 1989. 179pp.

Parallels the background and characters and of Lobel's books with those of his life. Covers working methods and influences. Analyzes his early illustrations for texts by others, and then those he wrote himself. Extensive bibliography. Index lists comments on illustrations in individual books.

751. ———. "The Artist's Journey and the Journey as Art: M.B. Goffstein's 'Grains of Sand.'" *Children's Literature in Education* 8, no. 4 (1987): 210–218.

While chiefly concerned with Goffstein as an author of books that he considers serious explorations of a symbolic "journey" of life, Shannon does discuss her illustrations as extensions of "her intimate voice." Mostly, however, a serious analysis of her prose.

752. Sheppard-Conrad, Connie. "The Enduring Appeal of Beatrix Potter." *Emergency Librarian* 16, no. 5 (May–June 1989): 21–25.

Brief notes on Potter's illustrations and their contribution to the appeal of her stories.

753. Sidorsky, Phyllis G. "Lisbeth Zwerger: Children's Book Illustrator." *Childhood Education* 69, no. 2 (Winter 1992): 86–88.

Describes Zwerger's studio and her early life, then briefly analyzes her works. Awards listed. Several b & w illustrations.

754. Silvey, Anita. "James Marshall (1942–1992)" *Horn Book* 69, no. 1 (January–February 1993): 4–5.

An editorial appreciation of the illustrator.

755. Sis, Peter. "The Artist at Work." *Horn Book* 68, no. 6 (November–December 1992): 681–688.

Sis describes his childhood and youth, his art training, the development of his style, his working method, and his influences. Three b & w illustrations.

756. Sleator, William. "An Illustrator Talks." *Publishers Weekly* 195 (February 17, 1969): 126–128.

This interview with Blair Lent asks a range of questions. Lent bases his answers on his belief that "the picturebook can be an art form," depending on how well the picture and the text work together. His art has evolved as print technology has made it possible for him to free himself from color separations. He believes that illustrating children's books is vital because the readers are at their most impressionable age.

757. Smith, Amanda. "Jon Scieszka and Lane Smith." *Publishers Weekly* 238 (July 26, 1991): 220–221.

In this interview "the irrepressible author/ illustrator duo unleash their wacky sense of humor on a growing legion of fans." They cover their collaboration. Lane details his palette and some ways he manipulates media.

758. Smith, Karen Patricia. "Merging Dreams and Consummate Realities: The Collaborative Ventures of Dick Roughsey and Percy Trezise." *Journal of Youth Services in Libraries* 2, no. 1 (Fall 1989): 34–42. and in *Where Rivers Meet: Confluence and Concurrents: Selected Papers from the 1989 International Conference of the Children's Literature Association.* May 11–14, 1989. Mankato, Australia: Mankato State University, 1989. Pp. 20–31.

A brief introduction to Aboriginals in Australia and to the early life of Roughsey, followed by the details of Roughsey's art training, his meeting with Trezise, and the start of their collaboration. The story content and the illustrations of three of the collaborative works are analyzed in great detail.

759. ———. "The Picture Storybook Art of Junko Morimoto." *Journal of Youth Services in Libraries* 5, no. 1 (Fall 1991): 55–65.

Briefly traces Morimoto's education, summarizes the plots of her eight picture books, and describes the variety of styles displayed in her illustrations for those seen at the Dromkeen Children's Literature Foundation exhibit in Australia in July 1989. The art of each book is analyzed and related to Japanese life and/or art, when relevant.

760. Smith, Lane. "The Artist at Work." *Horn Book* 69, no. 1 (January–February 1993): 64–70.

Describes his art training, his collaboration with Jon Scieszka, the role of pacing and timing in picture books, and how he makes his illustrations. Some b & w illustrations.

761. Smith, Linda Gramatky. "Little Toot Turns Fifty." *Horn Book* 65, no. 6 (November–December 1989): 746–747.

A note by Hardie Gramatky's daughter at the 50th anniversary of the publication of *Little Toot*, briefly recalls his life and the genesis of the tugboat story. B & w illustrations.

762. Solonen, Marja, and Maria Laukka. *Rudolf Koivu, 1890–1946*. Helsinki, Finland: Weilin & Goos, 1990. 83pp.

Text is in Finnish with some English translation and summary on the life and art of "the most loved among Finnish illustrators of children's books." B & w photos and many b & w and color illustrations.

763. Sonheim, Amy. *Maurice Sendak*. Boston: Twayne, 1991. 170pp.

Beginning with a biographical summary (including quotations from Sendak), Sonheim proceeds to the critical examination of Sendak's work and art that has more recently emerged, examining aspects of his visual and verbal style "that have not received much analysis." This includes a quite detailed examination of his early illustrations for the texts of others and then moves to books he wrote and illustrated. One chapter gives a detailed analysis of the trilogy and its stylistic verbal and visual elements. There are also chapters rich in conjecture and critical speculation on the rhythm of Sendak's prose and the "rhetoric" of the painter Runge and its relation to *Dear Mili*. A final chapter notes Sendak's influence on younger illustrators, especially Uri Shulevitz and Richard Egielski. There is an extensive list of references.

764. Sottomaya, Maria Jose. "BIB 1989 Golden Apple Award to the Portuguese Illustrator Manuela Bacelar." *Bookbird* 29, no. 1 (March 1991): 27–28.

Brief summary of the life and work of Bacelar, with a list of works. B & w illustrations.

765. Spencer, Isobel. *Walter Crane*. New York: Macmillan, 1975. 208pp.

Detailed account of his life and work includes his illustrations, especially the chapter "Colour work for Edmund Evans: Yellow Backs and Toy Books," pp. 39–63, and "Illustration up to 1890," pp. 76–100, which also discusses his contemporaries, including Greenaway and Caldecott.

766. Spielmann, M.H., and G.S. Layard. *Kate Greenaway*. Reissue of 1905 ed. New York: Benjamin Blom, 1968. 300pp.

Many facsimile sketches and notes from her letters. Pp. 265–284, "The Artist: A Review and an Estimate," analyzes her work.

767. Stan, Susan. "Donald Crews." *The Five Owls* 8, no. 1 (September–October 1993): 7–8.

A brief summary, with quotes from an interview, of Crews's work over the years, his two most recent books in particular, *Bigmama's* and *Shortcut*, which are about his early childhood experiences. Notes on how he and his wife Ann Jonas came to picture books.

768. Stander, Bella. "Nancy Ekholm Burkert." *Publishers Weekly* (July 28, 1989): 30.

Reports on Burkert's research, inspiration, and comments about her work for *Valentine and Orson*. Photo.

769. Steig, William. "The Artist at Work." *Horn Book* 69, no. 2 (March–April 1993): 170–174.

The author-illustrator discusses his childhood and family life, how he began illustrating and writing for children, and a bit about how he works. Two small b & w illustrations.

* *Story of a Book*. Holling C. Holling's *Pagoo*. Cited above as item 133.

770. Stott, Jon C. "Profile: Paul Goble." *Language Arts* 61 (December 1984): 867–873.

In an interview, Goble tells about his background, how he arrived in the United States and became interested in Native American culture, some individual books, and his life today. Some notes on the art and iconography. B & w portrait and illustrations.

771. Sullivan, Robert. "Oh, the Places He Went!" *Dartmouth Alumni Magazine* 84, no. 4 (Winter 1991): 19–43.

Traces Geisel's (Dr. Seuss's) life and career from early childhood, with some emphasis on his time at Dartmouth. Covers his early magazine and advertising work, his start in children's picture books, his work with early readers, and the major books and events of his life, with some quotes from Seuss and an analysis of his work. Many b & w and color photos, cartoons, and illustrations.

772. Svend Otto S. "On the Criticism of Illustrations."
    Bookbird (January 1986): 4–9.

    The illustrator talks about his role as he sees it. He
    states his own feelings about what he chooses to
    illustrate, the relationship between "fine art" and that for
    children's books, and generally what he hopes to
    accomplish. Photo, illustration.

773. Swanson, Mary T. *From Swedish Fairy Tales to American
    Fantasy. Gustaf Tenggren's Illustrations, 1920–1970.*
    Catalog of an exhibition. Minneapolis: University of
    Minnesota, 1986. 22pp.

    Catalog of an exhibition from the University Art
    Museum. Discusses Tenggren's life and analyzes his
    work. Includes a chronology, a checklist of the works in
    the exhibition, and many b & w illustrations.

774. Swinger, Alice K. "Profile: Ashley Bryan." *Language Arts*
    61 (March 1984): 305–311.

    A description of Bryan in his role as storyteller to an
    audience, notes on his life, and Bryan's own description
    of how he works to gather his words and to produce his
    images. Some discussion of individual books.
    Bibliography, b & w photos and illustration.

775. Sylvestrova, Marta. "Kveta Pacovska—A Magician of
    Modern Art." *Bookbird* 30, no. 3 (September 1992): 6–8.

    Describes the background of the Hans Christian
    Andersen Award winner during the Communist regime,
    the variety of her artwork, and her techniques for
    illustrating both books and picture books. Photo and b &
    w illustration.

776. Tafuri, Nancy. "The Artist at Work: Books for the Very
    Young." *Horn Book* 65, no. 6 (November–December
    1989): 732–735.

After a brief summary of her early life and training, Tafuri describes her start as an illustrator. She details the work of creating a book from start to finish. B & w illustration.

777. Tatham, David. "Winslow Homer: The Years as Illustrator." *Humanities* (March–April 1992): 22–25.

A brief account of Homer's career as an illustrator for the flourishing weekly magazines of the 1850s and 1860s, based on Tatham's book cited as item 777 above.

778. ———. *Winslow Homer and the Illustrated Book.* Syracuse: Syracuse University Press, 1992. 348pp.

In addition to discussion of all aspects of Homer's illustrations for magazines and books, Tatham specifically details the juveniles he did from 1857 to 1859 on pp. 34–59. In "The Illustrator's Eye," pp. 129–133, he talks more about his "picture-making." Some other aspects of his life are covered, but mainly book illustration is the concern here. Considerable attention is given to esthetic content and technical qualities, to the processes by which his drawings were translated into printed images. Many b & w illustrations. Plates on pp. 136–286.

779. Taylor, Ina. *The Art of Kate Greenaway: A Nostalgic Portrait of Childhood.* Gretna, La.: Pelican, 1991. 128pp.

Covers the artist's early life, time in art school, her breakthrough to become "the height of fashion," her relationship with John Ruskin, and her paintings and illustrations. A final chapter describes the "collectible" Greenaway. Carefully reproduced artwork on coated stock dominates the pages. A few b & w photos.

780. Taylor, Judy. *Beatrix Potter: Artist, Storyteller and Countrywoman.* New York: Warne/Viking Penguin, 1986. 224pp.

A very complete study of her life with details of her works. Little analysis of the pictures, however. Many b & w illustrations and photographs, twenty-eight color plates of her work.

781. ———, et al. *Beatrix Potter 1866–1943: The Artist and Her World.* London: Warne/Penguin, 1987. 223pp.

This companion to the Pierpont Morgan Library exhibition "Beatrix Potter: Artist and Storyteller," profusely illustrated with photographs and with reproductions of Potter's work in b & w and color, covers many aspects of her life and work. Joyce Irene Whalley's "The Young Artist and Early Influences," pp. 35–48, specifically treats her artistic development. Whalley and Anne Stevenson Hobbs's "Fantasy, Rhymes, Fairy Tales and Fables," pp. 49–70, includes comments on the illustrations as well as the stories in those Potter volumes. Judy Taylor does the same for "The Tale of Peter Rabbit," pp. 95–106, and Anne Stevenson Hobbs and Whalley join her for the analysis of "The Little Books" pp. 107–168.

782. ———, comp. *"So I shall tell you a story . . ." Encounters with Beatrix Potter.* London: Frederick Warne, 1993. 224pp.

Many writers discuss the importance of their encounters with Potter's work or with Potter herself, with little or no comment on her illustrations. Included are:

Maurice Sendak's "The Aliveness of Peter Rabbit," pp. 92–96, a paper delivered in 1965, defends Peter's story as full of life, blending fact and fantasy. He also comments on the quality of the illustrations.

Anne Stevenson Hobbs's "Beatrix Potter's Other Art," pp. 135–143, analyzes all of Potter's art, discussing the varying subjects, techniques, and historic development.

Rosemary Wells's "Sitting in Her Chair," pp. 144–150, reflects on Potter's influence from her childhood, and on the revelation of seeing Potter's original artwork. Wells analyzes Potter's work, the way she did it, and the conditions under which it was done.

Nicholas Garland's "Controlled Wool-Gathering: The Political Cartoonist and Beatrix Potter," pp. 151–159, points out the tempting parodies of Potter's work that are grist for the cartoonist's mill, and pictures of "good-natured Mockery."

783. ———. *That Naughty Rabbit: Beatrix Potter and Peter Rabbit*. New York: Warne, 1987. 96pp.

A sympathetic and complete story of the genesis and evolution of *Peter Rabbit* from an illustrated letter to foreign translations and a myriad of bits of merchandise (dolls, games, plates, napkins, etc.). Artistic and commercial details make this a particularly insightful analysis of the broader contemporary field of picture book publishing.

784. Tobias, Richard C. *The Art of James Thurber*. Athens: Ohio University Press, 1969. 196pp.

A serious study of the life and work of Thurber comments only on the words of his picture books. See "drawings" in the index for some notes on his pictorial art.

785. Tomes, Margot. "Why I Became a Children's Book Illustrator." *Horn Book* 65, no. 1 (January–February 1989): 36–38.

Tomes describes her childhood and seeks factors that contributed to her becoming an illustrator: She feels that her sense of isolation and the company of talented artists were strong reasons. Two small b & w illustrations.

786. *Tomi Ungerer: Storyteller.* 16mm color film. Video-cassette. Weston. Conn.: Weston Woods, no date. 21 min.

    The artist talks about his life and work and why he does controversial books. Scenes from the animated versions of his work are included.

787. "Top Dog." *People* 36, no. 11 (September 23, 1991): 83–84.

    Describes how Alexandra Day got the idea for the character that became the hero of her books about Carl the Rottweiler. Briefly covers Day's life and the dogs and people she uses for models. B & w photos.

788. Tudor, Tasha, and Richard Brown. *The Private World of Tasha Tudor.* Boston: Little, Brown, 1992. 134pp.

    Many full-page color photographs and color and b & w illustrations, but only a few from Tudor's picture books. The photos show Tudor's life through a year on the Vermont farm where she has "recreated an early Victorian world." Brief summary of her life with some insight into the person.

789. Turner, Robyn Montana. *Faith Ringgold.* Portraits of Women Artists for Children, series. Boston: Little, Brown, 1993. 32pp.

    This biography includes detailed notes on the artist's work, with brief mention of her picture books. In particular, the development of her painted quilts shows the source of her illustrations for *Tar Beach.* Many b & w photos and color illustrations of her art.

790. Van Allsburg, Chris. "David Macaulay: The Early Years." *Horn Book* 67, no. 4 (July–August 1991): 422–425.

    A tongue-in-cheek summary of Macaulay's childhood years, education, and start in picture books.

791. Van Stockum, Hilda. "Caldecott's Pictures in Motion." *Horn Book* 22 (March–April 1946): 119–125.

An artist's appreciative analysis of how Caldecott achieves a sense of motion in his illustrations, with b & w examples.

792. *A Visit with Bernard Waber.* Videocassette. Boston: Houghton Mifflin, 1993. 10 min.

Waber fills in the New York background of his stories about Lyle, shows his notebook where he keeps ideas he can use later, draws and paints, and finally reads about Ira, whose neighborhood is like the one in Philadelphia where Waber grew up.

793. Waugh, Dorothy. "Adrienne Adams, Illustrator of Children's Books." *American Artist* 29 (November 1965): 54–59, 74–75.

A very detailed analysis of her technique for both b & w and color illustrations, including the color separation process. Some notes on her life, her working method from receipt of manuscript through printing, and quotes from the artist. Many b & w illustrations.

794. ———. "Nonny Hogrogian, Decorator of Books for Children." *American Artist* 30 (October 1966): 52–57.

Many examples of Hogrogian's woodcut illustrations. Detailed descriptions of her technique of making the woodblocks. Notes on her life and some of her books.

795. Weber, Nicholas Fox. *The Art of Babar: The Work of Jean and Laurent de Brunhoff.* New York: Harry N. Abrams, 1989. 191pp.

Describes the life of the Brunhoffs at the time of Babar's creation, and how Laurent came to take him on after the death of his father Jean. The art of both is analyzed. Of particular importance are the many watercolor studies and black ink line drawings which demonstrate a combination of vital spontaneity with a sure sense of composition. Sumptuously illustrated with large and small, color reproductions of the original artwork and b & w drawings; also photos of the family.

* Weinstein, Frederic D. *Walter Crane and the American Book Arts, 1880–1915.* Cited above as item 77.

796. Wells, Rosemary. "The Artist at Work: The Writer at Work." *Horn Book* 63, no. 2 (March–April 1987): 163–170.

Wells tells how and where she works, how she began illustrating, where some ideas have come from, why she uses animal characters, and the relationship of story and illustration.

797. Weston, Annette H. "Robert Lawson: Author and Illustrator." *Elementary English* 47, no. 1 (January 1970): 74–84.

How he came to do some of his books, with quotations from the artist. Evaluation, pp. 82–83, includes discussion of his art. B & w portrait photograph, biographical sketch.

798. White, Colin. *Edmund Dulac.* New York: Scribner, 1976. 205pp.

One hundred eighty-one illustrations, thirty-two in color. Summary of his life and work. Illustrations for children not specified or analyzed separately.

799. White, David E. "A Conversation with Maurice Sendak." *Horn Book* 56 (April 1980): 145–155.

Discusses *Outside Over There*, the role of picture books for children and adults, Sendak's opinion of other picture books, and his future plans.

800. ———. "Profile: Trina Schart Hyman." *Language Arts* 60 (September 1983): 782–792.

Mainly Hyman's own words on her life and the reasoning behind some of her illustrations, including the controversial. Very illuminating and informative. Partial bibliography of her works year by year. B & w photo portrait and illustrations.

801. White, Gabriel. *Edward Ardizzone: Artist and Illustrator.* New York: Schocken, 1979. 191pp.

After a brief summary of Ardizzone's childhood, early life in London and start as an illustrator, White concentrates his comments on the work and a critical appraisal of style. Profusely illustrated on every page with b & w and six color, full-page illustrations.

802. *Who's Dr. Seuss? Meet Ted Geisel.* Sound Filmstrip. Videocassette. American School Publishers/SRA, 1980. 14 min.

Geisel talks about his life and work.

803. *Why Do You Write for Children? Children, Why Do You Read?* Proceedings of the 20th IBBY Congress, Tokyo. 1986. In English and Japanese. Tokyo: Japanese Board on Books for Young People, 1987. 542pp.

Picture books are not discussed except in Mitsumasa Anno's "Why I Write and Paint," pp. 81–87, in which he uses metaphors and references to other writers as well as personal anecdotes to explain the spiritual values that shape his creativity. No technical descriptions or discussions of his specific books, but he provides unique insights to help us better understand why he writes "for children who are the future." B & w photos.

804. Wildsmith, Brian. "Antic Disposition: A Young Illustrator Interviews Himself." *Library Journal* 90 (November 1965): 5035–5038; and *School Library Journal* 12 (November 1965): 21–24.

In a question-and-answer format the illustrator sums up his life, how he came to illustration, especially for children, and a bit about his aims as illustrator. B & w photo portrait and illustrations.

805. Wilkens, Lea-Ruth C. *Walter Crane and the Reform of the German Picture Book, 1865–1914.* Pittsburgh: University of Pittsburgh, 1973. University Microfilm No. 74–1452. 138pp.

Discusses how Crane's work was a catalyst in Germany. Two major exhibitions have been organized by German teachers' organizations to show this.

806. Wilms, Denise. "The Booklist Interview: Helen Oxenbury." *Booklist* (March 15, 1990): 1454–1455.

In answer to questions, Oxenbury summarizes her background and influences, her feelings about books for the very young, her method of work, and her ideas about picture books in general. B & w photo and illustrations.

807. Wood, Don, and Audrey Wood. "The Artist at Work: Where Ideas Come From." *Horn Book* 62, no. 5 (September–October 1986): 556–565.

The Woods describe the origins of several of their books and how the art and text work together toward the final product. B & w examples.

808. Yolen, Jane. "In the Artist's Studio: Dennis Nolan." *The New Advocate* 2, no. 1 (Winter 1989): 15–19.

After describing his studio, Yolen details Nolan's background and working method, with quotes about his work. B & w photo and illustrations.

809. Yorinks, Arthur. "Richard Egielski." *Horn Book* 63, no. 4 (July–August 1987): 436–438.

His collaborator's brief view and appreciation of Egielski's life and work.

810. Zemach, Margot. *Self-Portrait: Margot Zemach*. Reading, Mass.: Addison-Wesley, 1978. 31pp.

Zemach tells the story of her life very simply, from childhood on. She does not discuss her art, but it covers the pages. Profusely illustrated by the author.

811. ———, and Harve Zemach. "Profile of an Author and an Illustrator." *Top of the News* 27 (April 1971): 248–255.

In answering questions, Margot Zemach briefly fills in her background, and on pp. 251–252, she talks about how she came to, and feels about illustration. Their collaboration is also covered.

812. Zigany, Edit. "The Illustrator Eva Gaal." *Bookbird* 29, no. 4 (December 1991): 16, 21.

Describes the artist's life, her work in film animation, her development as an illustrator, and prizes won. Bibliography of books she has illustrated in the last ten years. B & w photo and two illustrations.

813. Zuckerman, Linda. "Don Freeman: An Editor's View." *Horn Book* 54 (June 1979): 273–281.

The editor's view of her relationship with Freeman and how they worked together. Includes his account of how he "found" the stories for the Corduroy books, and notes on his artwork for picture books and galleries.

814. Zvirin, Stephanie. "The Booklist Interview: David Macaulay." *Booklist* (July 1989): 1892–1893.

In answer to questions, Macaulay talks about how he came to children's books, the role of humor in his work, his feelings about nonfiction and the Caldecott, and his future plans. Photo and illustration.

815. ———. "The Booklist Interview: Jon Scieszka and Lane Smith." *Booklist* (September 1, 1992): 57.

After summarizing how they began to do children's books, the team details their work together on *The Stinky Cheese Man* and what may lie ahead. B & w photo.

PART VI

Guides and Aids to Further Research

816. *AB Bookman's Weekly.* Special Children's Book Issue, published yearly, usually in November to coincide with Children's Book Week.

    Includes articles about current publication and information about the market in general, including antiquarian and manuscript sales, and on collecting original art.

* Baer, Beverly, ed. *Children's Book Review Index.* See item 819 cited below.

* Beach, Barbara, ed. *Children's Book Review Index.* See item 819 cited below.

817. Best, James J. *American Popular Illustration: A Reference Guide.* Westport, Conn.: Greenwood, 1984. 171pp.

    Covers historic background, major illustrated works and their illustrators, the social and artistic content, the techniques, and introductory notes to each section. Works on children's picture books are included but must be sought out. Appendix 3, pp. 157–162, is a bibliography of illustrated books by author.

* Brenni, Vito J., comp. *Book Illustration and Decoration: A Guide to Research.* Cited above as item 12.

* Brown, Muriel W., and Rita Schuch Foudray. *Newbery and Caldecott Medalists and Honor Book Winners:*

Bibliographies and Resource Material through 1991. 2d ed. Cited above as item 424.

* Callaghan, Linda Ward. "Caldecott Citations: A Selective Bibliography." Cited above as item 176.

818. Entry deleted.

819. *Children's Book Review Index.* Detroit, Mich.: Gale, annual since 1975. Vol. 18, 1992, is edited by Neil E. Walker and Beverly Baer.

Cites all reviews of children's books (grades K–5) appearing in this publisher's *Book Review Index.* Of the periodicals currently indexed, about 150 review children's books. The arrangement is alphabetical by author. In earlier volumes, the illustrator's name is listed with the title. Beginning with the 1986 annual, there is also an index of illustrators.

820. *Children's Books: Awards and Prizes.* New York: Children's Book Council, revised biennially. 1992 ed. 404pp.

A listing of the prizes and their winners in the U.S. and the British Commonwealth with some international awards included. Illustrators are named only when the awards are specifically for illustration or design. In Appendix A, "Awards Classified," is a list of awards for illustration or design. Illustrators can be found in the index of persons.

821. Davis, Dorothy R., ed. *The Carolyn Sherwin Bailey Historical Collection of Children's Books: A Catalog.* New Haven: South Connecticut State College, 1966. 232pp.

From the 3,000 books, games and items in this collection, 1,880 are listed. The books were published in Great Britain and the United States from 1657. Some b & w illustrations.

822. Ellis, Alec. *How to Find Out About Children's Literature.* New York: Pergamon, 2d ed., 1968. 3d ed., 1973. 252pp.

     Includes chapters on the growing importance of children's literature; purpose in children's reading; and reading and child development. Details search strategies. Bibliographies must be searched by name of individual illustrator. Pp. 104–105 list British and international periodicals that include articles on illustrators. Includes list of Kate Greenaway winners, 1955–1971.

  * Estes, Glenn, ed. *American Writers for Children Since 1960: Poets, Illustrators, and Nonfiction Authors.* Cited above as item 221.

823. Ettlinger, John R.T., and Diana Spirt. *Choosing Books for Young People: A Guide to Criticism and Bibliography, 1945–1975.* Chicago, Ill.: American Library Association, 1982. 219pp. Vol. 2, *1976–1984.* Phoenix, Ariz.: Oryx Press, 1987. 152pp.

     An alphabetical annotated listing. Relevant sources must be found under "Illustration" and "Illustrators," or "Picture Books."

824. Field, Carolyn W., ed. *Special Collections in Children's Literature.* Chicago: American Library Association, 1982. 258pp.

     Lists special collections by subject. A directory lists them by state. References to collections are given. "Illustrations of Children's Books," pp. 97–100 gives names of individual artists, e.g., Potter, Petersham. Authors and illustrators not listed in the body of the work appear in an appendix.

825. Gottlieb, Robin. *Publishing Children's Books in America, 1919–1976: An Annotated Bibliography.* New York: Children's Book Council, 1978. 195pp.

One chapter, "Illustration, Design and Production," pp. 59–83, includes books and articles relevant to picture books and their history. Some on designers are listed under "Portraits of Designers and Production People," pp. 84–86.

826. Hannabuss, Stuart. "Sources of Information for Children's Book Illustration." *Journal of Librarianship* 13, no. 3 (July 1981): 154–171.

Many sources including British are listed, unfortunately in paragraph form, making retrieval very difficult. Appreciative comments for the researcher.

827. Haviland, Virginia, and Margaret N. Coughlan, comps. *Children's Literature: A Guide to Reference Sources.* Washington, D.C.: Library of Congress, 1966. 1st supp., 1972. 2d supp., 1977. Pages vary.

Some b & w illustrations included. These comprehensive annotated bibliographies cover all areas of children's literature. Of particular relevance to picture books are "Illustrating for Children," pp. 77–83, in the first supplement and pp. 109–117, in the second supplement; and "Critical Appraisals of Individual Illustrators," pp. 83–87, in the first supplement and pp. 117–125, in the second supplement. Sources on history and collections are also included.

828. Hendrickson, Linnea. *Children's Literature: A Guide to the Criticism.* Boston: G.K. Hall, 1987. 664pp.

Includes articles, books and dissertations from a wide range of sources, emphasizing the twentieth century. Part A, "Authors and Their Works," pp. 1–298, includes many illustrators in the alphabetical listing of subjects. Part B, "Subjects, Themes, and Genres," includes lists of sources under relevant subjects such as "Alphabet Books," pp. 306–307; "Art," p. 311; "Picture Books," pp. 477–495; "Toy Books," p. 553; "Wordless Picture Books," pp. 507–571.

There is an index of critics as well as of authors, titles, and subjects. Other subjects with references in the index include: children's preferences in picture books, fairy and folktale illustration, abstract illustrations, continuity in illustrations, endpaper illustration, photographic illustration, scratchboard illustration, woodcut illustration, picture book evaluation and reader response, and names of individual illustrators. This incredibly comprehensive work also covers British periodicals unavailable to the compilers of this bibliography.

829. Hoyle, Karen Nelson. "Special Collections and Archives: Scholarly Resources for Caldecott Award Research." *Journal of Youth Services in Libraries* 1, no. 2 (Winter 1988): 168–172.

Notes many places here and abroad that hold materials of all sorts relevant to the Caldecott winners and their work.

830. ———. "Treasure Houses to Share: Children's Literature Special Collections." *Journal of Youth Services in Libraries* 6, no. 4 (Summer 1993): 400–408.

Summarizes special collections of children's literature with notes on scope, history, physical plant, staffing and limitations, users, and funding of some of the best known. Some information specifically on picture books in these collections.

* Jones, Dolores Blythe, ed. *Children's Literature Awards and Winners: A Directory of Prizes, Authors, and Illustrators.* Cited above as item 457.

831. *The Kerlan Collection: Manuscripts and Illustrations for Children's Books.* Minneapolis: University of Minnesota, 1984. 432pp.

A checklist of the manuscripts and/or illustrations for over 4,950 books that are in the collection from 640 authors and/or 584 illustrators and 31 translators. Indexed by author, title, translator, illustrator, editor, and subject.

832. Lief, Irving P. *Children's Literature: A Historical and Contemporary Bibliography.* Troy, N.Y.: Whitston, 1977. 338pp.

Has sections on trends in various countries, on identifying old editions, old school books, and on authors, with listings of unpublished theses and magazine articles as well as books. "Children's Book Illustration" section includes: "The Art of Illustrated Children's Books," pp. 249–256; "Picture Books," pp. 256–259; "Illustrators of Children's Books" and "General Biographies and Critiques," pp. 259–261. Individual illustrators, pp. 261–297. Many foreign illustrators, also authors and references in non-English languages.

* Lima, Carolyn W., and John A. Lima. *A to Zoo: Subject Access to Children's Picture Books.* Cited above as item 43.

833. Meacham, Mary. *Information Sources in Children's Literature: A Practical Reference Guide for Children's Librarians, Elementary School Teachers, and Students of Children's Literature.* Westport, Conn.: Greenwood, 1978. 256pp.

The chapter "Illustrators, Authors and Awards," pp. 198–201, covers illustrators.

834. Monson, Diane, and Bette J. Peltola, comps. *Research in Children's Literature: An Annotated Bibliography.* Newark, Del.: International Reading Association, 1976. 96pp.

Index enables one to find articles on "Caldecott," "Illustrators," and "Picture Storybook." Many entries on using these books for reading purposes. Dissertations, journal articles, related studies and ERIC documents are included.

835. Nakamura, Joyce, ed. *Children's Authors and Illustrators: An Index to Biographical Dictionaries.* 4th ed. Detroit, Mich.: Gale, 1987. 799pp.

   More than 450 reference sources are indexed in this update of the series formerly edited by Sarkissian. Entries from previous editions have been updated, and pseudonyms and other name variants are included.

836. *The Newbery and Caldecott Awards: A Guide to the Medal and Honor Books.* Chicago: American Library Association, 1993. 137pp.

   Published yearly. Annotates all winning books. Brief notes on the illustrators. The 1992 edition included "Choosing the Newbery and Caldecott Medal Winners" by Bette Pelltola; the 1993 edition has Christine Behrmann's article on the media used in Caldecott winners cited above.

 * Pellowski, Anne. *The World of Children's Literature.* Cited above as item 57.

 * Peterson, Linda Kauffman, and Marilyn Leathers Solt. *Newbery and Caldecott Medal and Honor Books: An Annotated Bibliography.* Cited above as item 59.

837. Entry deleted.

838. Provenzo, Eugene F., Jr. "A Note on the Darton Collection." *Teacher's College Record* 84 (Summer 1983): 929–934.

   Describes contents of the collection.

839. Quimby, Harriet B., with Margaret Mary Kimmel. *Building a Children's Literature Collection: A Suggested Basic Reference Collection for Academic Libraries and a Suggested Basic Collection of Children's Books.* 3d ed. Bibliographic Essay Series, No. 7. Middletown, Conn.: Choice, 1983. 48pp.

Lists general texts, histories, sources on authors, specific picture book sources pp. 3–4, critical works, awards and prizes, international sources, other areas of interest, including books on parenting and how to write for children and young people. Lists include books by area (picture books, pp. 21–23) and both author and title indexes.

840. Rahn, Suzanne. *Children's Literature: An Annotated Bibliography of the History and Criticism.* New York: Garland, 1981. 451pp.

Books about picture books and their creators can be found in the section "Studies of Genres" in "Books for Children Under Five," pp. 78–80, with references to specific people in the later section on individual authors.

  * Roginski, James W. *Newbery and Caldecott Medalists and Honor Book Winners: Bibliographies and Resource Materials Through 1977.* Cited above as item 485.

841. Sarkissian, Adele, ed. *Children's Authors and Illustrators: An Index to Biographical Dictionaries.* 3d ed. Detroit, Mich.: Gale, 1981. 2d ed. 1978, 667pp.

More than 250 reference sources for biographical information are indexed in alphabetical order by name of author or illustrator followed by birth and death date and code letters for the sources of information. Includes list of titles indexed with abbreviations. For 4th ed., 1987, see Nakamura, Joyce cited above as item 835.

842. Sharkey, Paulette Bochnig. *Newbery and Caldecott Medal and Honor Books in Other Media.* New York: Neal-Schuman, 1992. 142pp.

Includes not only media productions of books, but listing of media about illustrators, pp. 79–88.

843. St. John, Judith. *The Osborne Collection of Early Children's Books, 1566–1910: A Catalogue.* Toronto: Toronto Public Library, 1958. 561pp.

   Reprinted 1975. Illustrated with many b & w examples of title pages and book illustrations and twelve color plates. The catalogue lists the books by types including "Nursery Rhymes and Alphabets" and "Movable and Toy Books." There is a list of illustrators and engravers.

844. ———. *The Osborne Collection of Early Children's Books, 1476–1910: A Catalogue.* Vol. 2. Toronto: Toronto Public Library, 1975. Pp. 563–1138.

   Books are listed by types as in volume one, but there is no index of illustrators or engravers. Includes some small b & w illustrations.

*   Tarbert, Gary C., ed. *Children's Book Review Index.* See item 819 cited above.

*   Walker, Neil E., ed. *Children's Book Review Index.* See item 819 cited above.

*   Woolman, Bertha. *The Caldecott Award: The Winners and the Honor Books.* Cited above as item 494.

PART VII

Some Collections and/or Repositories of Materials on Picture Books and Their Creators

Alice M. Jordon Collection. Boston Public Library.

A children's literature research collection that includes, in addition to print materials, correspondences, memorabilia, taped interviews, videotapes, etc.

Babbidge Library, Special Collections Department. University of Connecticut, Storrs.

Includes a recently donated collection of over 5,000 illustrated books and original art work by Richard Scarry for twenty-seven of his books.

Beinecke Library. Yale University, New Haven, Conn.

Some illustrations along with many manuscripts, letters, etc., of authors and illustrators of children's books.

Carolyn Sherwin Bailey Historical Collection of Children's Books. Southern Conn. State College, New Haven.

About 3,000 books and some other items from the early seventeenth century onwards.

Children's Literature Historical Collection. The State University of New York at Albany.

A collection of "inexpensive children's books of a popular nature" from the past.

Darton Collection. Teachers College, Columbia University, New York City.

Collection includes 1,400 titles, some English children's books published before 1850, a 1763 Newbery publication, pedagogical and other board games, scrapbooks, original sketches and watercolors by Kate Greenaway and others.

De Grummond Collection. University of Southern Mississippi.

"Largest collection of original children's literature material in the U.S."

Donnell Branch, New York Public Library, New York City.

Early illustrated books and some original art for picture books.

Dr. Seuss Collection. University of California at San Diego.

Memorabilia of twenty years, including 4,000 manuscripts, drawings, and other work.

Elizabeth Nesbitt Room. School of Library and Information Services Library, University of Pittsburgh, Penn.

Two hundred seventy-four historically notable children's books, including the work of a number of fine illustrators.

The Five Owls Collection. Hamline University, St. Paul, Minn.

A noncirculating examination library consisting of thousands of review copies sent to *The Five Owls* beginning in 1986.

Gail E. Haley Collection of the Culture of Childhood. Appalachian State University, Boone, N.C.

Includes games, toys, books, dolls, puppets, and other artifacts from many countries and cultures. Includes some of the linocuts, woodblocks, sketches, and finished artwork for Gail Haley's books.

George Glotzbach Collection. New Ulm, Minn.

Materials by and about Wanda Gag.

Kerlan Collection. University of Minnesota, Minneapolis.

More than 5,000 books are represented by manuscripts and/or illustrations donated by over 700 authors and/or illustrators and thirty-one translators, all of which document the stages in the production of the books over six decades. Over 40,000 children's books are also in the collection. Offers for classroom use audiovisual kits, including slides and videos of original art, and information on how books come from ideas.

Library of Congress Special Collection, Washington, D.C.

Some rare children's books including some illustrated books.

Mary Faulk Markiewicz Collection of Early American Children's Books. University of Rochester, N.Y.

More than 1,000 volumes, mainly for older children, but includes some picture books and alphabet books.

May Massee Collection. Emporia State University, Kans.

Books that Massee brought to publication; includes manuscripts and original art, and sketches by Robert McCloskey.

Mazza Collection. The University of Findlay, Ohio. Currently in the Shafer Library; will move in 1994 to the Virginia B. Gardner Fine Arts Pavilion.

Over 400 original art works by children's books illustrators. "The only teaching gallery in the world specializing in such art." Collection includes the books with the featured illustrations.

Morgan Library. New York City.

Many children's books, including early illustrated books.

The Osborne Collection of Early Children's Books. Toronto Public Library, Canada.

Several thousand books plus games, periodicals, toy books, etc., from the last 400 years in England; donated by Edgar Osborne in 1949. The collection has since been augmented by purchases and donations.

The Renier Collection of Historic and Contemporary Children's Books. Bethnal Green Museum of Childhood, a branch of the Victoria and Albert Museum, London.

"The largest special collection of children's books in the United Kingdom." Originally donated by Anne and Fernand Renier, but added to since. Includes about 80,000 books, periodicals, toys, and games from the sixteenth century to the present. "Ephemera featuring characters or illustrators from children's books are also part of the collection."

Rosenbach Collection. Free Library of Philadelphia.

A collection of rare children's books, with some original work by Maurice Sendak.

U.C.L.A. Research Library. Los Angeles.

Some manuscripts and materials by Dr. Seuss and Holling C. Holling.

University of Oregon, Eugene.

Papers of Maude and Miska Petersham.

Galleries Carrying Original Art Work of Illustrators:

The Elizabeth Stone Gallery, Birmingham, Mich.
Every Picture Tells a Story, Hollywood, Calif.

Index of Artists

Adams, Adrienne, 283, 348, 433, 459, 741, 793
Agee, John, 116
Ahlberg, Janet, 321, 385, 470
Alexander, Martha, 483
Alexov, Alexander, 588
Allen, Pamela, 141
Allen, Thomas B., 436
Ambrus, Victor G., 321, 456
Anfousse, Ginette, 229
Angelo, Valenti, 423
Anglund, Joan Walsh, 490
Anno, Mitsumasa, 303, 436, 473, 508, 803
Ardizzone, Edward, 158, 182, 338, 439, 448, 451, 456, 493, 509, 555, 801
Arnosky, Jim, 436
Artzybasheff, Boris, 423, 515
Aruego, Jose, 465, 728
Atwell, Mabel L., 149

Bacelar, Manuela, 764
Baker, Jeannie, 223
Baker, Keith, 568
Bang, Molly, 290, 470
Base, Graeme, 436, 558
Bayley, Nicola, 436, 470
Bemelmans, Ludwig, 158, 428, 448, 490
Berenstain, Michael, 480

Berenstain, Stan and Jan, 465, 480, 688
Bilibin, Ivan Y., 243, 581
Billout, Guy, 447
Bishop, Gavin, 470
Blake, Quentin, 321, 436, 470, 517, 720
Blegvad, Erik, 433, 518, 519
Blythe, Gary, 481
Bodecker, N. M., 518
Booth, Graham, 213
Boutet de Monvel, Maurice, 596, 638
Bradley, Luther Daniels, 200
Brett, Jan, 436, 727
Brewster, Patience, 436
Briggs, Raymond, 238, 303, 321, 530, 733
Brighton, Catherine, 430
Brooke, Leslie, 338, 451
Brown, Marc, 521, 687
Brown, Marcia, 221, 246, 253, 433, 459, 460, 462, 490, 650
Brown, Margaret Wise, 428
Browne, Anthony, 116, 144, 206, 321, 470, 663
Brunhoff, Jean de, 34, 158, 303, 426, 691, 795
Brunhoff, Laurent de, 303, 426, 493, 640, 691, 795
Bryan, Ashley, 470, 471, 473, 685, 774

Burgess, Gelett, 423
Burkert, Nancy Ekholm, 471, 488, 522, 523, 524, 768
Burningham, John, 321, 470, 482, 571
Burton, Virginia Lee, 158, 291, 335, 338, 423, 448, 525, 629
Byard, Carole, 440, 470

Caldecott, Randolph, 2, 41, 51, 64, 303, 338, 439, 459, 528, 545, 556, 633, 791
Carle, Eric, 436, 565, 630
Catalanotto, Peter, 436
Charlot, Jean, 433
Charuschin, Nikita, 701
Chen, Tony, 433
Chess, Victoria, 435
Chwast, Seymour, 447
Cleaver, Elizabeth, 213, 303
Climo, Shirley, 533
Cole, Babette, 469, 470
Collington, Peter, 470
Conover, Chris, 436
Cooney, Barbara, 116, 306, 433, 436, 459, 460, 462, 589
Cousins, Lucy, 649
Crane, Walter, 27, 41, 51, 58, 64, 77, 338, 765, 805
Crews, Donald 436, 440, 473, 483, 767
Cummings, Patricia, 435, 436, 440, 473, 484

Daugherty, James, 158, 423, 433, 622
D'Aulaire, Ingri and Edgar Parin, 428, 531, 610
Day, Alexandra, 787
de Angeli, Marguerite, 428, 448, 480, 546
Degen, Bruce, 560
Delessert, Etienne, 547

de Mejo, Oscar, 341
Demi (Charlotte Dumaresq Hunt), 483, 548
Denslow, W.W., 51, 598
dePaola, Tomie, 153, 184, 221, 436, 442, 480, 497, 505, 549, 603, 706
Desimini, Lisa, 449
Devlin, Harry, 433
Dewey, Ariane, 465
Diamond, Donna, 442
Dillon, Leo and Diane, 291, 435, 453, 462, 465, 551, 719
Drescher, Henrik, 436, 570
Du Bois, William Pene. *See* Pene du Bois, William
Dulac, Edmund, 51, 58, 64, 798
Duvoisin, Roger, 212, 221, 291, 433, 439, 445, 448, 490, 587

Egielski, Richard, 430, 435, 436, 809
Ehlert, Lois, 435, 436, 557, 579
Ehrlich, Bettina, 459
Eichenberg, Fritz, 246, 433, 442, 459
Emberly, Ed, 291, 294, 448, 459, 461
Ernst, Lisa Campbell, 435
Ets, Marie, 428, 448, 460, 490, 619
Eveno, Mach, 550

Feelings, Tom, 246, 435, 480, 569
Fisher, Leonard Everett, 221, 347, 436, 442, 572
Florian, Douglas, 725
Foreman, Michael, 321, 467
Frasconi, Antonio, 433, 573
Fraser, Lovat, 48
Frasier, Debra, 287
Freeman, Don, 433, 813

Gaal, Eva, 812

Gag, Wanda, 4, 158, 338, 423, 428, 459, 490, 577, 613
Galdone, Paul, 436
Gammell, Steven, 444
Gay, Marie-Louise, 229
Geisel, Theodor see Seuss, Dr.
Geisert, Arthur, 436
Gerrard, Roy, 436, 470
Gibbons, Gail, 442, 541
Gibbs, May, 584
Glaser, Milton, 447
Goble, Paul, 462, 473, 770
Goffstein, M.B., 221, 470, 665, 718, 751
Goode, Diane, 436, 470
Gorey, Edward, 162, 221, 433, 445, 744
Gramatky, Hardie, 428, 448, 710, 761
Greenaway, Kate, 41, 51, 64, 338, 426, 427, 432, 451, 490, 504, 564, 586, 607, 653, 766, 779
Grifalconi, Ann, 436, 488

Haas, Irene, 347
Hader, Elmer, 291, 448
Haley, Gail E., 89, 94, 461
Hardiyono, 425
Hawkes, Kevin, 481
Hedderwick, Mairi, 599
Heine, Helme, 436
Henkes, Kevin, 436, 561, 602
Hill, Eric, 575, 736
Hillenbrand, Will, 481, 667
Himler, Ronald, 436
Hoban, Tana, 480
Hofsinde, Robert, 610
Hogrogian, Nonny, 461, 487, 554, 794
Holesovsky, Frantisek, 227
Holling, Holling C., 133, 448
Homar, Lorenzo, 433
Homer, Winslow, 777, 778

Honey, Elizabeth, 141
Hughes, Shirley, 321, 469, 470
Hunt, Jonathan, 449
Hurlimann, Bettina, 722
Hutchins, Pat, 436, 469, 470
Hutton, Warwick, 436, 615
Hyman, Trina Schart, 184, 221, 436, 442, 462, 597, 616, 617, 677, 678, 742, 800

Ingraham, Erick, 436
Ipcar, Dahlov, 459, 734
Isadora, Rachel, 648

Jacques, Faith, 321
Jannemin, Bernard, 550
Jeffers, Susan, 436
Jonas, Ann, 436, 470, 484, 662
Joyce, William, 436

Kalman, Maira, 341, 535
Karrebaek, Dorte, 698
Keats, Ezra Jack, 221, 291, 306, 338, 433, 436, 448, 459, 460, 480, 566, 637, 703, 714
Keeping, Charles, 321, 456, 493, 627
Kellogg, Steven, 105, 221, 435, 467, 484, 559, 628
Kemble, Edward Windsor, 150
Kepes, Juliet, 459
Kipling, Rudyard, 58
Kitchen, Bert, 436
Koivu, Rudolf, 762
Kroll, Steven, 442
Krush, Joe and Beth, 480
Kuskin, Karla, 184
Kyte, Dennis, 729

Lawrence, John, 321, 488
Lawson, Robert, 158, 338, 423, 428, 432, 448, 490, 527, 538, 626, 797

Lear, Edward, 23, 51, 58, 64, 158,
    490
LeCain, Errol, 238
Lenski, Lois, 428, 448, 490, 591
Lent, Blair, 291, 433, 459, 461, 488,
    641
Le Tord, Bijou, 155
Lionni, Leo, 221, 304, 338, 433,
    436, 448, 488, 490, 499, 537,
    582, 645, 686
LLoyd, Errol, 470
Lobel, Anita, 436, 465, 723
Lobel, Arnold, 184, 221, 248, 433,
    436, 462, 465, 467, 480, 510,
    594, 605, 646, 647, 672, 735,
    739, 750
Locker, Thomas, 430
Low, Joseph, 433, 459
Lubin, Leonard, 484

Macaulay, David, 153, 221, 248,
    297, 341, 347, 471, 488, 503,
    534, 544, 606, 608, 790, 814
MacDonald, Suse, 436
Marshall, James, 153, 221, 436,
    623, 652, 670, 754
Mathers, Petra, 436, 673
Mavor, Salley, 287
Maxey, Dale, 445
Mayer, Mercer, 146, 221
McCloskey, Robert, 246, 291, 306,
    338, 428, 433, 448, 460, 480,
    490, 600, 737, 740, 745
McCully, Emily Arnold, 642
McDermott, Gerald, 91, 436, 459,
    461, 488, 679
McMillan, Bruce, 323
Mikolaycak, Charles, 246, 436,
    442, 444, 483, 695
Milhous, Katherine, 448
Minor, Wendell, 436
Mizumura, Kazue, 185
Monin, Yevgeny, 696

Montresor, Beni, 436, 460, 724
Moon, Sarah, 231
Morimoto, Junko, 759
Moser, Barry, 116, 150, 436, 471,
    699
Munro, Roxie, 436
Murawski, Marian, 507
Myller, Rolf, 483

Narahashi, Keiko, 436
Ness, Evaline, 221, 433, 459, 461,
    702
Nielsen, Kay, 51, 64
Niland, Deborah, 470
Nolan, Dennis, 808

Oakes, Bill, 436
Oakley, Graham, 470
Olsen, Ib Spang, 578
Ormerod, Jan, 436, 470
Otto S., Svend. *See* Svend Otto S.
Oxenbury, Helen, 321, 445, 470,
    482, 571, 708, 806

Pacovska, Kveta, 775
Parker, Nancy Winslow, 436, 730
Parker, Robert Andrew, 436, 447
Parnall, Peter, 433
Peet, Bill, 516, 713
Pene du Bois, William, 221, 433,
    523
Petersham, Maude and Mishka,
    291, 423, 428
Pienkowski, Jan, 321
Pierce, Leona, 433
Pinkney, Brian, 436, 440, 449, 473
Pinkney, Jerry, 435, 436, 601, 690,
    716, 717
Polacco, Patricia, 436, 666
Politi, Leo, 448
Potter, Beatrix, 23, 24, 51, 64, 158,
    283, 338, 426, 427, 451, 455,
    490, 513, 514, 635, 643, 658,

712, 748, 752, 780, 781, 782,
    783
Poulin, Stephane, 229, 562
Priceman, Marjorie, 449
Primavera, Elise, 483
Provensen, Alice, 303, 436, 462,
    465, 471
Provensen, Martin, 303, 436, 462,
    465
Pyle, Howard, 47, 48, 51, 158, 423,
    452, 474, 479, 498, 563, 585,
    676

Rackham, Arthur, 27, 51, 58, 64,
    338, 451, 590, 611, 683
Radunsky, Vladimir, 449
Rand, Ted, 436
Raskin, Ellen, 246, 433, 483, 707
Rayevsky, Robert, 436
Reid, Barbara, 436, 689
Rey, H.A., 254, 428, 448, 490
Ringgold, Faith, 287, 567, 789
Robbins, Ken, 470
Robinson, Charles and William
    Heath, 639
Rojankovsky, Feodor, 451, 460
Rose, Gerald, 445
Ross, Tony, 470
Roughsey, Dick, 758
Rounds, Glen, 436, 442
Russo, Marisabina, 436, 543

Say, Allen, 436, 671, 743
Scarry, Richard, 221, 490, 493
Schoenherr, John, 433, 436
Schulz, Charles, 661
Schwartz, Amy, 435, 436, 470, 669
Sendak, Maurice, 4, 65, 146, 147,
    153, 194, 221, 235, 246, 291,
    303, 306, 338, 364, 383, 426,
    433, 439, 446, 447, 448, 455,
    460, 480, 488, 490, 493, 495,
    501, 511, 529, 532, 539, 580,

593, 634, 636, 651, 654, 674,
    675, 681, 684, 692, 738, 747,
    749, 763, 799
Seuss, Dr., 4, 162, 194, 338, 357,
    448, 490, 493, 526, 540, 553,
    659, 771, 802
Sewell, Helen, 423
Sewell, Marcia, 436
Shepard, Ernest H., 51, 149, 459,
    631, 700
Shulevitz, Uri, 130, 221, 246, 291,
    436, 459, 461, 731
Sidjakov, Nicolas, 460
Simmonds, Posy, 470
Simont, Marc, 433, 460
Siow, John, 119
Sis, Peter, 436, 470, 755
Smith, Jessie Willcox, 65, 200, 479,
    704, 705
Smith, Lane, 223, 435, 436, 757,
    760, 815
Sorel, Edward, 447
Spier, Peter, 221, 462
Stanley, Diane, 436
Steadman, Ralph, 470, 721
Steig, William, 194, 221, 295, 461,
    488, 595, 604, 632, 726, 769
Steptoe, John, 436, 480, 625
Stevens, Janet, 442
Stevenson, James, 656
Svend Otto S., 578, 583, 621, 772
Sylvestre, Daniel, 229

Tafuri, Nancy, 436, 776
Tamsaar, Jaan, 620
Tarrant, Margaret, 149
Teague, Mark, 449
Tenggren, Gustaf, 609, 610, 773
Tenniel, John, 51, 58, 64, 477, 512,
    592
Thurber, James, 428, 697, 784
Tibo, Gilles, 229
Tomes, Margot, 484, 576, 785

Treloar, Bruce, 141
Tryon, Leslie, 481
Tudor, Tasha, 788
Tunis, Edwin, 459
Turkel, Brinton, 490

Ungerer, Tomi, 471, 490, 694, 786
Unzer-Fischer, Christa, 660

Van Allsburg, Chris, 153, 221,
    226, 291, 334, 430, 435, 444,
    462, 484, 614, 680
Vivas, Julie, 436

Waber, Bernard, 715, 792
Walsh, Ellen Stoll, 436
Ward, Lynd, 423, 428, 433, 448,
    459, 480, 488, 711
Warhola, James, 624
Watson, Richard Jesse, 436
Watson, Wendy, 682
Weisgard, Leonard, 459, 709

Wells, Rosemary, 495, 657, 796
Wick, Walter, 126
Wiese, Kurt, 423
Wiesner, David, 435, 436, 496,
    618, 655
Wildsmith, Brian, 321, 448, 456,
    488
Williams, Garth, 428, 433, 506, 668
Williams, Vera B., 347, 732
Wolff, Ashley, 436
Wood, Audrey, 746, 807
Wood, Don, 436, 746, 807
Wyeth, N.C., 48, 51, 65, 423, 452,
    459, 474, 479, 693

Yashima, Taro, 433
Young, Ed, 436, 470, 471, 520

Zelinsky, Paul O., 436, 470, 664
Zemach, Margot, 433, 436, 461,
    500, 810, 811
Zwerger, Lisbeth, 574, 753

Index of Authors, Editors, and Compilers

Abdullah, Cheryl, 420, 496
Abegg, Walter, 242
Abrahamson, Richard F., 140, 497
Adams, Adrienne, 283, 459
Adams, Bess Porter, 1
Adams, Gillian, 338
Agosta, Lucien L., 498
Agree, Rose, 499
Alberghene, Janice, 221
Alderman, Belle, 141
Alderson, Brian, 2, 238, 243, 284, 500, 501
Aliki, 82
Allen, Pamela, 141
Allender, David, 502
Althea (Althea Braithwaite), 83
American Institute of Graphic Arts, 142
Ammon, Richard, 503
Amor, Stuart, 227
Andersen, Anne, 143
Andersen, Hans Christian, 504
Anderson, Dennis, 505
Anderson, Joy, 221
Anderson, William, 506
Andreae, Christopher, 144
Andryszczak, Maria Ewa, 507
Anno, Mitsumasa, 803
Aoki, Hisako, 508
Apseloff, Marilyn, 145, 158, 338
Arakelian, Paul G., 146

Arbuthnot, May Hill, 401
Ardizzone, Edward, 182, 439, 448, 451, 509
Arnold, Arnold, 3, 461
Aubrey, Irene Elizabeth, 148
Austin, Susan R., 420
Averill, Esther, 451, 460
Avery, Gillian, 149
Avi, 158

Bader, Barbara, 4, 461, 462
Bailey, Diane, 511
Bang, Molly, 84
Barclay, Donald A., 150
Barr, John, 5
Barron, Pamela, 151
Barry, Florence, 6
Barto, Agnia, 227
Barton, Griselda, 684
Bassett, Lisa, 512
Bator, Robert, 7, 152
Bechtel, Louise Seaman, 445, 515
Behrmann, Christine, 85
Belden, Martha, 232
Benedict, Susan, 155
Beneduce, Ann, 100, 303
Benson, Ciaran, 156
Berridge, Celia, 157
Bertrand, Gerard, 210
Best, James J., 817
Bicknell, Treld Pelkey, 284

Bingham, Jane, 8, 158
Bird, Bettina, 63
Bishop, Rudine Sims, 155, 159
Bitzer, Lucy, 160
Blake, Quentin, 517
Bland, David, 9
Blegvad, Erik, 518, 519
Blumenthal, Eileen Polley, 161
Bodner, George R., 162
Bolton, Theodore, 423
Booth, Graham, 213
Borgens, Helen, 200
Bornens, Marie-Therese, 164
Bosma, Bette, 165, 166
Bostian, Frieda F., 167
Boston Museum of Fine Arts, 10
Brainard, Dulcy, 520
Braithwaite, Althea. See Althea
Bravo-Villasante, Carmen, 11, 227
Brenni, Vito J., 12
Briggs, Raymond, 238
Briley, Dorothy, 576
Brookfield, Karen, 86
Brown, Joseph Epes, 462
Brown, Marc, 521
Brown, Marcia, 168, 246, 253, 283,
    324, 459, 460, 462
Brown, Muriel W., 424
Brown, Richard, 788
Bryan, Ashley, 471
Bunanta, Murti, 425
Burkert, Nancy Ekholm, 471, 522,
    523, 524
Burley, Jennifer Q., 151
Burton, Virginia Lee, 525
Busbin, O. Mell, 169, 221
Butler, Francelia, 13, 170, 171, 172,
    173, 174, 175, 426, 526

Cain, Melissa, 192
Callaghan, Linda Ward, 176
Callahan, Joan F., 177
Canham, Stephen, 200

Caradec, Francois, 14
Carlisle, Lenore, 155
Carpenter, Humphrey, 427
Carroll, Joyce Armstrong, 178,
    179
Cart, Michael, 527
Carter, Juliet Mason, 332
Carus, Marianne, 528
Cascardi, Andrea E., 180
Casper, Franz, 241
Cass, Joan E., 181
Cech, John, 303, 428, 529
Chagnoux, Christine, 242, 243
Chambers, Aidan, 530
Chambers, Nancy, 182
Chapman, Diane L., 183
Chappell, Warren, 441, 451, 459
Chenery, Janet D., 462
Chester, Tessa Rose, 80
Chevalier, Tracy, 463
Cianciolo, Patricia, 187, 188, 189,
    190, 191, 227
Clarke, Grace Dalles, 87
Claverie, Jean, 36
Cleaver, Elizabeth, 213, 303
Clemons, Walter, 532
Clerc, Christiane, 36
Climo, Shirley, 533
Cobb, Nathan, 534
Cohen, Morton N., 303
Colby, Jean Poindexter, 88
Collier, Laurie, 468
Colvin, Marilyn, 497
Commire, Anne, 431, 432
Conant, Jennet, 535
Conrad, Barnaby, III, 536
Considine, David M., 193
Cooney, Barbara, 441, 459, 460,
    462
Cooper, Ilene, 537
Cornell, Robert W., 538
Cotham, John, 221
Cott, Jonathan, 15, 16, 194, 539

Coughlan, Margaret, 31, 827
Councell, Ruth Tietjen, 155
Cox, Alfred John, 17
Crago, Hugh, 195, 221
Crago, Maureen, 195
Crane, Walter, 18
Crichton, Jennifer, 540, 541
Cross, Jennifer Lynn, 196
Crouch, Marcus, 434
Cullinan, Bernice E., 197, 198, 199, 253
Cummings, Pat, 435, 542
Cummins, Julie, 436
Cutts, Alida von Krogh, 543

Dalby, Richard, 19
Dalgliesh, Alice, 451
Dalphin, Marcia, 324
Darling, Harold, 200
Darling, Richard L., 438
Darton, Frederick J. Harvey, 20, 201
Davis, Dorothy R., 821
Davis, Mary Gould, 545
De Angeli, Marguerite, 546
Debes, John L., 414
Delessert, Etienne, 36, 547
Demers, Patricia, 338
dePaola, Tomie, 202, 549
Despinette, Janine, 227, 550
Devereaux, Anne, 221
Devereaux, Elizabeth, 481
De Vries, Leonard, 21
Dillon, Diane, 462, 551
Dillon, Leon, 462, 551
Dirda, Michael, 203
Dobbs, Rose, 459
Dondis, Donis A., 204, 414
Dooley, Patricia, 205, 338, 676
Doonan, Jane, 206
Dorfman, Ariel, 207
Doyle, Brian, 22
Dressel, Janice Hartwick, 208

Driesson, Diane Z., 209
Durand, Marion, 210, 211
Durrell, Ann, 461, 554
Duvoisin, Roger, 212, 439, 445

Eastman, Jackie F., 338
Eckstein, Arthur, 132
Edwards, James P., 556
Edwards, Michelle, 90
Egoff, Sheila A., 213, 214, 439
Ehlert, Lois, 557
Ehrlich, Bettina, 441, 459
Eichenberg, Fritz, 246, 324, 459
Eisner, Elliot W., 215
Elleman, Barbara, 216, 217, 218, 558, 559
Elliot, Ian, 560, 561
Ellis, Alec, 822
Ellis, Sarah, 562
Elzea, Rowland, 563
Emberly, Barbara, 461
Emberly, Ed, 459, 461
Engen, Rodney, 564
England, Claire, 219
Estes, Glenn E., 321
Ets, Marie Hall, 460
Ettlinger, John R.T., 823
Eutsler, Nellvena Duncan, 221
Evans, Dilys, 222, 223, 224, 440, 471
Eyre, Frank, 225

Fakih, Kimberly Olson, 92, 568
Fasick, Adele M., 219
Feaver, William, 25
Feelings, Tom, 246, 569
Ferguson, Jesseca, 570
Field, Carolyn W., 824
Field, Elinor Whitney, 441, 475
Field, Louise Frances Story, 26
Field, Michele, 571
Field, Rachel, 47
Fisher, Crispin, 445

Fisher, Emma, 493
Fisher, Leonard Everett, 347, 572
Fogelman, Phyllis J., 462
Folmsbee, Beulah, 48
Ford, Elizabeth A., 226
Foreman, Michael, 467
Foster, Joanna, 283
Foudray, Rita Schuch, 424
Fox, Geoff, 227
Frank, Jerome P., 93
Fraser, James H., 27
Frederick, Heather, 574
Freedman, Russell, 442
Freeman, Graydon La Verne, 228
Freeman, Ruth Sunderlin, 228
Frith, Margaret, 575, 576
Fryett, Norma R., 459, 460

Gag, Wanda, 577
Gagnon, Andre, 229
Gainer, Ruth Strays, 230
Gankina, E., 443
Garland, Nicholas, 782
Garness, Susan, 221
Garrett, Caroline S., 95
Garrett, Jeffrey, 231
Gates, Frieda, 96
Gendrin, Catherine, 36
Georgiou, Constantine, 28
Gerber, Annyce, 235
Giff, Patricia Reilly, 232
Gill, Bob, 233
Glazer, Joan, 234
Glistrup, Eva, 578
Gmuca, Jacqueline, 221
Gobels, Hubert, 29
Goble, Paul, 462
Godden, Connie, 579
Godden, Rumer, 283
Godine, David, 347
Golden, Joanne M., 235
Goldenberg, Carol, 97
Goldsmith, Evelyn, 236, 237, 238

Goldstein, William, 580
Golynets, Sergei, 581
Gordon, Elizabeth, 462
Gordon, Lucy Latane, 582
Gordon, Stephan F., 98
Gormsen, J., 583
Gottlieb, Robin, 825
Gough, John, 584
Green, Roger Lancelyn, 585
Greenaway, Kate, 504, 586
Greene, Ellin, 264, 338, 587
Greenfeld, Howard, 99
Greenlaw, M. Jean, 244
Gregory, Richard, 238
Groff, P., 245
Gross, Gerald, 100
Grozdanov, Dimiter, 588

Haas, Irene, 347
Halbey, Hans A., 240
Hale, Robert D., 589
Haley, Gail E., 461
Hamilton, James, 590
Hamilton, Laurie, 591
Hammond, Graham, 227
Hancher, Michael, 592
Hands, Nancy S., 101
Hannabuss, Stuart, 826
Harman, Lauren, 141
Harms, Jeanne McLain, 102, 444
Harris, Muriel, 593
Harrison, Barbara, 246
Hart, Thomas L., 103
Harthan, John, 30
Hautzig, Esther, 460
Haviland, Virginia, 31, 242, 445,
    446, 827
Haywood, Carolyn, 200
Hearn, Michael Patrick, 243, 426,
    504, 594, 595, 596, 597, 598
Hearne, Betsy, 247, 248, 249, 250,
    348, 402
Hedderwick, Mairi, 599

Heffernan, Mary Ann, 221
Heins, Ethel, 158, 246, 251, 462, 600
Heller, Steven, 252, 447
Henderson, Darwin, 601
Hendrickson, Linnea, 828
Henkes, Kevin, 602
Hepler, Susan, 33, 603
Herdeg, Walter, 243
Hewins, Caroline Maria, 32
Hickman, Janet, 33, 155, 253
Higgins, James, 604
Hildebrand, Ann, 158
Hillier, Bevis, 631
Hirsch, Julie, 303
Hirschman, Susan, 605
Hoare, Geoffrey, 606
Hobbs, Anne Stevenson, 782
Hoffman, Miriam, 448
Hogarth, Grace Allen, 254, 283, 284, 459
Hogrogian, Nonny, 461
Hollinshead, Marilyn, 255
Holme, Bryan, 607
Holmes, Joseph O., 608
Holtze, Sally Holmes, 104, 256
Homes, A. M., 449
Honey, Elizabeth, 141
Hopkins, Lee Bennett, 450
Horning, Kathleen T., 257
Houfe, Simon, 258
Hoyle, Karen Nelson, 158, 609, 610, 829, 830
Hubbard, Ruth, 259
Huck, Charlotte S., 33
Hudson, Derek, 611
Hunt, Peter, 261, 338
Huntoon, Elizabeth, 612
Hurley, Beatrice J., 613
Hurlimann, Bettina, 34, 240, 241, 242, 243, 262
Hurt, Jeffry A., 263
Hurwitz, Laurie S., 614

Hutton, Warwick, 615
Hyland, Douglas, 452
Hyman, Katrin, 462
Hyman, Trina Schart, 462, 616, 617

IBBY. *See* International Board on Books for Young People
Inglis, Fred, 265
Ingram, Laura, 221
Inman, Sue Lile, 221
International Board on Books for Young People, 37
Ipcar, Dahlov, 459
Irvine, Joan, 106, 107
Irvine, Ruth R., 619
Ishii, Momoko, 284
Italiano, Graciela, 152
Itta, John Paul, 461
Ivy, Barbara, 266

Jaaksoo, Andres, 620
Jacobson, Frances F., 267
Jacques, Robin, 108
Jagusch, Sybille A., 38
Jakobsen, Gunnar, 621
Jalongo, Mary Renck, 268
James, Philip Brutton, 39
Jameyson, Karen, 269
Jan, Isabelle, 455
Jenkins, Patrick, 109
Jennett, Se-an, 110
Jensen, Virginia Allen, 111
Johnson, Diana L., 40
Johnson, Diane, 270
Johnson, Elizabeth, 461
Johnson, Paul, 112
Johnston, Margaret, 213
Jones, Cornelia, 456
Jones, Dolores Blythe, 457
Jones, Helen L., 626
Jones, Linda Harris, 41
Jones, Raymond E., 338

Jordan, Ann Devereaux, 53
Judson, Bay Hallowell, 271

Kalisa, Beryl Graham, 272
Kanerva, Arja, 458
Karrer, Mary K., 198
Katz, Elia, 273
Kaye, Marilyn, 248
Keats, Ezra Jack, 459, 460
Keenan, Hugh T., 221
Keeping, Charles, 627
Kehoe, Michael, 113, 114
Kellogg, Steven, 467, 628
Kemp, Edward C., 158
Kemp, Elaine, 158
Kepes, Juliet, 459
Kherdian, David, 461
Kibler, Myra, 221
Kiefer, Barbara, 253, 274, 275, 276,
    277, 278, 279, 280, 281
Kiefer, Monica Mary, 282
Kimmel, Margaret Mary, 839
Kingman, Lee, 283, 284, 459, 460,
    461, 462, 629
Kirkpatrick, D.L., 463
Kissel, Mary, 338
Klein, Robert F., 240
Klemin, Diana, 285, 286
Klingberg, Delores R., 630
Knox, Rawle, 631
Krahe, Hildegard, 243
Kraus, Robert, 461
Krier, Teresa, 338
Kroll, Steven, 632
Krull, Kathleen, 287
Kujoth, Jean Spealman, 464
Kunnemann, Horst, 241
Kurth, Heinz, 115
Kuskin, Karla, 288, 289, 465

LaBarbera, Kathryn, 290
Lacy, Lyn E., 291, 633
Lahr, John, 634

Lamb, Lynton, 292
Lamme, Linda Leonard, 234, 293
Landes, Sonia, 246, 635
Landow, George P., 40
Lanes, Selma, 294, 636, 637, 638
Langford, Sondra Gordon, 295
Lansing, Elizabeth, 460
Lapointe, Claude, 36
Larkin, David, 522, 639
Larrick, Nancy, 296
Latimer, Louise Payson, 48
Laughlin, Mildred, 297
Laukka, Maria, 458, 762
Laws, Frederick, 439
Lawson, Robert, 48, 451
Layard, G.S., 766
Lebrun, Yves, 36
Lechner, Judith V., 466
Lemieux, Louise, 298
Lemontt, Bobbie Burch, 221
Lent, Blair, 299, 459, 461, 641
Lenz, Millicent, 221
Le Tord, Bijou, 155
Lettow, Lucille J., 102, 444
Levine, Arthur, 642
Lewis, Claudia, 300
Lewis, John, 42, 233
Lewis, Marjorie, 301
Lief, Irving P., 832
Lima, Carolyn W., 43
Lima, John A., 43
Lindauer, Shelley L. Knudsen,
    302
Linder, Enid, 644
Linder, Leslie, 643, 644
Lionni, Leo, 304, 448, 645
Lipson, Eden Ross, 305
Livingston, Myra Cohn, 158
Lloyd, A.L., 461
Lloyd, Pamela, 467
Lobel, Arnold, 248, 462, 467, 646,
    647
Lodge, Sally, 287, 307, 648

Logan, Claudia, 649
Lontoft, Ruth Giles, 283
Loranger, Janet A., 462, 650
Lord, John Vernon, 238
Lorraine, Walter, 284, 308, 439, 459, 651
Low, Joseph, 459
Lucas, Barbara, 117
Lundin, Anne H., 653
Lunt, Dudley Cammett, 47, 459
Lurie, Stephanie, 309
Luther, Kenneth E., 200
Lystad, Mary, 44, 654

Macaulay, David, 248, 347, 462, 471, 655
MacCann, Donnarae, 310, 311, 312, 313, 314, 361, 656, 657
MacDonald, Eleanor, 315
MacDonald, Ruth K., 45, 158, 658, 659
Macy, George, 451
Madura, Nancy L., 46
Maguire, Gregory, 246
Mahne, Sabine, 660
Mahony, Bertha E., 47, 48. *See also* Miller, Bertha Mahony
Manna, Anthony L., 338, 601
Many, Joyce E., 316
Marantz, Kenneth, 152, 215, 317, 318, 338, 470, 662, 663, 664, 665, 666, 667
Marantz, Sylvia S., 319, 420, 470, 662, 663, 664, 665, 666, 667
Marcus, Leonard S ., 303, 668, 669, 670, 671
Marshall, James, 672
Marshall, Margaret Richardson, 320
Martin, Douglas, 118, 321
Martin, Rodney, 119
Marzollo, Jean, 120
Maschler, Tom, 238

Massee, May, 460
Mathers, Petra, 673
Matsui, Tadashi, 242, 243
Matthias, Margaret, 152
May, Jill P., 158, 676, 677, 678
Mayor, A. Hyatt, 433
McClellan, Constance Reed, 462
McCloskey, Robert, 246, 460
McCormick, Edith, 471
McCulloch, Lou, 49
McDermott, Gerald, 459, 461, 679
McElderry, Margaret, 471
McElmeel, Sharon M., 472, 473
McGee, Lea M., 322
McGillis, Roderick, 158
McKee, Barbara, 680
McLean, Ruari, 50
McMillan, Bruce, 323
McPherson, William, 681
McQuade, Molly, 682
McWhorter, George, 683
Meacham, Mary, 833
Meek, Margaret, 684
Mehren, Elizabeth, 691
Mercier, Jean F., 692
Mestrovich, Marta, 121
Meyer, Susan E., 51, 474, 693
Michel, Joan Hess, 694
Micklethwait, Lucy, 478
Mikolaycak, Charles, 246, 695
Miller, Bertha Mahony, 324, 451, 475. *See also* Mahony, Bertha
Mitchell, Florence S., 325
Mitgutsch, Ali, 122
Moebius, William, 326
Moir, Hughes, 192
Monin, Yevgeny, 696
Monson, Dianne L., 355, 834
Montana, Louis, 327
Montanaro, Ann R., 123
Montresor, Beni, 436, 460, 724
Moore, Anne Carroll, 364, 451
Moore, Kay, 333

Moran, Susan, 328
Morris, Charles Henry, 52
Morsberger, Robert E., 697
Mortensen, Heddi, 698
Moser, Barry, 471, 699
Moss, Elaine, 329
Moulton, Priscilla, 461
Moynihan, William T., 53
Muir, Marcie, 54
Muir, Percy, 55, 56
Munro, Eleanor C., 330
Murphy, Stuart J., 331
Myatt, Barbara, 332

Nakamura, Joyce, 468, 487, 835
Nazarevskaia, Nadezhda, 701
Neal, Judith C., 333
Nesbit, Elizabeth, 585
Ness, Evaline, 459, 461, 702
Neumeyer, Peter, 200, 334
Nicholson, George, 471
Nikola-Lisa, W., 703
Nisbet, John, 408
Nodelman, Perry, 200, 335, 336, 337, 338, 339
Noesser, Laura, 36
Nudelman, Edward D., 704, 705

O'Connell, Diane, 706
Olendorf, Donna, 431
Olmert, Michael, 124
Olson, Marilynn Strasser, 707
Ovenden, Graham, 477
Overton, Jacqueline, 47
Oxenbury, Helen, 708

Packard, Myrna, 340
Page, Diana, 141
Painter, Helen W., 709, 710, 711, 712
Paley, Nicholas, 341, 342
Pariser, David, 343
Parish, Anne, 451

Park, Dorothy M., 378
Parker, Ulla Hyde, 712
Parmegiani, Claude-Ann, 36
Patrick, Jean Streufert, 338
Paulin, Mary Ann, 344, 345
Peet, Bill, 713
Pellowski, Anne, 57
Peltola, Bette J., 346, 834
Peppin, Brigid, 58, 478
Perry, Erma, 714
Peterson, Linda Kauffman, 59
Pickering, Samuel F., 60
Pillar, Arlene M., 198
Pinkney, Jerry, 716, 717
Piotrowski, Mieczyslaw, 242
Pissard, Annie, 303
Pitz, Henry Clarence, 61, 349, 441, 479
Pohribny, Arsen, 240
Polette, Nancy, 350, 351, 352
Poltarnees, Welleran, 62
Porte, Barbara Ann, 718
Porter, Anna Newton, 460
Potter, Tony, 238
Potts, Lesley S., 221
Preiss, Byron, 719
Prentice, Jeffrey, 63
Prince, Diana M., 353
Pritchard, David, 303
Prosak-Beres, Leslie, 192
Protheroe, Pamela, 354
Provensen, Alice, 462, 471
Provensen, Martin, 462
Provenzo, Eugene F., Jr., 838
Puckett, Kathryn E., 362
Purves, Alan C., 355

Quimby, Harriet, 284, 839
Quist, Harlan, 240

Rahn, Suzanne, 303, 840
Ramseger, Ingeborg, 242, 722
Ramsey, Inez L., 356

Raskin, Ellen, 246
Ray, Gordon N., 64
Raymond, Allen, 723, 724, 725, 726, 727, 728, 729, 730, 731, 732
Raymond, Chet, 357
Read, Donna, 358
Reed, Marilyn, 253
Reed, Roger, 65
Reed, Walt, 65
Reef, Pat Davidson, 734
Reimer, Mavis, 338
Reinstein, P. Gila, 221
Rhoades, Jane, 359
Richard, Mari, 427
Richard, Olga, 311, 360, 361, 656
Richey, Virginia H., 362
Rixford, Ellen, 125
Roads, Clarice, 363
Roback, Diane, 126, 481, 735, 736
Roberts, Ellen E. M., 127
Robinson, Evelyn Rose, 364
Robinson, Moira, 482
Rochman, Hazel, 738
Roegiers, Patrick, 36
Roginski, James W., 424, 483, 484, 485
Rojankovsky, Feodor, 460
Roll, Dusan, 242, 243
Rollin, Lucy, 739
Rollock, Barbara, 486
Ronai, Kay, 141
Roop, Peter, 740
Rosenbach, A.S.W., 66
Rossi, Mary Jane Mangini, 232
Rotert, Richard, 426
Roxburgh, Stephen, 303, 347
Rudisill, Madel, 364
Rychlicki, Zbigniew, 241, 365
Ryder, John, 128, 240, 242, 366
Rynerson, Barbara Bagge, 155

Sadler, Philip A., 221

Sadowski, Eloise, 741
Sale, Roger, 67, 426
Samuels, Eva, 448
Sarkissian, Adele, 487, 841
Saul, Wendy, 742
Saxby, H.M., 367
Say, Allen, 743
Schatzmann, Jurg, 242
Schiff, Stephen, 744
Schmidt, Gary D., 745
Schuman, Patricia, 368
Schwarcz, Chava, 370
Schwarcz, Joseph H., 227, 369, 370
Seale, Doris, 376
Sebesta, Sam Leaton, 197
See, Lisa, 129, 746
Seiter, Richard, 221
Selden, Rebecca, 488
Sendak, Maurice, 246, 364, 371, 445, 460, 495, 748, 749, 782
Senick, Gerard J., 489
Seta, Teiji, 284
Shaner, Mary E., 53
Shannon, George, 750, 751
Sharkey, Paulette Bochnig, 842
Shepard, Ernest H., 459
Sheppard, Valerie, 372
Sheppard-Conrad, Connie, 752
Sherrill, Anne, 221
Short, Kathy G., 373
Shulevitz, Uri, 130, 246, 374, 375, 459, 461
Sicroff, Seth, 426
Sidjakov, Nicolas, 460
Sidorsky, Phyllis G., 753
Siemaszkova, Olga, 240
Silvey, Anita, 754
Simont, Marc, 460
Sis, Peter, 755
Slapin, Beverly, 376
Sleator, William, 461, 756
Smaridge, Norah, 490
Smedman, M. Sarah, 221, 488

Smith, Amanda, 757
Smith, Dora V., 68
Smith, Henrietta M., 358
Smith, Irene, 377
Smith, James A., 378
Smith, James Steel, 379
Smith, Janet Adam, 69
Smith, Karen Patricia, 758, 759
Smith, Lane, 760
Smith, Lillian H., 451
Smith, Linda Gramatky, 761
Smith, Nicole Gnezda, 380
Snyder, Jerome, 242
Solonen, Marja, 762
Solt, Marilyn Leathers, 59
Sonheim, Amy, 763
Soriano, Marc, 381
Sottomaya, Maria Jose, 764
Spaid, Elizabeth Levitan, 382
Spencer, Isobel, 765
Spielmann, M.H., 766
Spier, Peter, 462
Spirt, Diana, 823
Spitz, Ellen Handler, 383
St. John, Judith, 384, 843, 844
Stahlschmidt, Agnes D., 221
Stan, Susan, 131, 287, 767
Stander, Bella, 768
Steig, William, 461, 769
Steinfirst, Susan, 169
Stephens, Catherine, 385
Stephens, John, 386
Stewart, Robert, 140
Stewig, John Warren, 271, 387,
    388, 389, 390, 391, 392, 393,
    394, 395, 396, 397, 398
Stone, Bernard, 132
Stone, Wilbur Macy, 47
Stott, Jon C., 338, 399, 770
Street, Douglas, 221
Sullivan, Peggy, 400
Sullivan, Robert, 771
Sutherland, Zena, 401, 402

Svend Otto S., 772
Swanson, Mary T., 773
Swinger, Alice K., 774
Sylvestrova, Marta, 775
Szekely, George, 403

Tafuri, Nancy, 776
Targ, William, 70
Tatham, David, 777, 778
Taylor, Ina, 779
Taylor, Judy, 240, 780, 781, 782,
    783
Taylor, Mary-Agnes, 338
Telgrin, Diane, 431
Thorpe, James, 71
Thwaite, Mary F., 72
Tobias, Richard C., 784
Tomes, Margot, 785
Tompkins, Gail E., 322
Topor, Roland, 36
Toth, Bela, 227
Townsend, John Rowe, 73, 404
Treloar, Bruce, 141
Trignon, Jean de, 74
Tucker, Nicholas, 238
Tudor, Tasha, 788
Tuer, Andrew W., 75
Tunis, Edwin, 459
Turner, Robyn Montana, 789

Ulrich, Anna Katharina, 242, 243
Ungerer, Tomi, 471

Van Allsburg, Chris, 462, 790
Vandergrift, Kay E., 405
Van Stockum, Hilda, 459, 791
Vie, Francois, 36
Viguers, Ruth, 324

Wakeman, Geoffrey, 76
Waller, Jennifer R., 426
Ward, Lynd, 47, 48, 324, 459
Ward, Martha Eads, 491, 492

Warlow, Aidan, 684
Warthman, John Burns, 406
Watanabe, Shigeo, 407
Watts, Lynne, 408
Waugh, Dorothy, 793, 794
Weber, Nicholas Fox, 795
Weinstein, Frederic D., 77
Weisgard, Leonard, 459
Weiss, Ava, 134, 347
Weiss, Jacqueline, 480
Weitenkampf, Frank, 78
Weller, Joan, 409, 410
Wells, Rosemary, 136, 495, 782, 796
Weston, Annette H., 797
Whalen-Levitt, Peggy, 411
Whalley, Joyce Irene, 79, 80
White, Colin, 798
White, David E., 799, 800
White, Gabriel, 801
White, Mary Lou, 412
White, Maureen, 413
Whitney, Elinor, 47
Wiesner, David, 362
Wildsmith, Brian, 448, 804
Wilkins, Lea-Ruth C., 805
Willard, Nancy, 303, 462
Williams, Clarence M., 414

Williams, Helen E., 415
Williams, Vera, 347
Wilms, Denise, 806
Wilson, Rodger B., 137
Wilson, Trudy G., 416
Wintle, Justin, 493
Wolfe, Leo, 460
Wolff, Robert Lee, 81
Wood, Don and Audrey, 807
Woolman, Bertha, 494
Wroblewka, Danuta, 243

Yeager, Allan, 417
Yokoyama, Tadashi, 138
Yolen, Jane, 808
Yorinks, Arthur, 809
Young, Ed, 471

Zaum, Marjorie, 461
Zemach, Harve, 811
Zemach, Margot, 461, 810, 811
Zerfoss, Charlotte, 418
Zigany, Edit, 812
Zinsser, William, 495
Zipes, Jack, 303
Zuckerman, Linda, 576, 813
Zvirin, Stephanie, 814, 815
Zwicker, Marilyn, 139

Index of Titles

A to Zoo, 43
AB Bookman's Weekly, 816
"ABC and Counting Books," 242
About Books and Children, 1
"About Lovat Fraser," 47
"About Lucy and Tom," 451
"Abstraction in Illustration: Is it Appropriate for Children?", 208
"Accent on Art," 274
"Adrienne Adams: Illustrator of Children's Books," 793
"Aesthetic Literacy: Teaching Preschool Children to Respond to Book Illustrations," 380
"Africa in Picture Books: Portrait or Preconception?" 272
"Afterword: Children's Book Illustration in the Twentieth Century," 221
"Alexander Alexov: Illustration as an Art," 588
"Alice and Martin Provensen," 462
"Alive with Color," 579
"Aliveness of Peter Rabbit, The," 748, 782
All Mirrors Are Magic Mirrors: Reflections on Pictures Found in Children's Books, 62

"Alphabet Books: A Neglected Genre," 387
American Book Illustrators: Bibliographic Checklists of 123 Artists, 423
American Children Through Their Books, 1700–1835, 282
American Picture Books from Noah's Ark to the Beast Within, 4
American Popular Illustration: A Reference Guide, 817
American Writers for Children, 1900–1960, 428
American Writers for Children Since 1960, 221
America's Great Illustrators, 474
"Anita Lobel: Up From the Crossroad," 723
"Another Wonderland: Lewis Carroll's *The Nursery Alice*," 303
"Antic Disposition," 448, 804
"Are You Sure That Book Won the Caldecott Medal?", 257
Arnold Lobel, 750
Arnold Lobel (Filmstrip), 510
"Arnold Lobel," 462, 605, 672
"Arnold Lobel: An Appreciation," 594
"Arnold Lobel's Three Years with Mother Goose," 735

Art and Design in Children's Picture Books, 291

"Art and Language in Middle Childhood: A Question of Translation," 156

Art and Man, 147

"Art in Lois Lenski's Book *The Little Auto,* The," 591

Art of Art for Children's Books, The, 285

Art of Babar, The, 795

Art of Beatrix Potter, The, 644

Art of Children's Books, The," 129

"Art of Illustrating Books for the Younger Reader, The," 445

"Art of Illustration, The," 441

Art of James Thurber, The, 784

Art of Kate Greenaway, The: A Nostalgic Portrait of Childhood, 779

Art of Leo and Diane Dillon, The, 719

Art of Maurice Sendak, The, 636

Art of Nancy Ekholm Burkert, The, 522

"Art of Picture Books, The: Beautiful Treasures of Bookmaking," 160

"Art of the Contemporary Picture Book, The," 488

"Art of the Picture Book, The," 308

Arthur Rackham, 590

Arthur Rackham: His Life and Work, 611

"Arthur Rackham: The Search Goes On," 683

"Arthur Rackham and the Romantic Tradition," 173

"Arthur Rackham and *The Wind in the Willows,*" 451

"Arthur Rackham's *Fairy Book*: A Confrontation with the Marvelous," 338

"Artist and His Editor, The," 283

Artist and the Book 1860–1960, in Western Europe and the United States, The, 10

Artist and the Child: Exhibition of Children's Books and Original Illustration from the John D. Merriam Collection, The, 419

"Artist as Author, The," 684

"Artist at Work: Cardboard Cuts," 641

"Artist at Work, The" (Tomie dePaola), 549

"Artist at Work, The" (Kevin Henkes), 602

"Artist at Work, The" (Petra Mathers), 673

"Artist at Work, The" (Peter Sis), 755

"Artist at Work, The" (Lane Smith), 760

"Artist at Work, The" (William Steig), 769

"Artist at Work, The: The Art Director," 134

"Artist at Work, The: Books for the Very Young," 708, 776

"Artist at Work, The: Card Tables and Collage," 557

"Artist at Work, The: The Challenge of the Picture Book," 695

"Artist at Work, The: Characters Interacting with the Viewer," 716

"Artist at Work, The: Creating Nonfiction," 572

"Artist at Work, The: Illustrating the Classics," 699

"Artist at Work, The: The Importance of Humor," 521
"Artist at Work, The: A Sense of Place," 599
"Artist at Work, The: The Technique and the Artist's Vision," 569
"Artist at Work, The: The Writer at Work," 796
"Artist at Work, The: Where Ideas Come From, " 807
"Artist at Work, The: Woodcut Illustration" 702
"Artist, the Book, and the Child, The," 275
"Artist Profile: David Wiesner," 496
"Artistic Interpretation in the Fairytale Picturebook," 196
"Artists' Adventures in Wonderland," 144
"Artist's Journey and the Journey as Art, The," 751
Artists of a Certain Line, 366
"Artist's Other Eye, The: The Picture Books of Mitsumasa Anno" 303
Aspects of Victorian Lithography: Anastatic Printing and Photozineography, 76
"Astonished Witness Disclosed, The: An Interview with Arnold Lobel" 739
"Audrey and Don Wood," 746
Author Profile Collection, 420
Authors and Illustrators of Children's Books: Writings on Their Lives and Works, 448
Authors of Pictures, Draughtsmen of Words, 259
"Autobiographical Note, An," 448

"Ava Weiss and Vera Williams," 347

"Babar, Reborn in the U.S.A.," 691
"Back to Basics: Reevaluating Picture Books," 301
"Barbara Cooney," 460, 462
Beatrix Potter, 658
Beatrix Potter: Artist, Storyteller and Countrywoman, 780
"Beatrix Potter: Centenary of an Artist-Writer," 283
Beatrix Potter: A Private World, 513
"Beatrix Potter and Her Nursery Classics," 451
Beatrix Potter 1866–1943: The Artist and Her World, 781
Beatrix Potter Had a Pet Named Peter, 514
"Beatrix Potter's Other Art," 782
"Beatrix Potter's *The Tale of Peter Rabbit*: A Small Masterpiece," 338
"Before Images," 304
Behind the Covers: Interviews with Authors and Illustrators of Books for Children and Young Adults, 483
Behind the Covers Volume II, 484
"Ben, Mr. Popper and the Rabbits," 527
Ben Yitzak Award for Distinguished Illustration of a Children's Book, The 154
"Benchmarks for Illustrators of Children's Books," 441
"Beneath the Surface with *Fungus the Bogeyman*," 303
"Beni Montresor," 460
"Beni Montresor: Carmen, Cannes, and Caldecott," 724
"Berta and Elmer Hader," 448

Best of 3–D Books, The, 138
Best-Selling Children's Books, 464
"Bewicks, The: Thomas and John," 47
"Beyond Illustration: Information About Art in Children's Picture Books," 230
Beyond Words: Picture Books for Older Readers and Writers, 155
"BIB 1989 Golden Apple Award to the Portuguese Illustrator Manuela Bacelar," 764
Bibliophile in the Nursery, 70
Biennale of Illustrations Bratislava, 422
Bill Peet: An Autobiography, 713
Bill Peet in His Studio, 516
"Birds and the Beasts Were There, The: An Interview with Martin Provensen," 303
"Birthdays and Beginnings," 646
Black Authors and Illustrators of Children's Books, 486
"Bob McCloskey, Inventor," 460
Book, 86
"Book Artist, The: Ideas and Techniques," 324
"Book Artist, The: Yesterday and Tomorrow," 48
Book Design, 118
"Book Design," 102
"Book Illustration: Key to Visual and Verbal Literacy," 388
"Book Illustration: The State of the Art," 284
Book Illustration and Decoration: A Guide to Research, 12
Book of One's Own, A: Developing Literacy Through Making Books, 112
Book Takes Root, A, 113
"Booklist Interview: Graeme Base," 558

"Booklist Interview: Steven Kellogg," 559
"Booklist Interview: Leo Lionni," 537
"Booklist Interview: David Macaulay," 814
"Booklist Interview: Helen Oxenbury," 806
"Booklist Interview: Jon Scieszka and Lane Smith," 815
"Booklist Interview: Maurice Sendak," 738
"Bookmaking Made Simple," 120
Bookpeople: A First Album, 472
Bookpeople: A Multicultural Album, 473
Books Are by People: Interviews with 104 Authors and Illustrators of Books for Young Children, 450
Books by African-American Authors and Illustrators for Children and Young Adults, 415
"Books for Babies: Learning Toys or Pre-Literature," 145
Books for Children: Bibliography, 163
"Books from Parellel Cultures," 159
Books from Writer to Reader, 99
"Books, Illustrations and Child Development: How Much Are We Ever Likely to Know?", 238
"Books in the Classroom," 244
"Boris Artzybasheff," 515
"Bothering to Look," 246
Brain Power Through Picture Books, 350
Brandywine Tradition, The, 479
"Brandywine Tradition, The: Howard Pyle and N.C. Wyeth," 47
Bright Stream, The , 80

British Children's Authors: Interviews at Home, 456

British Children's Books in the Twentieth Century, 225

"Bruce Degen: Doing What He Likes Best," 560

Building a Children's Literature Collection: A Suggested Basic Reference Collection for Academic Libraries and a Suggested Basic Collection of Children's Books, 839

Butter at the Old Price: The Autobiography of Marguerite de Angeli, 546

"Caldecott Album, A," 612

Caldecott & Co., 371

Caldecott Award, The: The Winners and the Honor Books, 494

"Caldecott Citations," 176

Caldecott Medal Books: 1938–1957, 475

"Caldecott Spectrum, The," 462

"Caldecott Winners Are Picture Perfect," 216

"Caldecott's Pictures in Motion," 791

"Canadian Tribute to Leslie Brooke, A," 451

Carolyn Sherwin Bailey Historical Collection of Children's Books: A Catalog, 821

Case for Legibility, The, 128

Celebrating Children's Books, 248

Century of Children's Books, A, 6

"Changing Picture of Poetry Books for Children, The," 296

Child and His Book, The, 26

Child and His Picture Book, The, 228

"Child and the Picture Book, The: Create Live Circuits," 276

"Child as Parent to the Illustrator: Drawing and Painting with Words," 238

"Child Reading and Man Reading; Oz, Babar and Pooh," 426

Children and Books, 401

Children and Literature, 389

Children and Literature: Views and Reviews, 445

Children and Their Literature, 28

Children of the Northern Lights, 531

Children's Authors and Illustrators: An Index to Biographical Dictionaries, 835, 841

"Children's Book Art Attracts Collectors," 382

"Children's Book Illustration," 212, 330

Children's Book Illustration: The Pleasures and Problems," 439, 445

"Children's Book Illustration and Design," 436

"Children's Book Illustration in Britain," 242

"Children's Book Illustration in England," 240

"Children's Book Illustration in Poland," 241, 365

"Children's Book Illustration in Poland: A Landscape with a Rainbow," 243

"Children's Book Illustrators Play Favorites," 184

"Children's Book Production in the U.S.A.," 240

Children's Book Review Index, 819

Children's Book Showcase, 429

"Children's Books," 93, 142

Children's Books: Awards and Prizes, 820

Children's Books About Art, 266

"Children's Books in Britain: Divergent Styles and Occupational Highlights," 243

"Children's Books in Czechoslovakia: A Younger Generation Takes Over," 243

Children's Books in England: Five Centuries of Social Life, 20

"Children's Books in France," 240

"Children's Books in Japan: Rapid Growth and a Promising Future," 243

"Children's Books in Other Languages," 413

Children's Books International, 185, 186

Children's Books of the 19th Century, 49

Children's Books of Yesterday, 39

Children's Illustrated Books, 69

Children's Literature
Volume 1, 170
Volume 2, 171
Volume 3, 172
Volume 6, 173
Volume 12, 174
Volume 13, 175

Children's Literature: An Annotated Bibliography of the History and Criticism, 840

Children's Literature: Criticism and Response, 412

Children's Literature: A Guide to Reference Sources, 827

Children's Literature: A Guide to the Criticism, 828

Children's Literature: A Historical and Contemporary Bibliography, 832

Children's Literature: Theory, Research, and Teaching, 405

Children's Literature Awards and Winners: A Directory of Prizes, Authors and Illustrators, 457

Children's Literature from A to Z: A Guide for Parents and Teachers, 399

Children's Literature in the Classroom, 253

Children's Literature in the Elementary School, 33

Children's Literature in the Reading Program, 197

Children's Literature Review: Excerpts from Reviews, Criticism and Commentary on Books for Children and Young People, 489

Children's Picture Book, The, 127

"Children's Picture Books: Into the Second Century," 312

"Children's Picture Books Today," 241

"Children's Preference in Picture Book Illustration," 390

"Children's Preferences for Color Versus Other Qualities in Illustration," 364

Children's Preferences for Traditional and Modern Paintings, 273

"Children's Responses to Illustrations in Picture Books," 227

"Children's Responses to Illustrations of Poetry," 227

"Children's World of Ludwig Bemelmans, The," 448

Child's First Books, The: A Critical Study of Pictures and Texts, 311

ChildView: Evaluating and Reviewing Materials for Children, 219

Choosing Books for Children: A Commonsense Guide, 247

Choosing Books for Young People: A Guide to Criticism, 823

"Choosing the Caldecott Medal Winners," 346

"Choosing the Caldecott Winner: Fifth Graders Give Their Reasons," 391

"Chris Van Allsburg," 462, 614

"Cite the Source," 249

Closer Look at Peter Rabbit, A, 635

Cobwebs to Catch Flies: Illustrated Books for the Nursery and Schoolroom 1700–1900, 79

"Colleagues and Co-Conspirators," 628

Collected Perspectives: Choosing and Using Books for the Classroom, 192

"Color Separation," 283

"Coming Attractions," 430

Comparison of the Works of Walter Crane, Randolph Caldecott and Kate Creenaway and Their Contributions to Children's Literature, A, 41

"Computerized Children's Literature," 267

"Concerned Criticism or Casual Cop-Out?", 368

Contemporary American Illustrators of Children's Books, 433

"Contemporary Children's Book Illustration in Czechoslovakia," 242

Contemporary Illustrators of Children's Books, 47

"Continuous Narrative Technique in Children's Literature, The," 227

"Controlled Wool-Gathering: The Political Cartoonist and Beatrix Potter," 782

"Conversation with Maurice Sendak, A," 799

"Conversation with Mitsumasa Anno, A," 508

"Converstion with Tomie dePaola, A," 706

"Conversations: Robert McCloskey," 740

"Conversations: Susan Hirschman," 131

Cool Web, The, 684

Cousin Beatie: A Memory of Beatrix Potter, 712

"Creating Children's Books at the Rochester Folk Art Guild," 139

Creating Jack and the Bean Tree, 89

"Creating a Picture Book," 533

"Creation of a Picture Book," 439, 509

"Creative Reading: Young Adults and Paperback Books," 328

Creative Uses of Children's Literature, 344

Critical Approach to Children's Literature, A, 379

"Criticism of Artwork in Children's Picture Books," 169

Criticism, Theory, and Children's Literature, 261

"Cult of Peter Pan, The," 149

"Daddy, Talk! Thoughts on Reading Early Picture Books," 303

Dahlov Ipcar/Artist, 734

"Dancing to a Different Tune,"
    648
"David Macaulay," 347
"David Macaulay: The Early
    Years," 790
David Macaulay in His Studio, 544
"David Wiesner," 655
"Decade of Books, A: A Critic's
    Response, " 462
"Deceptive Beetles," 238
"Degrees of Freedom," 265
"Delinquent Youth Write and
    Illustrate Their Own Books,"
    103
"Demi: Drawing and Writing,"
    548
"Description of a Select Group of
    Six Fifth Grade Students'
    Response to Picturebooks,
    A," 209
"Design and Typography of
    Children's Books, The," 97
"Design in Communication," 414
"Developing the Beginning
    Reading Process with Picture
    Books," 187
"Dialogue on Illustrating, A," 482
"Diane Dillon," 462
*Dictionary of British Illustrators:
    The Twentieth Century*, 478
*Dictionnaire des ecrivains pour la
    jeunesse: Auteurs de la langue
    français*, 37
"Discovering Art Through
    Picture Books," 217
"Distinction in Picture Books,"
    324
"Don Freeman: An Editor's
    View," 813
"Donald Crews," 767
Dora's Book, 90
"Dorte Karrebaek, the Danish
    Illustrator," 698

"Douglas Florian: Keeping a
    Balance Between Simplicity
    and Reality," 725
*Down the Rabbit Hole: Adventures
    and Misadventures in the
    Realm of Children's Literature*,
    294
Dr. Seuss, 659
"Dr. Seuss and Dr. Einstein," 357
Dr Seuss from Then to Now, 553
"Dr. Seuss Turns 80," 540
"Dr. Seuss' *The 500 Hats of
    Bartholomew Cubbins: Of Hats
    and Kings*, 338
"Drawing Out William Steig,"
    595
"Dream Weaver," 535
*Dromkeen: A Journey into
    Children's Literature*, 63

"E" Is for Everybody, 351
*Early American Children's Books
    with Bibliographic Descriptions
    of the Books in His Private
    Collection*, 66
*Early Children's Books and Their
    Illustration*, 23
"Ed Emberly," 461
"Ed Young," 520
"Editor's Comments, An," 347
Editors on Editing, 100
Edmund Dulac, 798
"Educating the Eye," 471
Edward Ardizzone, 555
*Edward Ardizzone: Artist and
    Illustrator*, 801
"Edward Ardizzone's *Little Tim
    and the Brave Sea Captain*: An
    Art of Contrasts," 338
"Edward Gorey and the Tao of
    Nonsense," 744
"Effect of Art Style on Children's
    Picture Preferences," 356

Ellen Raskin, 707

Emerging Authors and Illustrators in the '80s: Noteworthy Contributions to Children's Literature, 444

"Emily Arnold McCully," 642

"Emotional Impact of Books by Molly Bang, The," 290

"Emperor's New Clothes, The," 392

Empire's Old Clothes, The, 207

"Enamoured of the Mystery," 246

"Enduring Appeal of Beatrix Potter, The," 752

English Children's Books, 1600–1900, 55

English Illustration: The Nineties, 71

"Enjoying Festivals with Katherine Milhous," 448

Enjoying Illustrations, 220

"Enriching the Arts and Humanities through Children's Books," 197

Eric Carle: Picture Writer, 565

"Eric Hill and His Dog Spot," 736

Etienne Delessert, 547

"European Picture Book, The," 324

"Evaline Ness," 461

Evolution of a Graphic Concept: The Stonecutter, 91

"Exhibition in Memory of Bettina Hurlimann, An," 722

"Expanding Market for Children's Book Illustrations, The," 327

Experiencing Children's Literature, 355

Experimental Visual Literacy Program in Schools, An, 393

Exploring the Art of Picture Books, 363

"Extraordinary Vision, An," 222

"Extraordinary Vision, An: Picture Books of the Nineties," 223

Ezra Jack Keats, 566

"Ezra Jack Keats," 460

"Ezra Jack Keats: Author and Illustrator," 448

"Ezra Jack Keats: In Memoriam," 637

"Ezra Jack Keats' *The Snowy Day*: The Wisdom of a Pure Heart," 338

Fabulous and Familiar: Children's Reading in New Zealand, Past and Present, 24

"Fairies Come into Their Own, The," 47

Fairy Tales and After: From Snow White to E.B. White, 67

Fairy Tales, Fables, Legends and Myths: Using Folk Literature in Your Classroom, 165, 166

"Fairytale Book, A: Exploration into Creating an Art Form," 95

Faith Ringgold, 789

Faith Ringgold: The Last Story Quilt, 567

Famous Author-Illustrators for Young People, 490

Fantastic Illustration and Design in Britain, 1850–1930, 40

Fantastic Paintings of Charles and William Heath Robinson, The, 639

Fantasy: The Golden Age of Fantastic Illustration, 58

Fifteen Centuries of Children's Literature, 8

Fifth Book of Junior Authors and Illustrators, 256

*Fifty Years of Children's Books,
1910–1960,* 68
*Fin de Siecle: Illustrators of the
'Nineties,* 258
"First the Word: An Editor's
View of Picture Book Texts,"
309
*Flipbook Animation and Other Ways
to Make Cartoons Move,* 109
"Flowers for a Birthday—Kate
Greenaway, March 17, 1846,"
451
Flowers of Delight, 21
"Flying Starts," 481
"Flying Starts: New Faces of
1989," 449
"Four African-American
Illustrators," 440
"Four or Fourteen or Forty," 155
*Fourth Book of Junior Authors and
Illustrators,* 256
"Frasconi's Brio with a Book,"
573
"French Canadian Picture Books
in Translation," 229
"French Children's Books: Cult of
the New v. the Old
Favorites," 243
"French Illustrators Bernard
Jannemin and Mach Eveno,
The," 550
"Fresh Vision of Lucy Cousins,
The," 649
"From Caldecott to Caldecott,"
460
*From Dr. Mather to Dr. Seuss: 200
Years of American Books for
Children,* 44
"From Lascaux to Hi-Tech," 202
"From Mallards to Maine: A
Conversation with Robert
McCloskey," 600

"From Our Correspondent in
Utopia," 246
From Picture to Picture Book, 122
From Primer to Pleasure in Reading,
72
*From Swedish Fairy Tales to
American Fantasy: Gustaf
Tenggren's Illustrations 1920–
1970,* 773
"Functional Approach to
Illustrations in Children's
Books—The Work of
Frantisek Holesovsky, A,"
227
"Fungus Encore," 530
"Future Evolution of the Art of
the Picture-Book, The," 242

*Gail E. Haley: Wood and Linoleum
Illustration,* 94
"Gail E. Haley," 461
"Garth Williams," 668
"Garth Williams after Eighty,"
506
"Genesis of a Picturebook, The,"
137
"Genius of Arthur Rackham,
The," 451
"Gentle World of Ezra Jack Keats,
The," 714
"Gerald McDermott," 461
"German Illustrator Christa
Unzer-Fischer, The," 660
"German Picture-Book Gains
Ground, The," 240
"German Picture-Books—A Ray
of Hope for Children in an
Unkind Age?", 243
"German Picture-Books of the
19th Century," 242
"Give All Ages a Look at a
Mother Goose Book," 372

"Glimpses of an Artist: Adrienne Adams," 741

Golden Age of Children's Book Illustration, The, 19

Golden Age of Fantastic Illustration, The, 58

"Good, the Bad and the Appropriate, The," 343

Good Books to Grow On, 180

"Good Picture Book Should . . . , A," 248

"Graphic Gallery," 239

Graphis, 240, 241, 242, 243

"Great Catalogs, The," 200

"Grimm Reaper, The," 532

Growing Pains: Diaries and Drawings for the Years 1908–1917, 577

Guide de litterature pour la jeunesse: Courants, problemes, choix d'auteurs, 381

"Gustav Tenggren's Golden Anniversary," 609

"Hang the Children—What About the Books?", 238

"Heightening the Perceptive Abilities of Middle School Art Students Through the Use of the Picturebook," 353

Histoire de la litterature enfantine, de la Mere l'Oye au Roi Babar, 74

Histoire de la litterature enfantine en France, 14

Historia de la Literatura Infantil Espanola, 11

History of Australian Children's Book Illustration, A, 54

History of Australian Children's Literature, A, 367

History of Book Illustration, A: The Illuminated Manuscript and the Printed Books, 9

History of Children's Book Illustration, A, 80

History of the Illustrated Book, The Western Tradition, The, 30

History of the Newbery and Caldecott Medals, A, 377

History of the Tale of Peter Rabbit, 643

Holiday House: The First Fifty Years, 442

"Holling C. Holling: Author and Illustrator," 448

Horn Book Reflections on Children's Books and Readings: Selected From Eighteen Years of the Horn Book Magazine, 1949–1966, 441

Horn Book Sampler on Children's Books and Reading: Selected from Twenty-Five Years of Horn Book Magazine, 451

How a Book Is Made, 82

How a Picture Book Is Made, 105

"How Children Respond to Art," 335

"How Does Perception Develop?", 238

"How I Found 'The Treasure'," 246

"How Jonah and the Great Fish Began," 615

"How Picture Books Mean: The Case of Chris Van Allsburg," 334

"How Picture Books Work," 200, 336

"How the Caldecott Changed My Life—Twice," 461

"How to Create a Successful
  Nonfiction Picture Book,"
  248
*How to Find Out About Children's
  Literature,* 822
"How to Make a Picture Book,"
  288
How to Make Pop-Ups, 106
How to Make Super Pop-Ups, 107
*How to Write, Illustrate and Design
  Children's Books,* 96
How Writers Write, 467
Howard Pyle, 498, 563, 585
"Howard Pyle and His Times,"
  48
*Howard Pyle and the Wyeths: Four
  Generations of American
  Imagination,* 452
"Howard Pyle Commemorative,"
  676
*Human and Anti-Human Values in
  Children's Books,* 260
*Hundert Alte Kinderbucher, 1870–
  1945,* 29

"I Immerse Myself in This Fairy-
  Tale World," 696
"I Knew It Would Happen," 730
"I See Me in the Book," 270
"I Spy," 126
"Idea to Image: The Journey of a
  Picture Book," 303
Illustrated Book, The, 78, 286
Illustrated Children's Books, 5
"Illustrated Poem, The," 315
"Illustrated Sendak, The," 511
"Illustrating Books for Children,"
  364
*Illustrating Children's Books: A
  Guide to Drawing, Printing,
  Illustrating, and Publishing,*
  101

*Illustrating Children's Books:
  History, Technique, Production,*
  61
"Illustrating Handel," 155
*Illustrating in the Third Dimension:
  The Artist Turned Craftsman,*
  453
"Illustrating *The Water of Life*,"
  616
Illustration: Aspects and Directions,
  233
"Illustration as Interpretation:
  Trina Hyman's Folk Tales,"
  677
"Illustration from a Publisher's
  Point of View," 238
Illustration of Children's Books, The,
  52
Illustrations in Children's Books,
  188
"Illustrations Today in Children's
  Books," 451
*Illustrator and the Book in England
  from 1790–1914, The,* 64
*Illustrator as Storyteller, The:
  Caldecott Medal and Honor
  Books, 1938–1984,* 264
"Illustrator Eva Gaal, The," 812
*Illustrator in America, 1880–1980:
  A Century of Illustration,* 65
"Illustrator Talks, An," 756
"Illustrators, Books and Children:
  An Illustrator's Viewpoint,"
  157
Illustrators at Work, 108
Illustrator's Notebook, The, 459
*Illustrators of Alice in Wonderland
  and Through the Looking Glass,
  The,* 477
*Illustrators of Books for Young
  People,* 491, 492
Illustrators of Children's Books, 35

*Illustrators of Children's Books,
1744–1945,* 48
*Illustrators of Children's Books,
1946–1956,* 324
*Illustrators of Children's Books,
1957–1966,* 283
*Illustrators of Children's Books,
1967–1976,* 284
"Illustrator's Viewpoint, An," 441
"Illustratorship: Key Facet of
Whole Language
Instruction," 293
Image and Maker, 200
L'image dans le livre pour enfants,
210
*Images a la page: Une Histoire de
l'image dans les livres pour
l'enfants,* 36
"Images and Ideas: Picture Books
for All Ages," 277
*Imagineers, The: Writing and
Illustrating Children's Books,*
141
"Impact of Phototechnology on
the Illustrations in
Picturebooks, The," 46
"Impressions of Sendak," 593
"In Search of the Perfect Picture
Book Definition," 402
"In the Artist's Studio: Dennis
Nolan," 808
*"In the Beginning Was the
Word . . ." The Illustrated Book
1967–1976,* 284
*Information Sources in Children's
Literature: A Practical
Reference Guide for Children's
Librarians, Elementary School
Teachers, and Students of
Children's Literature,* 833
*Innocence and Experience: Essays
and Conversations on
Children's Literature,* 246

Innovators of American Illustration,
447
"Interactions About Text and
Pictures," 316
"International Palette of Swiss
Children's Books, The," 243
"Internationally Derived
Standards for Children's
Picture Books," 313
"Interpreted Well Enough," 150
"Interview with Amy Schwartz,
An," 669
"Interview with Ann Jonas," 662
"Interview with Anthony
Browne, An," 663
"Interview with David Wiesner,
An," 618
"Interview with Eric Hill," 575
"Interview with Henrik
Drescher," 570
"Interview with IRA Book Award
Winner Marisabina Russo,
An," 543
"Interview with Jerry Pinkney,
An, 601
"Interview with Leo Lionni, An,"
582
"Interview with Maurice Sendak,
An," 439, 651
"Interview with Paul O.
Zelinsky," 664
"Interview with Svend Otto S.
The Famous Danish
Illustrator," 583
"Introducing Art History through
Children's Literature," 325
"Introduction to Art: Children's
Books, An," 403
"Introduction to Picturebook
Codes," 326
*Introduction to the World of
Children's Books, An,* 320

"Invention and Discoveries: An
     Interview with Ann K.
     Beneduce," 303
"Irene Haas," 347
"It Adds Up to Magic: Jeanne and
     Bill Steig," 726
Ivan Bilibin, 581
"Ivan Y. Bilibin: The Leading
     Illustrator of Children's
     Books in Pre-Revolutionary
     Russia," 243

"Jaan Tamsaar: An Illustrator
     from Estonia," 620
"Jacket IS Overture," 580
James Daugherty, 622
"James Marshall," 670
"James Marshall (1942–1992),"
     754
James Marshall in His Studio, 623
James Thurber, 697
"James Warhola: Science Fiction
     to Pumpkinville," 624
"Jan Brett: Making It Look Easy,"
     727
"Japanese and American Picture
     Books . . . Similarities and
     Differences," 407
"Japanese Picture-Book in Past
     and Present, The," 242
"Japanese Sensibility in Picture
     Books for Children, The,"
     361
"Jessie Willcox Smith," 200
*Jessie Willcox Smith: A
     Bibliography*, 705
*Jessie Willcox Smith: American
     Illustrator*, 704
"John Burningham and Helen
     Oxenbury," 571
"John Steptoe," 625

*Jon Locke and Children's Books in
     Eighteenth-Century England*,
     60
"Jon Scieszka and Lane Smith,"
     757
"Jose Aruego: From Law Books to
     Kids' Books," 728
"Judging Art for Children," 255
Jump over the Moon, 151

Kate Greenaway (Greenaway), 586
Kate Greenaway (Spielmann), 766
Kate Greenaway: A Biography, 564
Kate Greenaway Book, The, 607
"Kate Greenaway's *A Apple Pie*:
     An Atmosphere of Sober
     Joy," 338
*Kate Greenaway's Original
     Drawings for the Snow Queen*,
     504
"Kate Greenaway's Vision of
     Childhood," 653
"Keith Baker," 568
*Kerlan Collection, The: Manuscripts
     and Illustrations for Children's
     Books*, 831
*Khudozhnik v Sovremennoi Detskoi
     Knige*, 443
"Kids' Books You Can Enjoy,"
     252
"Kveta Pacovska—A Magician of
     Modern Art," 775

"L. Leslie Brooke's *Johnny Crow's
     Garden*: The Gentle Humor of
     Implied Stories," 338
"Language, Discourse, and
     Picture Books," 386
Laurent de Brunhoff, Daydreamer,
     640
"Learning from Illustrations," 236
*Legibility in Children's Books: A
     Review of Research*, 408

"Leo and Diane Dillon," 462

"Leo Dillon," 462

Leo Lionni at the Library of Congress, 645

"Leo Lionni's *Swimmy*: Undetailed Depth," 338

"Leonard Everett Fisher," 347

Leonard Weisgard: Exponent of Beauty," 709

"Leslie Brooke," 451

Lewis Carroll by Roger Lancelyn Green; E. Nesbit by Anthea Bell; Howard Pyle by Elizabeth Nesbit, 585

Lion and the Unicorn, The, 303

"Lionni's Artichokes: An Interview," 412, 499

"Lisbeth Zwerger: Children's Book Illustrator," 753

Literature and the Child, 199

Literature and the Young Child, 181

Literature for Children in England and America from 1646 to 1774, 45

"Little Toot—Hero," 448, 710

"Little Toot Turns Fifty," 761

Lively Art of Picture Books, 306

"Load of Old Nonsense, Edward Lear Resurrected by Four Publishers, A," 445

"Lois Lenski: Children's Interpreter," 448

"Long Live Babar!" 303

"Look Again: Picture Books Are More Than Pictures," 232

"Look at the Creative Process, A," 116

"Looking Beyond Picture Book Preferences," 278

"Lost Art, A," 652

"Lotus Blossom—Or Whodunit, The?", 246

Lotus Seeds: Children, Pictures and Books, 168

"Louder Than a Thousand Words," 152

"Luther Daniels Bradley: Guide to the Great Somewhere-or-Other," 200

"Lynd Ward: Artist, Writer, and Scholar," 711

Major Authors and Illustrators for Children and Young Adults, 468

Making a Book, 83

"Making Dimensional Illustrations," 125

"Making of a Crossover, The," 307

Making of a Picture Book, The, 119

Making of Books, The, 110

Making of the Book, The, 17

"Making Picture Books," 525

Making Picture Books, 469

Making Picture-Books: A Method of Learning Graphic Sequence, 98

Man Who Invented Snoopy, The, 661

"Marc Simont," 460

"Marcia Brown," 462, 650

"Margaret and H.A. Rey," 448

"Margot Tomes: Three Editors' Perspectives," 576

"Margot Zemach: A European Perspective," 500

"Marguerite L. de Angeli: Faith in the Human Spirit," 448

"Marian Murawski, Winner of the BIB '89 Grand Prix," 507

"Marie Hall Ets," 460

"Marie Hall Ets—Her Picture Storybooks," 448, 619

"Mary McNeer Ward and Lynd Ward," 448

"Master of Line, A," 631
Masterworks of Children's Literature, 15
    Vols. 1, 2: *The Early Years, 1550–1739*, 13
    Vols. 3, 4: *The Middle Period, 1740–1836*, 7
    Vols. 5, 6: *The Victorian Age, 1837–1900*, 81
    Vol. 7: *Victorian Color Picture Books*, 16
    Vol. 8: *The Twentieth Century*, 83
"Maurice Before Max," 501
"Maurice Boutet de Monvel: Master of the French Picture Book," 596
Maurice Sendak, 763
"Maurice Sendak," 460, 536, 529
"Maurice Sendak: Off the Page," 529
Maurice Sendak—1965, 674
"Maurice Sendak and the Blakean Vision of Childhood," 173, 426
"Maurice Sendak in Profile," 681
"Maurice Sendak, King of All Wild Things," 194, 539
"Maurice Sendak with Paul Vaughn," 675
"Maurice Sendak's *Where the Wild Things Are*: Picture Book Poetry," 338
"May Gibbs—Australia's Greatest Children's Writer," 584
"M.B. Goffstein: An Interview," 665
"Me and Blake, Blake and Me," 246
"Media Used in Caldecott Picture Books, The," 85

"Medium of Wordless Picture Books, The," 416
"Meet Ashley Bryan: Storyteller, Artist, Writer," 685
"Meet Dennis Kyte: A Modern-Day Aesop," 729
"Meet Kevin Henkes: Young Man on a Roll," 651
Meet Leo Lionni, 686
Meet Marc Brown, 687
Meet Stan and Jan Berenstain, 688
Meet the Artist: Barbara Reid, 689
Meet the Caldecott Illustrator: Jerry Pinkney, 690
Meet the Newbery Author: Arnold Lobel, 510
Meilikuvia/Images, 458
"Merging Dreams and Consummate Realities," 758
"Meteoric Career of Ed Emberly, The," 448
Mid-Century Child and Her Books, A, 32
Modern Book Illustration in Great Britain and America, 201
"Modern Picture Books and the Child's Visual Sense," 227
More Creative Uses of Children's Literature, 345
"Mother Goose's Garnishings," 445
"Mouse in the Corner, the Fly on the Wall, The," 289
"Movable Books—A New Golden Age," 140
"Mr. Ruskin and Miss Greenaway," 426
Mr. Shepard and Mr. Milne, 700
"Musings," 589
"Musings of a Walking Stereotype," 743
"My Books for Children," 448
"My Goals as an Illustrator," 253

"My Work as a Children's
Illustrator," 627

"Nancy Ekholm Burkert," 768
"N.C. Wyeth," 693
"New Children's Books—Or
Parents' Books?—in France,"
242
"New Golden Age of Kids'
Books, The," 203
"New Look of Children's Picture
Books, The," 183
"New Trends in Children's Books
in Germany," 242
"New Trends in Czechoslovak
Children's Books," 240
"New Textures in Children's
Book Art," 287
*New York Times Parent's Guide to
the Best Books for Children,
The,* 305
*Newbery and Caldecott Awards: A
Guide to the Medal and Honor
Books,* 836
*Newbery and Caldecott Medal and
Honor Books: An Annotated
Bibliography,* 59
*Newbery and Caldecott Medal and
Honor Books in Other Media,*
842
*Newbery and Caldecott Medal
Books: 1956–1965,* 460
*Newbery and Caldecott Medal
Books: 1966–1975,* 461
*Newbery and Caldecott Medal
Books: 1976–1985,* 462
*Newbery and Caldecott Medalists
and Honor Book Winners:
Bibliographies and Resource
Materials through 1977,* 485
*Newbery and Caldecott Medalists
and Honor Book Winners:*

*Bibliographies and Resource
Materials through 1991,* 424
"News from Down Under," 269
"News from the North," 562
"Nicolas Sidjakov," 460
"Nikita Charuschin: A Leningrad
Artist," 701
"N.M. Bodecker: A
Reminiscence," 518
"Nonny Hogrogian," 461, 554
"Nonny Hogrogian, Decorator of
Books for Children," 794
Notable Canadian Children's Books,
148
"Note on the Darton Collection,
A," 838
"Notes on Japanese
Picturebooks," 240, 241
"Notes on the International
Picture-Book Scene," 243

"Object Lesson, The:
Picturebooks of Anthony
Browne," 206
*Of the Decorative Illustration of
Books Old and New,* 18
"Oh, the Places He Went!" 771
On Children's Literature, 455
"On the Criticism of Illus-
trations," 772
"On the Mysteries of Reading
and Art," 215
"On Using Balloons Sparingly,"
167
"Once-Upon-a-Time Artist in the
Land of Now," 742
"One Hundred Years of
Illustrations in French
Children's Books," 211
"One Man's Art of Bookmaking,"
104
One Ocean Touching, 213
"One Wonders," 283

*Only Connect: Readings on
    Children's Literature,* 439
*Openhearted Audience, The: Ten
    Authors Talk About Writing for
    Children,* 446
"Osborne Collection of Early
    Children's Books, The":
    Highlights in Retrospect, 384
*Osborne Collection of Early
    Children's Books, 1566–1910,
    The: A Catalogue,* 843
*Osborne Collection of Early
    Children's Books, 1476–1910,
    The: A Catalogue, Vol. 2,* 844
*Oxford Companion to Children's
    Literature, The,* 427

*Pages and Pictures from Forgotten
    Children's Books,* 75
"Patricia Polacco," 666
"Paul Goble," 462
"Peepo Ergo Sum? Anxiety and
    Pastiche in the Ahlberg
    Picture Books," 385
"Perestroika and Picture Books,"
    121
"Personal Visions," 717
"Peter Spier," 462
"Photographer or Photo-
    Illustrator," 323
"Photography in Children's
    Books: A Generic
    Approach," 303
"Picture Book, The: Art for
    Children," 418
"Picture Book, The: Bridge from
    Potter to Picasso, " 318
"Picture Book Animals: How
    Natural a History?" 303
"Picture Book Art: Evaluation,"
    218

"Picture Book as Art Object, The:
    A Call for Balanced
    Reviewing, " 152, 317
Picture Book Comes of Age, The, 370
*Picture Book Design Conference:
    From Conception to
    Consumption,* 347
"Picture Book Genesis: A
    Conversation with Maurice
    Sendak," 749
Picture-Book World, 262
*Picture Books: Elements of
    Illustration and Story,* 348
*Picture Books: Integrated Teaching
    of Reading, Writing, Listening,
    Speaking, and Thinking,* 178
Picture Books: The Symposium, 715
"Picture Books: What Do Reviews
    Really Review?" 394
"Picture Books About Blacks,"
    314
"Picture Books, Art and
    Illustration," 461
"Picture Books as Artform," 213
"Picture Books as Contexts for
    Literary, Aesthetic, and Real
    World Understanding," 279
"Picture Books as Literature," 246
"Picture Books as Portable Art
    Galleries," 466
"Picture Books for All the Ages,"
    253
Picture Books for Children, 189, 190
"Picture Books for Children," 656,
    657
"Picture Books for Children Who
    Are Masters of Few Words,"
    117
"Picture Books for Chinese
    Children," 161
Picture Books for Gifted Programs,
    352

Picture Books for Looking and Learning, 319

"Picture Books for Older Children," 409

Picture Books for Young People, 9–13, 329

"Picture Books of M.B. Goffstein, The," 718

"Picture Books That Explain," 541

"Picture Books Today," 460

"Picture Equals How Many Words?, A," 303

"Picture Play in Children's Books: A Celebration of Visual Awareness," 411

"Picture Preferences of Children and Young Adults," 332

"Picture Storybook Art of Junko Morimoto, The," 759

Picture This, 84

"Picturebook as the Central Focus of an Elementary Art Curriculum, The," 177

"Picturebook for the Blind, A," 111

Pictures and Stories from Forgotten Children's Books, 3

Pied Pipers, The: Interviews with the Influential Creators of Children's Literature, 493

Pipers at the Gates of Dawn: The Wisdom of Children's Literature, 194

"Planting Inflammatory Ideas in the Garden of Delight," 100

"Playful Art of Maurice Sendak, The," 634

Pleasures of Children's Literature, The, 337

Pleins feux sur la litterature du jeunesse au Canada français, 298

"Polish Illustrators and the Children's Book," 242

"Poem Picture Books and Their Uses in the Classroom," 234

Pop-up and Movable Books: A Bibliography, 123

"Post-Modern Alphabet, The," 162

"Postmodernist Impulses and the Contemporary Picture Book," 341

"Preference Oriented Guide for Selecting Picture Books, A," 263

Prelude to Literacy: A Preschool Child's Encounter with Picture and Story, 195

Preparing Art for Printing, 132

"Present and Future Evolution of the German Picture-Book," 241

"Price of Being an Artist, The," 213

"Prickles Under the Frock: The Art of Beatrix Potter," 426

"Primary Art Objects," 383

Primer of Visual Literacy, A, 204

Print a Book, 115

Private World of Tasha Tudor, The, 788

"Problems Brought About by 'Reading' a Sequence of Pictures," 164

Proceedings of the First National Conference on Visual Literacy, 414

"Profile: Ashley Bryan," 774

"Profile: David Macaulay," 503

"Profile: Eric Carle," 630

"Profile: Paul Goble," 770

"Profile: Tomie dePaola: A Gift to Children," 603

"Profile: Trina Schart Hyman,"
    800
"Profile of an Author and an
    Illustrator," 811
Profiles in Literature, 480
"Psychological Relationships
    Between Text and
    Illustration," 227
"Publisher Adds to the Dialog,
    A," 347
"Publisher's Odyssey, A," 451
"Publisher's Perspective, A," 87,
    254
*Publishing Children's Books in
    America, 1919–1976*, 825
Puzzle of Books, The, 114

Quentin Blake with Heather Neill,
    720
"Questions to an Artist Who Is
    also an Author," 446, 448

Ralph Steadman with Peter Fuller,
    721
Randolph Caldecott, 556
"Randolph Caldecott," 439
*Randolph Caldecott, 1846–1886: An
    Appreciation*, 545
"Randolph Caldecott, Father of
    the Modern Picture Book,"
    528
*Randolph Caldecott, the Man Behind
    the Medal*, 633
"Randolph Caldecott's Picture
    Books," 338
Raymond Briggs with Barry Took,
    733
*Reading, the Arts, and the Creation
    of Meaning*, 215
Reading Pictures, 395
*Readings About Children's
    Literature*, 364

Readings in Children's Literature,
    482
"Rearrangements of Memory: An
    Interview with Allen Say,"
    671
*Reflections on Literature for
    Children*, 426
"Remembering Caldecott: *The
    Three Jovial Huntsmen* and the
    Art of the Picture Book," 303
*Republic of Childhood, The: A
    Critical Guide to Canadian
    Children's Literature in
    English*, 214
"Research: An Adventure," 155
*Research in Children's Literature:
    An Annotated Bibliography*,
    834
Research into Illustration, 237, 238
"Respect the Source," 250
"Response of Children in a
    Combination First/Second
    Grade Classroom to Picture
    Books, The," 280
"Response of Primary Children to
    Picturebooks, The," 281
Responses to Children's Literature,
    227
"Resurrection Twins:
    Implications in *Two Bad
    Ants*," 226
"Richard Egielski," 809
*Rise of Children's Book Reviewing in
    America, 1865–1881, The*, 438
"Robert Lawson: Author and
    Illustrator," 448, 797
"Robert Lawson: For All
    Children, " 538
*Robert Lawson, Illustrator: A
    Selection of His Characteristic
    Illustrations*, 626
"Robert Lawson's *The Story of
    Ferdinand*: Death in the

Afternoon or Life Under the
Cork Tree?" 338
Robert McCloskey, 745
Robert McCloskey (Video), 737
"Robert McCloskey: Master of
Humorous Realism," 448
"Robert McCloskey's *Make Way
for Ducklings*: The Art of
Regional Storytelling," 338
*Roger Duvoisin (1904–1980) The
Art of Children's Books*, 587
"Roger Duvoisin—Distinguished
Contributor to the World of
Children's Literature," 448
"Romance and Realism: Pyle's
Book Illustrations for
Children," 676
Rudolf Koivu, 762

"Scribbles, Scrawls, and
Scratches," 703
"Searching for the Master Touch
in Picture Books," 300
"Second Gaze at Little Red
Riding Hood's Trials and
Tribulations A," 303
"Second Look, A: Joan of Arc,"
638
"Second Look, A: *Lion*, " 523
"Second Look, A: *The Real Thief*,
295
Self-Portrait: Erik Blegvad, 519
Self-Portrait: Margot Zemach, 810
Self-Portrait: Trina Schart Hyman,
617
"Semiotic Perspective of Text, A,"
235
Sendak, 747
"Sendak on Sendak," 692
"Seuss as a Creator of Folklore,"
526
"Shape of Music, The," 364

"Should Picture Books and
Children Be Matched?", 245
"Show-and-Tell Tale(s) of the
Great Explainer, The," 534
"Show Me the Way to Go Home,"
647
*Signal Approach to Children's
Books, The*, 182
*Signposts to Criticism of Children's
Literature*, 152
Sing a Song for Sixpence, 2
"Sitting in Her Chair," 782
*Sixth Book of Junior Authors and
Illustrators*, 256
"Sky Father, Earth Mother: An
Artist Interprets Myth," 679
Smithsonian Book of Books, The, 124
"So I Shall Tell You a Story . . ."
Encounters with Beatrix Potter,
782
Society and Children's Literature, 27
"Some Second Graders' Verbal
Responses to the Picturebook
as Art Object," 340
Something About the Author, 431
*Something About the Author
Autobiography Series*, 487
"Something Old, Something
New: Children's Picture
Books in Poland," 310
"Sophisticated Picturebooks," 410
"Sources of Information for
Children's Book
Illustration," 826
"Special Collections and
Archives: Scholarly
Resources for Caldecott
Award Research," 829
*Special Collections in Children's
Literature*, 824
"Steig: Nobody Is Grown-up,"
632

Stepping Away from Tradition: Children's Books of the Twenties and Thirties, 38

Story and Picture in Children's Books," 441

Story Books: Integrated Teaching of Reading, Writing, Listening, Speaking, Viewing, and Thinking, 179

Story of a Book, 133

"Storytelling Through Art: Pretense or Performance?" 251

"Strange Balance of Joy and Pain, A," 246

"Study of Picture Preferences of Caldecott Award Winners and Runners-up by Fourth, Fifth, and Sixth Grade Children, A," 406

"Surprised by Joy: The World of Picture-Books," 213

"Svend Otto S., Winner of the Nordic Prize," 621

"Swiss Picture-Book Today, The," 240

"Tale of Callie Kott, A," 400

"Tale of the Mandarin Ducks, The," 551

"Talk with Lisbeth Zwerger, A," 574

Talking with Artists, 435

"Talking with Artists," 542

"Taming the Wild Things," 654

"Teachers Using Picture Books," 253

"Teaching Art," 359

"Teaching Visual Literacy Through Wordless Picture Books," 358

"Teaching with Picture Books," 143

Telling Line, The, 321

"Ten from the Decade: Visually Significant Picture Books and Why," 396

Tenniel Illustrations to the Alice Books, The, 592

"Text and Illustration: A Stylistic Analysis of Books by Sendak and Mayer," 146

"Text and Illustration in Emblem Books," 227

That Naughty Rabbit: Beatrix Potter and Peter Rabbit, 783

"There's Much More to the Picture Than Meets the Eye," 152, 299

"They Never Give Up: Indonesian Writers and Illustrators," 425

"Thoughts on Children's Books in Poland," 240

Three Centuries of Children's Books in Europe, 34

"Three Scandinavian Contributions to American Children's Literature," 610

Through Indian Eyes, 376

"To the Children with Love, from Leo Politi," 448

Tomi Ungerer: Storyteller, 786

"Tomie dePaola: Children's Choice," 497

"Tomie dePaola, Tough and Tender Storyteller," 505

"Top Dog," 787

Touchstones: Reflections on the Best in Children's Literature. Vol. 3: Picture Books, 338

"Tradition and Internationalism in the Swiss Children's Book," 242

"Treasure Houses to Share: Children's Literature Special Collections," 830

Treasure Seekers and Borrowers: Children's Books in Britain, 1900–1960, 434

Treasury of American Book Illustration, A, 349

Treasury of the Great Children's Book Illustrators, A, 51

"Trends in Caldecott Award Winners," 397

"Trina S. Hyman," 678

"Trina Schart Hyman," 462

"Tuppence Colored," 47

Twentieth Century Book, The, 42

Twentieth-Century Children's Writers, 463

"Two Danish Illustrators," 578

"Two Illustrators Can Be Better Than One," 465

"Tying up the Talent," 92

"'Ubiquitous' Trina Schart Hyman, The," 597

"Unfinished Portrait of an Artist," 460

"Uri Shulevitz," 461

"Uri Shulevitz: For Children of All Ages," 731

"U.S. Children's Books in a Changing World," 242

"Use Wordless Picture Books to Teach Reading," 191, 412

Using Picture Books with Children: A Guide to Owlet Books, 417

"Valentine and Orson," 524

"Van Allsburg: From a Different Perspective," 680

"Vera B. Williams: Postcards and Peace Vigils," 732

"Very Brief Talk . . . ?, A," 238

"Very Hungry Caterpillar Meets Beowolf, The, "333

Very Truly Yours, Charles L. Dodgson, 512

Vexed Texts: How Children's Picture Books Promote Illiteracy, 354

Victorian Book Design and Colour Printing, 50

Victorian Illustrated Books, 56

"View From the Island, A: European Picture Books 1967–1976," 284

"Virginia Burton's *The Little House*: Technological Change and Fundamental Verities," 338

"Virginia Lee Burton's Dynamic Sense of Design," 448, 629

Visit with Bernard Waber, A, 792

"Visit with Tomi Ungerer, A," 694

"Visual and Verbal Literacy," 398

"Visual Language of the Picture Book, The," 360

"Visual Learning Strategies," 331

"Visual Literacy: Exploring Art and Illustration in Children's Books," 373

"Visual Literacy and Children's Books," 193

"Visual Literacy Through Picture Books K–12: A Curriculum Approach," 297

Walter Crane, 765

Walter Crane and the American Book Arts, 1880–1915, 77

Walter Crane and the Reform of the German Picture Book, 1865–1914, 805

"Walter Crane's *The Baby's Opera*: A Commodious Dwelling," 338

"Wanda Gag—Artist, Author," 613

"Wanda Gag's *Millions of Cats*: Unity Through Repetition," 338

"Way David Macaulay Works, The," 698

Ways of the Book Illustrator in Britain, The," 292

Ways of the Illustrator, 369

Well-Built Book, The, 135

"Wendy Watson," 682

"What Is a Picture Book?" 374, 375

"What Is in a Picture?" 271

"What Manner of Beast? Illustrations of *Beauty and the Beast*," 200

When We Were Young: Two Centuries of Children's Book Illustration, 25

"Where the Old Meets the New: The Japanese Picture Book," 284

"Who Thunk You Up Dr. Seuss?" 448

"'Whoa! Nigel, You're a Wild Thing'," 155

Who's Dr. Seuss? Meet Ted Geisel, 802

Who's Who of Children's Literature, The, 22

Why Do You Write for Children? Children, Why Do You Read?, 803

"Why I Became a Children's Book Illustrator," 785

"Why I Write and Paint," 803

"Why the Books of Harlan Quist Disappeared—Or Did They?" 342

"Wild Washerwomen, Hired Sportsmen, and Enormous Crocodiles," 517

"Will Hillenbrand," 667

"William Steig," 461

"William Steig: Champion for Romance," 604

"William Steig at 80," 502

"Window in the Book: Conventions in the Illustration of Children's Books, The," 205

"Winslow Homer: The Years as Illustrator," 777

Winslow Homer and the Illustrated Book, 778

"With a Jeweler's Eye," 246

"'With Murderous Ending, Shocking, Menacing . . . ': Sarah Moon's Little Red Riding Hood 10 Years After," 231

Word Music and Word Magic: Children's Literature Methods, 378

Wordless/Almost Wordless Picture Books, 362

"Wordless Books," 302

"Wordless Picture Books Are for Older Readers Too," 322

"Wordless Picture Books—The Medium Is the Message," 224

Words about Pictures: The Narrative Art of Picture Books, 339

"Words and Pictures," 136

"Work of David Macaulay, The," 606

Work of E.H. Shepard, The, 631

World of Children's Literature, The, 57

Worlds of Childhood: The Art and Craft of Writing for Children, 495

Writers for Children: Critical Studies of Major Authors Since the Seventeenth Century, 158

Writing, Illustrating and Editing Children's Books, 88

Writing with Pictures: How to Write and Illustrate Children's Books, 130

Written for Children, 73

Written for Children: An Outline of English-Language Children's Literature, 404

"W.W. Denslow: The Forgotten Illustrator," 598

Yankee Doodle's Literary Sampler of Prose, Poetry and Pictures, 31

Yesterday's Authors of Books for Children: Facts and Pictures About Authors and Illustrators of Books for Young People from Early Times to 1960, 432

Young Children and Picture Books: Literature from Infancy to Six, 268